# ORGANIZATION FOR TREATMENT

*A Comparative Study of Institutions for Delinquents*

David Street

Robert D. Vinter

Charles Perrow

FOREWORD BY MORRIS JANOWITZ

THE FREE PRESS, *New York*

COLLIER-MACMILLAN LIMITED, *London*

112591

The research on which this book is based was supported by research grant M-2104 from the National Institute of Mental Health, Public Health Service. The study was based in the School of Social Work, University of Michigan, and the preparation of the volume was aided by the Center for Social Organization Studies, University of Chicago.

Collier-Macmillan Canada, Ltd., Toronto, Ontario

Library of Congress Catalog Card Number: 66-17696

*Second Printing November 1968*

# FOREWORD

　　To describe a research study as ambitious is indeed risky. It has an immediate ring of pretension, and it carries the implication that the study's objectives, although valid, could not be achieved. But this monograph is ambitious if the word can still be taken at its face value.

　　First, it deals with a central issue in organizational theory, that is, evaluation of the effects of those institutions that have the goal of changing human personality and human values so that their clients can participate effectively in the larger society. The authors studied a specific type of organization, the juvenile correctional institution, but they cast their problem in general terms. They were fully aware of the need for more adequate criteria to judge the performance of "people-changing organizations," as prisons, mental hospitals, and the like are called in this study. It has been traditional to approach the issue of effectiveness by seeking concrete and specific measures of behavior that are supposed to reflect changes that will persist long after the individual has left the institution. It is necessary to conduct research using such a format, but the technical and theoretical elements are often confounding. It is most difficult to obtain the matched samples that are required, especially those of persons who have not had the specific institutional experiences, and to get the necessary follow-up information. More fundamentally, such a research design must focus as much on the impact of the large society as on specific consequences of the particular "people-changing" institution.

　　Street, Vinter, and Perrow therefore pursue a more direct and

phenomenological approach, one that fuses hard social-science data with subtle moral and policy considerations. The effects of an institution are in part to be judged by the human climate and the immediate social situation that the institution is able to generate. One does not have to be a moral philosopher to subscribe to the notion that the best correctional institution is to be found in a society that does not have correctional institutions. In the real world, however, these institutions exist, and they vary in their goals and norms. The variations in outlook of their administrators and the resulting attitudes of the inmates are profound. The researchers have succeeded in recording and quantifying these differences.

But this perspective for evaluating performance runs much deeper. Correctional institutions, like mental hospitals and other such people-changing institutions, have moved toward the goals of treatment and rehabilitation. With the growth of this social movement, there has developed a persistent criticism of "two-person" psychotherapy and traditional case methods. Although these attacks have surface validity, they overlook the factors that have produced this social movement and the resistances it still must meet. The movement toward treatment and rehabilitation is grounded in many considerations, humanistic, political, religious, and professional. Concepts derived from psychoanalysis and dynamic psychology have been crucial elements.

These concepts can be thought of as value or belief systems that influence conceptions of treatment. This research is based on the assumption that these belief systems have the capacity to influence not only individual behavior but also the behavior of whole organizations. The empirical results are clear cut. Treatment belief systems do mold correctional institutions in ways that make them different from institutions whose administrative leaders are not committed to treatment strategies. The results move the organizations predominantly in a desirable direction. Because there are differences in conceptions of treatment, the question of which is the most appropriate emerges. The findings here indicate that group or milieu strategies are not automatically superior to individual treatment, for a basic issue is the capacity of the institution to implement its goals, whatever they may be.

Second, this study is ambitious because it directly confronts the deceptively simple notion of the "total institution" offered by Erving Goffman. Clearly, people-changing organizations are special institutions

because of the overlap of place of "work" and place of "residence." And clearly such institutions have more often than not served to deprive and degrade human beings, particularly when the institutions have reflected rigid and repressive external social structures. But the mono-lithic character of the total institution can be called into question on purely a priori grounds. Empirically as well, the facts do not seem to fit the total institution model. Social workers have observed and created benign institutions, in which, for at least some inmates, life chances and levels of self-esteem are superior to those the inmates have had in the outer world. Sociologists have pointed to those residential institutions —from the monastery to the artists' colony—in which the group-based individual is able to perform at a more adequate level than he could as a detached person. Is this atmosphere not what is meant by a "Bohemia," and should the university to some degree not be thought of as having selected features of the total institution that enhance creativity by fending off to some degree pressures from the outside world? (The struggle to locate the student and faculty in the immediate environs of the campus is nothing more than an effort to create a part of a total institution).

In research terms, the issue is to examine and to explain the varia-tions within and among residential institutions. Again, the data are noteworthy. As the goals of organizations change under the impact of treatment concepts, staff attitudes, inmate orientations, and inmate lead-ership structures alter. With the growth of treatment goals, it is possible to speak of a pluralistic institution, rather than of a total institution, and to use the language of the political scientist to describe leadership, power balance, coalition formation, and communications patterns.

Third, perhaps the most ambitious aspect of this study is its com-prehensive scope. It is not a pilot study, a preliminary report, or an ex-ploratory project—although the central hypotheses will of course have to be replicated. The prison has a long tradition in sociology as a focus for research in depth. One of the first studies, Donald Clemmer's *The Prison Community*, was not only remarkably insightful but remains a landmark in research on social organization precisely because the whole institution was studied.

The present research design sought to probe old fashioned and new fashioned correctional institutions in depth and at the same time to collect the types of systematic data required for precise comparisons.

It is comparative in that it encompasses six different institutions, which vary widely in their goals. It is comprehensive in that it encompasses all strata from the top administrators to the rank-and-file cadres. It is "in depth" in that each organization is studied from a variety of observational vantage points at two points in time. It has an experimental element in that there was a conscious effort to modify and change these institutions by means of an intensive training seminar. The seminar made available to the key administrator of each institution major findings collected during the first "wave" of research. It served as a technique for collecting additional data from the executives, and it served as a device for promoting organizational change. A period of approximately one year elapsed between the first and second waves of the field investigation. The pattern of change that was stimulated served to underline the basic hypotheses. In effect, the institutions that stressed conformity remained fixed while substantial changes were underway in the treatment institutions.

Fourth, implications for policy and professional practice derive from the volume's scope. The authors do not strongly emphasize a distinction between "basic" and "applied" research. Reliance on this distinction would lead to an "engineering" model of social research, in which there is a search for specific answers to particular operating questions. The engineering model sees the development and testing of hypotheses as a relatively self-contained process by and for social scientists. The results of such investigation must then be translated by others who have special skills in applying social science. By contrast, this research follows the "enlightenment" model. Although it is concerned with specifics, it focuses on developing a fundamental understanding of the institution jointly by both the social scientists and professional practitioners. In the enlightenment model, there is a continuity of interest and interaction between the researcher and the practitioner. Theoretical formulations have merit because the hypotheses are precise and sharp enough so that links between theory and data can be checked by both the social scientist and the professional, each using his own criteria. Furthermore, at every possible point, the authors seek to present the definitions of the situation as seen by the actors involved. The richness of detail is designed not to exaggerate deviant cases but to represent the institutional context. Without this detail, the hypotheses would lose their full import.

Some examples can illustrate a convergence of theory and practice

as it emerged in the natural history of this project. As the authors shared their findings with the executives, the most pervasive impact was to develop in the executive an understanding of the extent to which they were operating with a deficit of information and of how they could, with their own resources, develop more information about their own inmates and organizations. The social scientists were in effect implanting an empirical perspective.

The materials presented on changes reveal the direct and forthright manner of some of the executives who sought to probe more deeply into the operations of their organizations as a result of this research. As executives, their first commitment was to manage their institutions, so that sheer work pressures plus organizational constraints limited their capacity to overcome the deficit of information. In the end, it was abundantly clear to the research group that the task of developing adequate information cannot be accomplished by an individual executive alone. It is a professional responsibility that requires an outside perspective. An organizational audit that would periodically collect the types of data gathered in this study in a manner similar to an annual fiscal audit of a business company is obviously needed—although the research effort hardly succeeded in stimulating such an institutional development.

As the authors shared their findings with administrators and other social scientists, basic issues in the strategy of change for the correctional system had to be faced. In this process, they had to address themselves more and more directly to the social and economic costs of modifying the correctional institution. In the first instance, they were concerned with determining whether or not changes in goals had any discernible consequences. Because the researchers were concerned with treatment, they were most interested in those organizations that had the most radical programs, but the comparative approach required them to collect data on the full range of correctional institutions. It is thus possible to recast the research question: At what costs can what changes in correctional institutions be made? What types of change are most feasible, economically and organizationally?

Obviously, as an institution moves from the custodial format to treatment, more resources are required. Institutions that have abandoned custodial practices and do not have the resources for treatment are described by the authors as fitting a re-education or development model.

Is it therefore possible to describe the "input" and "output" ratios, that is, to examine the patterns of change in inmate attitudes as more resources are made available? Is there, so to speak, an optimum point? The research project collected detailed information on staff-inmate ratios that, along with other measures, gives a picture of costs or inputs. In turn, the details of attitudes, patterns, and leadership structures of the inmates supply useful measures of the results or the outputs. The authors supply an argument and set of criteria for evaluating whether or not these attitudes are compatible with the goals of rehabilitation, criteria that the reader must evaluate for himself. The relevance of these measures of outcome is enhanced because the social-background factors do not systematically influence the impact of the institutional experience.

The costs and efforts of shifting from an obedience and conformity model to a benign (or re-education/development) model are relatively limited, whereas the costs of taking the next step from the benign to the treatment institution require marked increases in finances and human efforts. The shifts in inmate attitude patterns that result from movement between the custodial and the benign organizations are sharp and clear, however, whereas the added increment that comes in the further movement to a treatment format (casework or group milieu) may be rather limited. This formulation does not overlook the operational problems in managing a benign institution and the necessity for such an institution to have a sufficient orientation to rehabilitation, so as to make it truly benign and not merely a camouflage for custodial patterns.

The implications for national policy are clear. The first priority is to modify existing institutions into the "midpoint"—that is, into effective re-education/development models. This shift is feasible, and the results are observable and direct. The treatment type of institution must still be considered an experimental institution. It is an organization that can succeed on the basis of imaginative personal leadership, but it is one that has yet to solve its operational and administrative problems.

National goals must be seen in terms of the size of the inmate population and types of correctional institutions that exist throughout the United States. At the time of the 1960 census, there were approximately 45,000 youngsters in state training schools for delinquents or comparable private institutions. Of these, more than 38,000 were in public

institutions. In addition, there were approximately 33,000 people under twenty years of age in federal and state penitentiaries, state prisons and reformatories, and local jails and workhouses. To this number should be added the more than 12,000 in detention homes or diagnostic and reception centers. In all, we were dealing with a population very close to 90,000 people at any one time. (The actual numbers of different people staying in these institutions over a twelve-month period would be much larger.) Given the age distribution of the population of the United States, the absolute number is likely to increase even if the delinquency rate remains constant.

There is no adequate body of data on the types or quality of programs to be found in correctional institutions throughout the nation. Yet on the basis of a variety of sources, especially measures of staff/inmate ratios, we estimate that at least half of public institutions are basically custodial (obedience/conformity format) and have only limited features of the re-education/development format. At least another 25 per cent of the institutions have moved to the re-education/development level, whereas the remainder have substantial features of the treatment organization. A high priority in the "war against poverty" should be the national goal that correctional institutions achieve the minimum re-education/development format. Correctional institutions have to be viewed as agencies for dealing with the consequences of poverty. These goals are likely to be achieved only if there are special programs for training personnel, many of whom should be recruited from low-income groups.

Although it is essential to emphasize the differences among correctional institutions, these institutions are still to be viewed as a group having common characteristics. A close examination of the materials of this research leaves a powerful impression of the lack of knowledge that the administrators have of the fates of their inmates after they leave the institutions. The bureaucratic element is not so much the social distance between administrators and clients as it is the lack of knowledge, in human terms, about outcomes after inmates are released. More adequate reporting and supervision of the inmates are obviously needed, but this observation is superficial and almost misleading.

The correctional institution, like other residential people-changing organizations, envelops its inmates. If it has an impact, it does so precisely because the experiences it creates are different from the ex-

periences in diffuse and multiple structures the inmates have had in the outer world. Yet the inmate is being prepared to return to this outer world. The weaknesses that have been uncovered in the casework approach to client treatment should not obscure the essential fact that this approach has been sensitive to the requirement that the individual has to be returned to live in this outer world and has to be prepared to operate with his own personal resources.

The contemporary revolution in expectations about correctional institutions not only emphasizes rehabilitation but also creates more realistic expectations about the changes that can and should be wrought in human personality. The result is a reaffirmation of the need to create group structures in the community to accommodate the released inmates. The "halfway-house" concept is an important expression of the goals that have to be achieved. A halfway house is based on the assumption that it is desirable to have more experience of the benign or treatment institution in a setting closer to the real world. It also implies that the society seeks some date of termination, after which the former delinquent is no longer different from the population at large and is prepared to live in the open society.

But the concept of the halfway house seems partial and in a sense unrealistic. The arrangements for transition from the correctional institution to the community might better be thought of as an "open house." The open-house concept implies that a released inmate cannot be confronted with the notion of a termination date for transition. He must become a member of a transitional community or an open organization that will permit his involvement or withdrawal as long as it is appropriate.

The open house is both residential and nonresidential. It is a subcommunity in a world in which the control of personal affect is increasingly relevant to life chances. It is an institution that is permanent and valid and not merely transitional. The delinquent, like the ex-soldier, will never be separated from his special experience. His differences cannot be denied. The delinquent cannot be rewarded for his deviant behavior, but he is certain to remain an ex-inmate in his own mind—just as much as the ex-concentration camp inmates persist in their social solidarity. The social forms appropriate for ex-inmates are difficult to anticipate, but these people should not be denied the right of

association as a special interest group within the framework of the law.

The task of the social researcher and the professional is to reach beyond the immediately attainable to present, if you will, an utopian objective but one that is paradoxically grounded in reality. Even if the bold programs of community development and new forms of social control being sponsored by the federal government succeed in drastically reducing delinquency, the problems of deviant behavior will persist. Even if correctional institutions move toward treatment-oriented goals and are highly successful, the need for open houses will persist and, in fact, will grow.

Here is what is meant by a "mass society." It is a society that recognizes the moral worth of each human being. The meaning is that, for the first time in human history, society is prepared to deal with the specific problems not only of the privileged but also of all (the whole mass). For the delinquent, this advance means not only increasing the opportunity for rehabilitation but also building institutions that give the person who has damaged himself and/or has been damaged by society an organizational base from which to manage his participation in the larger society.

The acknowledgments that are due are the result of the fact that this book is a collective product. It is based on data gathered in a field study that was directed by Robert Vinter and myself. The project was sponsored by a generous research grant (Grant M-2104) from the National Institute of Mental Health, United States Public Health Service, to the School of Social Work, The University of Michigan. This project also had its elements of individual scholarship, which resulted in a variety of personal research reports and publications. The publications on the treatment aspects of correctional institutions made possible by this and related grants are listed in Appendix E.

The original objectives and theoretical orientation that guided the research design and the data collection were presented in the article by Robert Vinter and myself, "Effective Institutions for Juvenile Delinquents: A Research Statement," *Social Service Review*, 33 (June, 1959). Robert Vinter and Charles Perrow, associate study director, supervised the data collection and the administration of the project. The other responsible staff members were Rosemary Conzemius Sarri, Mayer

Zald, and David Street, each of whom participated in the original analysis work. All three authors wrote various chapters of this volume— including alternative versions. The task of putting together the materials fell most heavily on David Street.

*Morris Janowitz*

Center for Social Organization Studies
University of Chicago

# CONTENTS

Foreword    v
List of Tables    xix
List of Figures    xx

## Part One. Introduction

Chapter   1. CHARACTER OF THE CORRECTIONAL
INSTITUTION FOR JUVENILES     3
The People-Changing Organization    3
The Juvenile Correctional Institution    7

Chapter   2. ORGANIZATIONAL VARIATIONS     16
Theoretical Framework    17
Research Design    22
Sketches of the Institutions    26

## Part Two. Executive Strategies

Chapter   3. THE EXECUTIVE:
FORMULATIONS OF GOALS     45
Executiveship    45
Goal Definition    48
Obedience/Conformity Institutions    49
Re-education/Development Institutions    53
Treatment Institutions    57
Contrasts among Types    63

*Chapter* 4. THE EXECUTIVE:
EXTERNAL STRATEGIES 67
Obedience/Conformity Institutions 69
Re-education/Development Institutions 75
Treatment Institutions 79
Contrasts among Types 86

*Part Three. Executive and Organization*

*Chapter* 5. INTERNAL STRATEGIES AND
STAFF ORGANIZATION 93
Obedience/Conformity Institutions 94
Re-education/Development Institutions 96
Treatment Institutions 98
Contrasts among Types 103
Findings on Organizational Structure 106

*Part Four. The Staff*

*Chapter* 6. STAFF PERSPECTIVES 137
Perspectives on Goals 137
Perspectives on Delinquents 142
Views of Rehabilitative Potential 146
Perspectives on Jobs and Careers 148

*Chapter* 7. STAFF-INMATE RELATIONS 151
The Daily Round 153
Differentiation 159
Authority Relations 161
Rewards and Sanctions 166
Control over Inmate Association 174
Problems of Implementation 177

*Part Five. The Inmates*

*Chapter* 8. INMATE PERSPECTIVES 195
Organizational Effectiveness 195
Propositions 198

Findings on Inmate Perspectives    199
Length of Stay and Perspectives    209
The Impact of Background Attributes    212

*Chapter* 9. THE INMATE GROUP    222
A Theoretical Scheme    223
Interpersonal Relations    227
Integration and Perspectives    230
Inmate Solidarity    232
Inmate Leadership    238
Findings on a Maximum-Security Unit    245
Summary of Findings    249

*Part Six. Organizational Change*

*Chapter* 10. CHANGE BETWEEN SURVEYS    257
The Executive Seminar    257
Measures of Stability and Change    264
*Chapter* 11. CONCLUSIONS    278
Overview of the Study    278
The Implementation of Treatment    279

*Appendixes*

*Appendix* A. THE STAFF QUESTIONNAIRE    285

*Appendix* B. SCALE AND INDEX CONSTRUCTION
FOR STAFF DATA    306

*Appendix* C. THE INMATE QUESTIONNAIRE    310

*Appendix* D. FACTOR ANALYSIS AND INDEX
CONSTRUCTION FOR INMATE DATA    321

*Appendix* E. PUBLICATIONS AND DISSERTATIONS
CONNECTED WITH THE RESEARCH    325

Index    327

2.1. Goals, Sizes, and Auspices of the Sample Institutions   24
5.1. Ratios of Inmates to Staff   106
5.2. Staff Background Characteristics   108
5.3. Staff Perceptions of Power in the Executive Core   122
5.4. Staff Perceptions of the Influence of Major Groups   125
6.1. Staff Perceptions of Institutional Purposes   138
6.2. Staff Perceptions of Institutional Purposes, by Education   139
6.3. New Treatment Programs vs. Containment, in Closed Institutions   141
6.4. Staff Attitudes Toward Delinquents   144
6.5. Additional Staff Attitudes Toward Delinquents   146
6.6. Staff Optimism About Inmate Change   147
7.1. Staff Beliefs About Running and Surveillance   158
7.2. Staff Agreement that All Boys Should Get the Same Discipline for Breaking Rules   159
7.3. Staff Agreement that Inmates Must Do What They Are Told and Do It Quickly   162
7.4. Staff Perception of Executive's Expectations in Handling and Relating to Inmates   165
7.5. Staff Scores on Sanctions Index   171
7.6. Staff Views on Best Way for an Inmate To Get Along   173
7.7. Staff Views on Groups and on Inmates Keeping to Themselves   176
7.8. Staff Scores on Prisonization Scale   176
8.1. Inmate Perspectives on Institution and Staff   200
8.2. Inmate Views on Food, Smoking, and Program   202
8.3. Inmate Views on Staff Supervision   203
8.4. Inmate Views on Adaptation to the Institution   205
8.5. Inmate Views on Self   206
8.6. Inmates' Knowledge of Staff Judgments About Them and Expectations About Stay   208
8.7. Inmate Background Attributes, from Institutional Records   214
8.8. Specific Breakdowns of Most Serious Offense in Record   216
8.9. Inmate Scores on Index of Perspectives on Institution and Staff, by Selected Background Characteristics   218
9.1. Inmate Social Relations and Perspectives on Other Inmates   229

9.2.   Integration into the Inmate Group and Perspectives   231
9.3.   Perceptions of Inmate Uncooperativeness   233
9.4.   Norms Against "Ratting" to Staff   234
9.5.   Integration and Scores on "Ratting" Index   235
9.6.   Inmate Solidarity   236
9.7.   Leadership and Perspectives   241
9.8.   Inmate Perceptions of Leaders   243
9.9.   Maxwell: Inmate Perspectives   247
9.10.  Maxwell: Impact of Integration on Perspectives   247
9.11.  Maxwell: Inmate Solidarity and Views on "Ratting"   248
10.1.  Changes of 10 Per Cent or More on Comparable Staff Questions from Survey I to Survey II   265
10.2.  Changes of 10 Per Cent or More on Comparable Inmate Questions from Survey I to Survey II   266

B.1.   Scale of Normal Relations   307
B.2.   Scale of Understanding   307
B.3.   Scale of Discipline   307
B.4.   Prisonization Scale   308
D.1.   Factor Loadings of .4 and Above   322

## LIST OF FIGURES

5.1.   Formal Organization at Dick   115
5.2.   Formal Organization at Regis   116
5.3.   Formal Organization at Bennett   116
5.4.   Formal Organization at Mixter   118
5.5.   Formal Organization at Inland   119
5.6.   Formal Organization at Milton   121
5.7.   Perceived Tension Between Staff Groups   128
8.1.   Lengths of Stay and Proportions Positive on Index of Perspectives on Institution and Staff in Closed Institutions   210
8.2.   Lengths of Stay and Proportions Positive on Index of Perspectives on Institution and Staff in Open Institutions   211

PART ONE

# Introduction

*Chapter 1*

# CHARACTER OF THE CORRECTIONAL INSTITUTION FOR JUVENILES

## THE PEOPLE-CHANGING ORGANIZATION

To understand many of the dominant sociological features of juvenile correctional institutions we must realize that these institutions share, in greater or lesser degree, the characteristics of a general organizational type. We shall call this type the "people-changing" organization.

All complex organizations use people to pursue their tasks, but people-changing organizations work not only with or through people but also *on* them. People constitute the *raison d'être* of these organizations, and, as our label suggests, the desired product is a new or altered person. People-changing organizations can be contrasted with organizations that produce, distribute, or service inanimate objects or symbols. The latter may have important consequences for their members' statuses, role-orientations, identities, and personalities, but these alterations are usually incidental, personal, or instrumental. In people-changing organizations the alterations are the primary end.[1]

Conceived in this way, the term "people-changing" encompasses a broad variety of organizations, ranging from the monastery (which cleanses the soul while teaching the outward signs of grace) to Menninger's (which restructures the personality), and even to the House of Venus (which reshapes buttocks and identity simultaneously). Included in the type are schools and universities; such youth groups as the Boy Scouts, which attempt to inculcate moral standards of behavior; churches, especially those that seek to "save" or remake the individual rather than simply to sustain his beliefs; military academies, where youths are segregated from previous ties and given new identities;

organizations that train people in the arts of human relations, insofar as new attitudes and behavior patterns must be effected; and the numerous organizations that attempt to alter deviant behavior.

People-changing organizations vary in the extent, direction, and difficulty of the change pursued. The change sought may be only symbolic, as when a new title is the only "real" product of an education but leads its possessor to occupational promotion and concomitant changes in style of life and orientation; it may involve new skills, ranging from the narrow and technical to the broad, social, or intellectual, or it may require entirely new attitudes, values, and standards of behavior. When we look at organizations that achieve or attempt to achieve the most thoroughgoing change, we see—with few exceptions—that these organizations are performing functions crucial to the maintenance of social control. Compared with most tasks of serving people, change is both difficult and expensive; often it requires considerable time (perhaps twenty-four hours a day for years), and generally it can occur only with community-wide or society-wide legitimation and resources. Schools, mental hospitals, prisons, reformatories, and juvenile correctional institutions are the principal organizations involved in these tasks.

## Characteristics of the People-Changing Organization

Despite the heterogeneous nature of this class, the organizations within it have several important differentiating characteristics:

First, because the materials to be worked on are human rather than non-human, various techniques of handling are ruled out under the general imperative that humans are to be regarded as ends in themselves and under the extension of humanitarian values and pressures.

Second, because humans are self-activating, reactive, and capable of wide variations in response, special measures often must be taken to limit their capability to frustrate change. The organization must focus on the behavior, interests, orientations, and motives of those persons who constitute its lowest echelon. There is constant danger of unanticipated response, as evidenced by prison riots or collective disturbances in mental hospital wards or classrooms. The focus on control is most prominent in the *closed* people-changing organization—the state mental hospital, the prison, the work camp, the reformatory—where the

persons to be changed are present involuntarily. Ostracized from the normal community, these persons require incarceration and extensive regulation of their individual and collective behavior. Further, the closed people-changing organization takes on the attributes of a community; it is a "total institution"[2] in which sustenance activities are fully as central as those connected with people-changing itself.

Third, the self-energizing characteristics of the human material, along with the assumed importance of each individual, provoke a continuing strain between the tendencies to bureaucratize and to particularize. On the one hand persons and behaviors may be perceived as mostly non-uniform, resulting in a proliferation of non-routinized, individualized modes of operation, with consequent difficulties in organizing operations. On the other hand events may be defined principally in gross categories of inmate characteristics and behaviors, with resultant difficulties in predicting individual behavior. In addition, whatever the basic viewpoint, the tendency toward non-uniformity is so great that the organization must delegate considerable discretion and authority to lower-level staff members, who otherwise would be unable to deal with the unpredictable events and the variant characteristics of the persons to be changed. Because of this, supervision of staff is especially problematic.

Fourth, in comparison with the technologies of most other work organizations, that of people-changing is little standardized, agreed upon, or objectively demonstrable.[3] In other work organizations the tractability of the material, the comparative irrelevance of cultural definitions, and the possibility of experimentation under controlled conditions ordinarily make it possible to establish relatively effective technologies. For obvious reasons this is not true in the people-changing organization, where the technology consists in a variety of human-relations techniques. The ends sought in people-changing have an abstract quality; there is difficulty not only in proving one technique more successful than another but also in assessing performance even given a particular technology. At present widely different technologies compete in virtually all people-changing organizations. Further, there is much borrowing among types: For example, military models are often used in correctional organizations, as are various technologies prevalent in case-work agencies and mental hospitals.

Fifth, the characteristic just discussed invites another attribute of

these organizations: Belief systems play a dominant role in organizing action, providing answers to the questions of what behavior needs changing and why, how the behavior originated, and how the change can be made. In the church, for example, activities will vary with whether the officials believe that "backsliding" is caused by a lack of friendly, sincere contact with church officials, by an absence of attractive social and recreational activities within the church, by economic deprivation and insecurity, by an absence of intense emotional or spiritual experience generated during services, or by the work of evil associates.

Finally, to the extent that these organizations are agencies of social control they are subject to continuing surveillance by publics and groups outside the organization. The surveillance is made in terms of humanitarian values and various beliefs about people-changing, apprehension about the deviance of persons to be changed and the extent to which they are, in fact, affected, and concern with the moral status of organizations that "work people over." The people-changing organization often resists surveillance because public concepts of proper means of changing behavior are so diverse that some outside groups will object to whatever means are utilized and because some means proposed by outsiders will be completely inappropriate or unreal. Thus the wall around the prison serves to keep the public out as much as to keep the inmates in.

### Socialization and Resocialization

People-changing organizations that emphasize *socialization* seek to prepare persons for their roles and consider the process of doing so a "natural," expected, developmental thing. Persons to be changed are presumed to be at least minimally committed to the task and generally ready for it. People-changing organizations that emphasize *resocialization* presume deviance on the part of the persons to be changed and do not consider the change as developmental. Instead, they assume that deviant forms of behavior must be eradicated; something must be *undone* before something can be done. The staffs of resocialization organizations, having evidence of the person's failure to behave in prescribed ways, cannot assume his cooperation or the support of his normal environment and must concern themselves with a wider range of behaviors, experiences, and intentions. As the presumption of deviance also implies an

assumption of incompetence or incorrect motives in at least some areas of behavior, the person to be changed must be managed until the change occurs.

Most people-changing organizations exhibit some mixture of the two processes, although ordinarily one will predominate. Thus, schools are primarily socializing organizations, phased in with other events in the student's life which contribute to his adoption of approved values and roles. To the extent that teachers feel the family or peer groups have been deficient, however, they may also attempt to resocialize. Indeed, teachers in urban slum areas may consider this their primary task. As we shall see, personnel in some juvenile correctional institutions feel their primary task is not to remake or restructure the personality but to provide a setting where the normal processes of socialization can take place. Because resocialization is thought to require more intensive effort and isolation from previous relationships, resocialization agencies frequently are total institutions, wherein the individual is subject to surveillance and efforts at changing his behavior twenty-four hours a day.

Obviously, there are large differences among types of people-changing organizations. Some seek to socialize individuals, others to resocialize them; some constitute total societies and some control only a fraction of the individual's daily life; some deal with voluntary clients or members, others with involuntary ones; some hold their charges for life, others until some change is effected, and still others until an arbitrary term or age is reached; and some seek broad and pervasive changes, others alterations in a limited segment of the person. Nevertheless, as we have indicated, the class as a whole has many distinctive characteristics.

## THE JUVENILE CORRECTIONAL INSTITUTION

The juvenile correctional institution shares with other people-changing organizations such characteristics as a heavy dependence upon belief systems that overcome the problems of uncertain technology. Like prisons, mental hospitals, and other closed organizations involved in resocialization, it is charged with containing a largely involuntary population of those ostracized from the community for deviant behavior and

with producing changes that will guarantee more conventional behavior upon their return to the community.

These organizations all are specialized descendants of the conglomerate institution in which local communities incarcerated a wide variety of deviants.[4] Until well into the nineteenth century paupers, adult and juvenile offenders and the mentally ill were housed together indiscriminately. Confinement of these diverse populations was, in turn, a modification of earlier and more severe responses to their deviance: maiming, driving-off, exile, outlawry, indenture, and execution. Institutional confinement of persons viewed as threats to the community—and sometimes to themselves—came with public disavowal of harsh and vengeful practices and a placement of higher valuation on individual life. Confinement was viewed as a severe deprivation but one that achieved the necessary protection of the community while avoiding the earlier excesses.

It is important that from the beginning, institutionalization was conceived as having rehabilitative value, whatever protectionist and deterrent functions were also served. Philosophies of reformation were developed more fully as deviant populations were differentiated and confined separately. From the opening of the first separate institutions for wayward youth in the United States during the 1820s, the assumption was that the inmates, because they were juveniles, could be rehabilitated. Deprivation of personal freedom, removal from the community, and managed confinement under various degrees of isolation were all believed necessary to *modify* the deviant or his behavior so that he could be returned to conventional society. These techniques remain the essential features of highly differentiated institutional programs in contemporary society, as do the dual purposes of modifying the deviant while protecting the community.

## The Unilateral Strategy

Intrinsic to the tradition of institutional care is the assumption that the institution, largely by itself, can accomplish the desired change in patterns of deviance. Prisons, mental hospitals, and institutions for juvenile delinquents are still much alike in their commitment to the strategy that people-changing must take place under conditions of custody. Although the practices of these institutions have become more

sophisticated and certainly more benign, they still are premised largely on the belief that these practices can be effective when coupled with deprivation of freedom and removal from the community.

In large part this unilateral strategy has been thrust upon the institutions, at first as an approximation of exile, later as a manifestation of community rejection of its deviants (if only for the brief period of their confinement), as well as the high specialization of tasks in modern society. Legal offenders, juvenile and adult alike, are viewed as persons who violate dominant values and drain off resources that might otherwise be used for more worthwhile purposes. Negative attitudes toward the deviants readily expand to include the organizations responsible for changing them. Although public disfavor may be greater for the adult prison than for the juvenile institution, it is nonetheless a dominant theme for the latter agency. Disfavor extends to the institutions' modes of operation, especially when these do not appear to guarantee secure custody, and to its apparent effectiveness, particularly as assessed by recidivism rates. Critical opinions of people who live immediately adjacent to the institution and of groups who have frequent contact with the organization may be especially crucial. For these persons the institution's operations are much more visible; they usually have a direct if not personal interest, and their disapproval can be couched in terms appealing to such salient values as citizen safety. Such negative judgments, local and abroad, provide a rationale to keep the resources of these organizations at a minimum level.

General disfavor and local criticism generate strong pressures to emphasize custodial functions. Coping with public opinion and controlling relations with the environment become compelling tasks for the administrators. Questions of boundary-crossing by inmates tend to be critical, so that officials generally exercise cautious control of these events. Such tendencies heighten the isolation of the institution, further reducing opportunities for more expansive relations involving the gradual reintegration of the inmates in the community. This problem is indicated by the difficulties which "halfway houses" now being established in the mental health and correctional fields encounter in overcoming community skepticism. These agencies represent an effort to stage the reintegration process and, as a result of special efforts, are being treated with relative tolerance by communities. Residents of houses constitute only a very small proportion of all released patients and

inmates, however, and usually they are carefully selected and certified as "ready" to return to community life under close management.

Also contributing to the unilateral strategy is the conception of the juvenile institution as the terminal stage in the sequence of the delinquent's movement through police, courts, and other agencies dealing with offenders. Each agency has its special responsibilities, and juveniles typically receive few or no post-confinement services, much less concurrent intervention in their family or community. (A youth may be apprehended for misconduct, but this constitutes a new cycle, albeit at a heightened level.) The geographical isolation of many correctional institutions and the fact that they remove the offender from his community further reinforce the unilateral strategy.

At the same time, the institution is never wholly closed or unrelated to the flow of community events. On the current scene there are examples of programs that do not entirely isolate the delinquent from the community, and some of the institutions we studied engaged in such programs. Nevertheless, the unilateral strategy is dominant in most contemporary institutions and strong in all of them.

*Inward Perspectives*

The isolation of committed offenders and the assignment of independent responsibility for rehabilitation to the institution induce a time-limited and internally oriented perspective within the organization. Information about the behavior of former inmates after their release or other data that might be used to evaluate the efficacy of programs are seldom available. As a result, behavior and adjustment within the organization become the primary criteria of successful change. Requirements for performance vary widely among different types of institutions, but each institution must make the assumption that adequate response in terms of its internal criteria signals readiness for return to community life. Conformity and accommodation in the immediate present easily become the primary measures of success, supported by residual emphases on coercion and deprivation. The relevance of all this for inmate "reformation" and subsequent conduct in the community is largely ignored, or disputed on the assumption either that the inmate has automatically and permanently been changed or that he cannot be changed at all. Lacking feedback about the degree of carry-over or stabilization

of change, staff members encounter little challenge to their perspectives.

Reinforcing this emphasis on inmate adjustment as the criterion for success are activities involved in controlling populations of involuntary residents, most of whom have demonstrated their capability for deviant and sometimes assaultive behavior. In the adult prison this emphasis customarily results in a sense of constant jeopardy and of a need for continuous surveillance among the staff. Perhaps because of age differences, the sense of omnipresent danger is muted within the juvenile institution. Surveillance procedures are generally less elaborate, although personnel believe they must be ever watchful and at least potentially in firm control. The personal histories of many committed delinquents may suggest that they cannot be trusted and that they have little motivation to cooperate unless pressed. The purely managerial requirements for coping with large numbers of persons on a twenty-four-hour basis—scheduling, moving, and feeding them—also induce concern with immediate and visible activity. Behavior that upsets these routines, violates rules, or disturbs others will monopolize attention.

The nature of institutional regimes and demands are of central importance, for the ways these define the offender's experience and condition his future behavior within the organization's boundaries constitute the primary means by which the institution pursues its goals. The inward focus of the closed institution has another important consequence: the withering effect upon the staff of twenty-four-hour-a-day exposure to the inmates. Especially in the resource-deprived institution the low pay, the odd working hours, and the threats felt to personal security may produce disenchantment, apathy, or hostility.

*Technologies and Personnel Cadres*

In the century since construction of the first public institution for delinquents, a variety of rehabilitative philosophies have contended with and partially succeeded each other. At various times institutional regimes have emphasized farming, military discipline, vocational training, or homelike cottage life, and traces of every approach can be found in contemporary institutions. Each was based on distinctive notions about causes and cures; each was in keeping with the dominant beliefs and theories about people-changing of its time; each was introduced as an advance over some earlier model, presumably being both more humani-

tarian and more effective in achieving desired change; and each posed its own requirements for physical facilities, architecture, the qualifications and activities of staff, and daily routines. To the extent that these models required unattainable resources, generated conflicts among personnel, or involved the institution in debates over their value, pressures formed that threatened institutional stability and led to modifications in programs. The most potent forces impelling modifications in programs and defining new models have been changes in values, which have proscribed severely punitive methods, and the development of theories of human behavior that have posed new alternatives or vitiated earlier ones.

In recent decades the rapid growth of the behavioral sciences and mental health professions has also had a significant effect upon institutional models. These disciplines have developed specialized knowledge thought relevant to rehabilitation, have reaffirmed the goal of change and given a new insistence to its feasibility, and have provided some specially trained cadres. The number of trained professionals—social workers, psychologists, psychiatrists, educators with special commitments —has been so limited that professionals have been thinly distributed. Nevertheless, working in elite, publicized institutions or through government agencies and professional associations, they have had great influence. They have succeeded in defining new models of operation, usually in the direction of ameliorating repressive conditions and emphasizing permissive and positive relations with the inmates. The professionals' values are little colored by traditional perspectives, and are at variance with the predominantly working-class orientations of lower-level institutional personnel.

The introduction of professionals directly into institutions has been gradual. In some institutions, particularly smaller ones, professionals have been able to rise to executive positions, but by and large their authority has been limited. Often they prefer to maintain their distinctive expertise by adhering to such conventional professional roles as classroom teaching or two-person therapy. Also, the professionals who take positions within institutions often submit to the realities of care and custody as defined by the non-professionals and cease to play an innovative or even broadly professional role.[5] Nevertheless, more and more persons with professional skills are working in these organizations

and their power is becoming pervasive and effective even in some large state institutions.

## Multiple Goals and Indeterminate Means

Research on the correctional institution typically has been addressed to contradictions between the requirements of the goals of confinement (custody) and of change (rehabilitation). Underlying this duality of orientation has been the difficulty in giving objective assessment to the effectiveness of competing institutional means—a problem that we have suggested constitutes a major characteristic of the people-changing organization.

Several sources of difficulty arise in judging effectiveness in the case of the juvenile correctional institution. First, the relatively ambiguous dual goals generate conflict and uncertainty both inside and outside. Various staff groups and special publics may give different interpretations to "rehabilitation" and "custody" and propose different priorities. Second, whatever the particular balance of official purposes, the generality and ambiguity of these goals fail to provide a clear-cut basis for deriving specific operational patterns—thereby stimulating contention over the most appropriate types of interaction between staff and inmates. Third, the relative absence of feedback information about the inmates' subsequent behavior prevents a choice of means based on demonstrable outcomes. Recidivism rates have been utilized, but the effects of the institutional experience are usually confounded with the influences of other social systems in which the releasees act. Moreover, crude rates of recommitment cannot be used to assess the relative efficacy of differentiated practices within the institution.

These difficulties in judging effectiveness have a number of important consequences. We have suggested that the organization must develop an inferential way of making assessments. Perspectivism and an emphasis on ideologies are heightened and, because personnel subgroups adhere to somewhat different belief and value systems, there is likely to be conflict. This gives additional impetus to the focus on immediate inmate behavior. The process can be seen as a tendency toward goal displacement through an overemphasis on means. In more traditional institutions the shift of attention to internal processes results in an

emphasis on procedures for control and stability and on protective architecture. In institutions where treatment-oriented cadres are dominant, the result is an emphasis on clinical processes, diagnostic refinements, and the enhancement of professional skills. In time, these operational patterns can become self-validating, with questions about utility treated as direct challenges to the integrity of the organization. Planned innovation to increase institutional effectiveness is thus impeded by difficulties in defining means as well as ends.

*Organizations in Change*

We have seen how distinctive patterns, commitments, and dilemmas have emerged in the juvenile institution by virtue of its membership in the people-changing class and its special career in Western and American society. Our discussion has also suggested the empirical existence of a range of organizations that differ in their adaptations to processes of social change. All are affected by the rise in humanitarian values, which has raised standards generally, moved many institutions from correctional to social welfare or mental health auspices, and precluded the use of extremely repressive means; by the emergence of new social technologies and specialized personnel groups, which has generated a new optimism and furnished professional cadres claiming to have the keys to successful organizational transformation; and by a rising general demand, especially in a period of great public concern with delinquency, for rationalization of operations and higher levels of performance, which has placed many new pressures on these organizations.

As a result of such forces, the secular trend has been toward treatment. Yet, as in Riesman's metaphor for colleges and universities, change across these institutions resembles less a straight line than a "snake-like procession . . . the head of which is often turning back upon itself . . . while the middle part seeks to catch up with where the head once was."[6] Change in correctional practices always has tended to be cyclical. Only isolated cases of institutions patterned after the adult prison remain, but frequently the move toward the treatment model has been piecemeal and tenuous.

Adaptation and change involve finding some solutions to various problematic issues. In contrast to the "total institution" view which emphasizes the commonalities of various people-changing organizations,

we shall develop a framework for understanding their differences in terms of the ways these issues are dealt with in different types of organization. This analysis will be based on a comparative study of several correctional institutions for male juvenile offenders. The basic theoretical problems of our research were to characterize the juvenile institution as a type of organization undergoing change, to analyze and explain major variations in organizational patterns within this type, and to assess and account for the outcomes of these patterns. The substantive concern stimulating our study was for the conditions necessary to create and maintain a precarious social structure, the "treatment-oriented" correctional institution.

## NOTES

1. We use the label "people-processing" to refer to a set of organizations similar to people-changing organizations in many respects but involved principally with the problem of adaptation—relating people to sustenance and welfare. These organizations also focus on people, but mainly to service them and to change their environments, not to change the persons themselves.

2. Erving Goffman, "On the Characteristics of Total Institutions," in Donald R. Cressey (ed.), *The Prison: Studies in Institutional Organization and Change* (New York: Holt, Rinehart and Winston, 1961), pp. 15–106.

3. On problems of the technology of mental hospitals, see Charles Perrow, "Hospitals: Technology, Structure, and Goals," in James G. March (ed.), *Handbook of Organizations* (Chicago: Rand McNally, 1965); and on several points made here, see Robert D. Vinter, "Analysis of Treatment Organizations," *Social Work*, 8 (July, 1963), 3–15.

4. For a history of these organizations, see Mayer Zald, "Multiple Goals and Staff Structure: A Comparative Study of Correctional Institutions for Juvenile Delinquents," unpublished Ph.D. dissertation (The University of Michigan, 1960), pp. 6–11; and for an earlier statement of the major characteristics of this type of organization, see Zald, "The Correctional Institution for Juvenile Offenders: An Analysis of Organizational 'Character,'" *Social Problems* 8 (Summer, 1960), 57–67.

5. For the classic statement of this phenomenon, see Harvey Powelson and Reinhard Bendix, "Psychiatry in the Prison," *Psychiatry*, 14 (February, 1951), 73–86.

6. David Riesman, *Constraint and Variety in American Education* (Garden City: Doubleday, 1958), p 35.

# Chapter 2

# ORGANIZATIONAL VARIATIONS

From the beginning of our research our basic questions had to do with variations in organizational goals. We were interested in the consequences of different goals—especially traditional custodial ends as against modern rehabilitative goals—for organizational structure, staff perspectives and behavior toward the inmates, and inmate behavior. Our aim was to classify institutional goals in as parsimonious a fashion as possible and then to assess how far such a scheme could carry us in predicting various organizational outcomes. Another aim was to investigate possible contradictions between goals and to discover ways in which structured conflicts might arise as new goals are introduced. We also were intrigued with the sources of organizational goals, the conditions under which different goals can be implemented, the effects of implementing treatment goals only partially, and the ways in which relationships of the institution to the parent organization and the local community might influence organizational goals and behavior.

The development of these questions essentially involved the explication of the concept and implications of organizational goals coupled with an institutional analysis of the juvenile institution. As our research progressed, we became aware that we were also dependent upon a voluntaristic theory of organizational behavior rooted in the activities of the executive. Here goals are clearly problematic. We ask how the goal-setting and decision-making functions of the executive, analyzed in terms of *executive strategies* formulated and executed in interaction with organization and environment, influence the organization's fate. Our aim is to develop concepts focusing on the executive as a way of grasping complex and interactive organizational processes.

## THEORETICAL FRAMEWORK

*Substantive Implications of Goals*

Reference to goals has always been central to the study of complex organizations. In the Weberian tradition, the bureaucracy is distinguished from other groups under the criterion that it maximizes rational orientation toward goals or, as put by Parsons, that it exhibits a "primacy of orientation to the attainment of a specific goal."[1] Students of organization have frequently analyzed the processes by which organizations succeed or fail in attaining their goals or suffer displacement of goals. In the pursuit of these and other problems a variety of conceptions of goals have emerged, all useful in understanding organizational behavior and all complementary to some extent in that each focuses on a different point of an end-means hierarchy. The major conceptions are[2]

*Goals as official mandates.* Goals are analyzed for their scope and complexity and as a yardstick against which effectiveness can be assessed, or studied as a focus for organizational activity under a rational model of organization.[3]

*Goals as outputs to external agents.* Goals are identified with functions performed for the larger society[4] or, at a less global level, with outputs to those who legitimate the organization and supply it with resources. This view, focusing on relationships with publics and controlling agents, emphasizes the recurring necessity of defining and creating goals.[5]

*Goals as personal and group commitments.* Goals are seen as the implementation of the executive's values, perhaps determined broadly outside the organization but "internalized" or specified through the executive; or they are seen as the ends and values of the cadre that is dominant among various competing interest groups, including the executive group.[6]

*Goals as the essential constraints built into the organization.* Constraints flow from the basic task of the organization[7] or from the particular sets of commitments, competencies, and predispositions it has accumulated.[8]

Only the last of these conceptions begins to indicate the potentials that analysis of the substantive implications of goals offers for the comparative study of organizations. Bureaucracies cannot be understood purely as social systems; it is necessary also to look at the culture—at the content expressed in goals, which defines certain arrangements and

activities as appropriate.[9] Organizations have been classified into types by their very general goals,[10] but we suspect that the prime utility of an analysis of the substantive implications of goals will be found in distinguishing among organizations that are similar in most respects.

Our approach, although recognizing the relevance of the diverse aspects of goals we indicated, is to identify them with the conception of the organization's task held by the members whose positions make their definitions of events authoritative.[11] Their conception of task is expressed in their views of the organization's desired end-product, the "materials" it must work with,[12] the ideal and practical requirements of the task, and the organization's distinctive competencies for it. The goals imply and set limits upon the organizational technologies seen as appropriate. Thus goals define alternative sets of social relations between staff and inmates as required or preferred.

Operationally, this approach will lead us to develop models of organizations classified by their goals. Both to satisfy our definition and to avoid problems of slippage and tautology, we shall characterize the goals of each organization—in the final analysis and to the extent possible—wholly on the basis of what the executive indicated were his goal conceptions, as manifested in his strategies for action.

### Sets of Beliefs and Goals in the Juvenile Institution

In order to classify the goals of juvenile correctional institutions we must look at various sets of beliefs. These give organizational activities substance empirically. They specify "who" the inmates are, what they did that got them into trouble, why they became deviant, what their current orientations are, and how to change them. The beliefs, derived from the larger society and certain subsystems such as professional groups, also are generated and reconciled in the day-to-day operations of the organization. The major sets, ordered on a continuum from those making simple assumptions about the production of change to those making complex assumptions, are

*Incarceration and Deprivation.* The mechanism is basically deterrence. The organization provides experiences leading to a decision by the inmate to end his deviance. This system involves a simple pleasure-pain psychology in which the inmate will do so only if he sees its bad consequences. The inmate may be seen as willfully deviant, so that he

must consciously decide to change, or as deficient in intelligence and human or moral qualities although capable of being conditioned to respond satisfactorily. The principal model here is the prison, where a well-tested technology of custody, deprivation, and order implies the view that the inmates understand and will change only through force and punishment. (In the prison, however, many personnel may "backslide" into the view that the inmates are not likely to change at all.) The prison model assumes that conformity within the institution indexes conformity after release.

*Authority and Obedience.* It is assumed that the inmate must learn to submit his own willfulness to the authority of others. This, too, is a simple view of man, but it is more complex than the previous one. Applied to the juvenile delinquent, it assumes that the inmate has not heretofore learned respect and obedience; the family is inevitably the villain.

*Learning.* The assumption is that good habits must be learned in several areas of behavior. In the case of the juvenile delinquent, it assumes that he has not learned the correct habits because of a disorganized home life and social environment. The most clear-cut model involving learning is, obviously, the academic and vocational school. The school uses mass handling, surveillance, order, and custody, but the means of change are the acquisition of skills, knowledge, mental discipline, and responsible work performance. In the case of delinquents, the inmates are thought to lack an appreciation for the rewards of knowledge, skill, and industry, and it is believed that a structured environment will give them the skills and habits for adult life. The measures of success here are the mastery of skills and hard work. Two other important models, the military academy and the institution preparing persons for religious orders, stress both the belief systems of authority-obedience and learning.

*Socialization.* Socialization as a belief system is even more complicated; the notion is that of "nurturance." All aspects of behavior are to be changed. In contrast to the first two systems, this system and, to an extent, the learning system see the production of change as more normal than abnormal. The major model here is the family, adapted to the juvenile institution through the cottage parent system. The technology uses withdrawal of affection, unwritten norms, and sometimes mild physical punishment. There is little mass handling, considerable indi-

vidualization of rewards and penalties, and an assumption of normal development in a secure, supportive, patterned environment. It is assumed the house parent system will provide a healthy substitute for the family, especially with the younger inmates. Performance in a "well-rounded" variety of activities is the criterion of success.

*Therapy.* Belief in therapy returns to the presumption of thorough-going deviance but embodies very complex assumptions about what to do about it. Previous socialization is seen not as simply inadequate but as deviant. The deviance is thought to be deep-seated, and the other belief systems we have enumerated are thought to be superficial. Rehabilitation is to take place through extensive changes in character and personality. There are two major submodels, one individual and the other milieu. The first stresses therapy, counselling, and casework—two-person analytic techniques. Under this model, custody and control are to be reduced to the manipulation of affect and the threat to transfer the inmate to a less permissive institution, and there is little mass handling and much individualization of rewards and punishment. The inmate is seen as one suffering from the classic psychoanalytic problems: neuroses, character disorders, and so on. The milieu model, developed in some experimental mental hospitals, uses more group handling, although custody and order are not to be stressed; and it seeks to work through manipulation of the psychological and social environment to reinforce accepted norms and to isolate and reduce deviant norms. The problems are seen as deriving from the inmate's beliefs, definitions of the situation, and ways of reacting to stimuli—expressions of his personality, although not necessarily indicating mental illness. Both models are highly dependent upon psychologically or psychiatrically trained professionals; the models discussed earlier, although they may require the use of professionals for screening and classifying inmates or working with exceptional cases, are outside contemporary psychology, psychiatry, or social work. For evidence of change, the therapy model requires an individualized scrutiny of motives and feelings.

These sets of beliefs imply a number of variations in organizational goals and activities depending upon which set or combination of sets is adopted. With due respect to the excess meaning and oversimplification that the words "custody" and "treatment" may entail, we find it useful to define a rough continuum of organizational types on the basis of these terms. The continuum refers to the organization's dominant

goals and runs parallel to our ordering of belief systems by the comlexity of their assumptions about change. At the custodial end, incarceration, deprivation, obedience, and authority are emphasized; and at the treatment pole, therapy.

## Institutional Models

The analysis of beliefs and goals allows us to define a set of three major organizational models, ranged along the custody-treatment continuum, into which we shall be able to classify the six organizations we have studied according to their goals.

*Obedience/conformity.* Habits, respect for authority, and training in conformity are emphasized. The technique is *conditioning.* Obedience/conformity maintains undifferentiated views of its inmates, emphasizes immediate accommodation to external controls, and utilizes high levels of staff domination with many negative sanctions. It is the most custodial type of juvenile institution presently found in the United States, for humanitarian pressures have eliminated the incarceration-deprivation institution as a viable empirical type.

*Re-education/development.* Inmates are to be changed through *training.* Changes in attitudes and values, acquisition of skills, the development of personal resources, and new social behaviors are sought. Compared to the obedience/conformity type, this type provides more gratifications and maintains closer staff-inmate relations.

*Treatment.* The treatment institution focuses on the psychological *reconstitution* of the individual. It seeks more thoroughgoing personality change than the other types. To this end it emphasizes gratifications and varied activities, with punishments relatively few and seldom severe. In the individual treatment-variant considerable stress is placed on self-insight and two-person psychotherapeutic practices. In the milieu treatment-variant attention is paid to both individual *and* social controls, the aim being not only to help the inmate resolve his personal problems but also to prepare him for community living.

In addition to these three types a special case, the *mixed goal* type, played a large role in our thinking prior to our intensive fieldwork. This type would emphasize custody and treatment goals simultaneously. As it turned out, none of the institutions—even the one we shall call "Mixter"—was clearly a mixed goal type. As notions of *degree*, however,

mixed goals and bifurcation will have clear import for some of the analysis.

*Outcomes: Basic Assumptions and Hypotheses*

Consideration of the character of the juvenile institution, the substantive implications of goals, and executive behavior suggests the following guiding propositions:

1. The substantive characteristics of goals will have consequences for many aspects of organizational behavior, including staff perceptions of institutional purpose and beliefs about the inmates, day-to-day operating patterns, and staff modes of authority in handling the inmates. Use of the typology of institutional models ranked along the rough custody-treatment continuum on the basis of goal emphases will provide a way to discern these consequences.

2. Organizational goals are made operational through the activities of the executive, whose essential task is to develop strategies reconciling dilemmas involved in relating the organization to its environment, explicating its goals, and defining staff roles and tasks. The strategies developed will influence not only the content of organization activities but also the structure of authority and power, the degree of coordination and interdependence among staff groups, and the level of conflict in the organization.

3. Different organizational types, having variant ways of controlling and attempting change in the inmates, will give rise to different inmate responses. Specifically, staff-inmate authority relations, rewards and sanctions, and levels of control should induce more cooperative, positive, and change-oriented inmate behavior and perspectives toward the organization, staff, and self in treatment-oriented organizations than in the obedience/conformity and re-education/development institutions.

4. Differences in organizational type will also have consequences for the patterns of social relations and leadership that emerge among the inmates. These in turn will have further impact upon the behavior and perspectives of the inmates with regard to the institution, staff, and self.

## RESEARCH DESIGN

The research was comparative, inclusive, and to some extent longitudinal. We studied a non-random sample of six institutions, selected to

maximize differences in goals but including both public and private and large and small organizations. The study was inclusive in embracing all major levels of organizational activity along with relevant groups external to the institutions. It was longitudinal not only in that we attempted to reconstruct the histories of these organizations but also in that we collected the major bodies of our data at two points in time, although only a year apart.

*Selecting Institutions*

We studied only institutions for boys because the majority of institutions in the country are for males alone, more is known about delinquency among boys than girls, and our analysis would be much easier without sex contrasts. Four of the organizations were in the same northern state and the others were in different regions of the country, one in a southern border state.

Selection began with an analysis of information on all institutions that received over half their inmates under court commitments for delinquency in the state in which we eventually studied four organizations. We rated the institutions on inmate-staff ratios, classifications of their official goal statements, and reports made by licensing officials. These measures seemed to give a rough indication of commitment to custodial or treatment philosophies; and, after high correlations were found among the indices, we established a composite rating and selected four institutions apparently representing a good range of goals and sizes. We studied three of these, but when we found that one small custodial institution was *very* small and located in a remote area of the state, we substituted another that a state official persuaded us was more custodial than our ratings had indicated. Unfortunately, the official had confused this institution with a custodial detention home—but by the time we found out it was a benign institution stressing training it was too late to change the sample, and we ended up without a really custodial small institution.

The other three institutions from this state represented a good range of goals, but only one was large. We decided then to select two large public institutions from other states, preferably ones near the extremes of the goal continuum. Various persons with knowledge of the national corrections field assisted in making the final selections. In the end we

settled on one institution known to use physical punishment freely and thought typical of many resource-poor state institutions with very limited programs for rehabilitation, plus a treatment institution whose reputation was supported by its goal statements, brochures, and staffing patterns.

Ranked on the custody-treatment continuum and classified by the institutional types we came to assign to them, the institutions are represented by fictional names in Table 2.1. The first letters of each name

### Table 2.1—Goals, Sizes, and Auspices of the Sample Institutions*

| | SIZE AND AUSPICES | |
|---|---|---|
| Goals | Large Public | Small Private |
| Obedience/conformity | Dick (235) Mixter (400) | |
| Re-education/development | | Regis (55) Bennett (35) |
| Treatment | Milton (180) | Inland (65) |

\* Approximate numbers of inmates in parentheses.

serve as a mnemonic device, representing the first letters of the characteristic goal.[13]

*Dick* (for Discipline)—A large public institution with no treatment program, whose staff felt no lack because of it, that concentrated on custody, hard work, and discipline.

*Mixter* (for Mixed Goals)—A very large public institution that to an extent emphasized both custody and treatment. It attempted some measure of treatment but presented to most boys an environment of surveillance, frequent use of negative sanctions, and other corollaries of custody. A few months after the first field study of Mixter, it established a separate small maximum security unit, *Maxwell* (for Maximum Security), in another part of the state. We were able to make some study of the early development of this unit.

*Regis* (for Religious and, in Latin, Rules)—A small institution run by a religious order. It emphasized full scheduling of the day's work, study, and recreational activities together with indoctrination and enforcement of the virtues of authority and religiosity. This was one of the two institutions where the inmates went off the grounds daily to attend classes with ordinary parochial or public school children.

*Bennett* (for Benign)—A quite small private institution that, like Regis, stressed neither modern treatment techniques nor custodialism and sent its boys off grounds to school each day. Inmates lived in a firm but rather home-like environment.

*Milton* (for Milieu Therapy)—A fairly large public institution. The clinical staff had much power, influenced the non-professional staff to provide the inmates with considerable freedom of behavior, and provided a round of "therapeutic experiences."

*Inland* (for Individual Therapy)—A small private "residential treatment center" in which the clinicians were in virtually complete control. They allowed much freedom to the inmates while stressing the use of psycho-therapeutic techniques to attempt to bring about major personality change.

In the course of the research it became clear that there was an additional dimension we had not sought. Both re-education/development institutions, Regis and Bennett, were open, sending their inmates out of the institution each day, and thus differentiating the organizations.

## Research Techniques

Major field work was done from 1958 through 1960. The project began with preliminary observation and interviewing in Mixter and Inland. Access was gained to all institutions by getting in touch with the executives. At Mixter and Dick we contacted the parent organizations as well. We explained the research and assured officials that no clerical assistance from the institution would be required, that the study would be conducted with minimum disruption of routine, and that the institution, staff, and inmates would not be named. Executives were aware that knowledgeable persons might be able to identify particular institutions, but they were mainly concerned with insuring that the general public could not. No institution selected for study refused to participate, and in all but one there was full formal cooperation. In the latter case we ultimately were able to pursue all research plans but occasionally had to proceed very slowly, negotiating individual steps carefully.

Initial explorations in each organization consisted of informal interviews with members of the executive core and other staff members and inmates. These contacts revealed enough about the formal and informal structure, official terms, and local argot to enable preparation of staff and inmate questionnaires for the first of two intensive studies of each

institution. These studies involved administration of the questionnaires, formal and informal interviewing including lengthy conversations with the executive, observation, and coding of data from files. Between the intensive surveys, held twelve months apart in each institution, we revised the questionnaires and maintained contact through occasional visits and "executive seminar" feedback sessions. All institutions agreed to participate in the second survey, and so the cycle repeated, following virtually the same data collection procedures, except that we did not obtain staff questionnaire responses at Regis and Bennett the second time.

Neither staff nor inmate questionnaires asked the respondent's name. Staff members filled theirs out individually, usually in free moments on the job. Inmates completed theirs in groups generally of fifteen to thirty-five boys, with the researchers usually reading each question aloud slowly and twice. At least 85 per cent of the staff in each institution in the first survey and 72 per cent in the second returned their questionnaires, and almost all the inmates completed the questionnaires in both surveys. We were reasonably satisfied with the adequacy of our data collection procedures.[14]

In our presentation of findings it ordinarily is irrelevant whether the data came from the first or second survey; we usually do not distinguish between the two, except in Chapter 10, where we focus on changes between surveys on comparable items. In the main we analyze staff questionnaire results from the first survey, when the questionnaire was administered in all institutions, and inmate questionnaire results from the second survey, when the questionnaire had been enlarged and improved. Findings on items asked both times are reported without qualification only if the same organizational differences emerged from each.

For details of research procedures, the reader should consult the appendices: Appendix A presents and discusses the staff questionnaire, Appendix C the inmate questionnaire; Appendix B describes the construction of scales and indices from staff data; Appendix D discusses factor analyses and index construction made on the inmate data.

## SKETCHES OF THE INSTITUTIONS

For readers interested in the backgrounds and characteristics of the institutions we present brief individual descriptions—accounts that also

illustrate some of the pressures for and adaptations to change ex
the juvenile corrections field.

### Dick (Discipline)

Dick was a large public institution located in a rural area of a border
state, with heavy unemployment, a declining population, and an
economy of agriculture, mining, and some manufacturing. The state
had few large cities, and most inmates came from depressed mining
areas. Levels of education and health service in the state were low compared to the rest of the nation, and especially low compared to the two
other states in which sample institutions were located.

The institution occupied several hundred acres of land that included
a large farm and a coal mine. There were no fences, and well-kept
grounds, rolling hills, and widely spaced buildings gave Dick a pleasant
air. Most of the buildings were old. Two new cottages and a gymnasium
had been built since World War II. There were five living units for
inmates. The largest was the top floor of a three-story industrial arts
building (a structure otherwise unused at the time of our first survey)
that served as a dormitory for up to eighty of the oldest boys. Another
sixty could be accommodated in a wing of the administration building.
An old frame house housed the thirty-five youngest and smallest boys,
and the two newer cottages contained forty to forty-five boys each.
Married couples were in charge of the three cottages; only men worked
in other living units.

Dick was created by act of the legislature in the 1890s. In 1939 it
had a population of 465 boys. The armed services soon took many of
these boys, so that by 1943 the population had declined to 222. Despite
a rise in the delinquency rate in the state, the inmate population remained roughly the same up to the time of our study. This was because
the institution began discharging boys when they reached eighteen, if
they had appropriate homes, and reducing length of stay (on the average
to between ten and eleven months when we did our study), and because the state's population had declined.

Dick operated under a state board responsible for all charitable and
penal institutions. Although some agencies in the state operated under
a merit system this department did not, so that institutional staffing was
subject to political patronage. Theoretically the patronage system did

not include the academic teachers, but in practice it seemed to do so. The party in power had won control of the state government, after many years out of office, shortly before our study began. Almost three quarters of the staff, including the executive, had come to the institution since the political change. Most of the remaining personnel who were members of the opposition party were removed over the next two years. Dick was the only state institution in the study that did not operate under some form of civil service procedure.

Dick also was the only institution studied that still operated a farm. Older boys, not in school, supplied its stable work force, with other boys working during peak periods of harvesting and canning. Reports in the 1940s indicated that the farm then produced about 70 per cent of the food used by the institution, and statistics from one year showed that 36 per cent of the dollar-value of the yield had been sold outside the institution. Statistics were not available for the study period, but it was apparent that the farm was still economically important.

The institution maintained an accredited academic school, but inmates were not required to attend it after reaching sixteen, and few pursued schooling beyond the ninth grade. At the time of our first survey the vocational education program was very limited, but during the period of our study the executive managed to secure funds for some additional vocational teachers. Although the academic school emphasized the teaching of skills, the farm and other work programs (grounds, kitchen, maintenance, and the like) did not.

The formal aims of the institution had remained roughly the same over the last two decades. A 1943 report to the legislature said the purpose of the institution was "to offer an opportunity for . . . rehabilitation [through changing] the thinking of these youth by offering purposeful activity through education, wholesome recreation and practical work on the farm and in the shops." This statement was repeated in most subsequent reports. There were two important changes over these decades, however. First, reliance on the military model was reduced. Earlier, boys were drilled and marched in cadence, cottage parents were referred to as "commanders" (as they still were in the two largest cottages), "outline boys" (who managed the other boys under staff supervision) were given considerable power to punish other inmates, and sanctions were stronger. In this change Dick's history followed that of many state institutions for delinquents.

Second, the institution, running counter to general trends, abandoned even the minimal use of clinical or social work professionals. The 1943 report noted the presence of a full-time psychologist doing diagnostic and classification work and teaching remedial classes, and proclaimed that "social casework is carried on. Boys are given an opportunity to discuss and work through their problems privately with a sympathetic person, trained and experienced in the field." By the time of our study, there had been no psychologist, even on a consulting basis, for several years, and the social work staff consisted of one person without college training (the executive said he would not hire a *trained* social worker) aided by the counselling activities of the chaplain. This change, coupled with the fact that the farm was still playing a large role in the program for inmates, indicates that Dick, relatively isolated geographically, was largely unaffected by changes taking place in many state institutions.

## Mixter (Mixed Goals)

Mixter was a public institution, the largest and oldest organization studied, and generally considered the "last resort" in the northern industrial state—one with many private institutional facilities—that it served. It was located in a pleasant residential section not far from the center of a fairly large city. Mixter housed its approximately four hundred boys in fourteen old and drab cottages. Boys lived in groups of from sixteen to thirty-three. Most cottage groupings were based on age and size similarities, but four were reserved for special groups: the reception cottage, the cottage for "emotionally disturbed" boys, the cottage for certain of the "chronic truants" and others requiring close controls, and the cottage for older "aggressive" boys. Mixter had a relatively large proportion of urban, multiple-offense delinquents and was under the jurisdiction of a state department that also had authority over most social welfare matters.

Mixter's history is in some ways prototypical of the development of the correctional institution for delinquents in the United States. Mixter was affected sharply by the deterioration of its buildings, which resulted from fiscal difficulties, and by conflicts arising out of changing definitions of child care and welfare. At one time or another the institution emphasized farming, military training, and industrial training. With time its controls shifted from a major reliance on corporal punishment to more benign sanctions. In its later years it added psychological,

psychiatric, and case-work services, but without making extensive use of these technologies.

Mixter was founded in the mid-nineteenth century, before the decades of most rapid development of institutions in this country. When the city grew, enclosing Mixter, the state sold some of the institution's newly valuable land and the farm program became restricted to work on a small truck garden. The growth of the city accompanied the industrialization of the state, a rapid expansion of the population, and an increase in the delinquency problem. About 1925 a new field house was constructed, and the administration building was remodeled, but no new cottages were built thereafter despite the fact that several had to be closed as fire hazards. In 1932 the institution housed about seven hundred boys, but by 1940 the condemnation of buildings reduced the number to 460. Starting in 1945 the postwar rise in delinquency was taking its toll: To accommodate the same numbers, Mixter gradually had to reduce the average stay of inmates from nineteen months to seven and a half months at the time of our study.

The last four decades at Mixter testify to the difficulties of eradicating punitiveness. In 1925 a former state police officer became executive, banned corporal punishment, and attempted to operate a program based on firmness and training. By 1940 he had become isolated from his staff and skeptical of the possibilities either of changing his staff or of gaining more resources from the state and cooperation from the community. Especially troublesome were the cottage parents, who seemed to use whatever sanctions they considered necessary to attain strict control. The executive criticized them for a lack of common sense and understanding but found no way to curb their power. Early in his regime this executive had opened the doors of the disciplinary cottage so that its boys could go to other buildings for schooling or other activities, believing that this would force the cottage parents to work more intensively with the boys. He also started an athletic program that he believed cut down disciplinary problems. By the end of his tenure, however, the disciplinary cottage was closed again.

The year 1941 marked the beginning of a decade of upheaval at the institution—a period in which major efforts were made to build a consistent, non-repressive program. It started when a national leader in correctional reform was called in to evaluate operations. His first report, on cottage life and discipline, led to the executive's resignation. The

successor was given a broad mandate for reform: He was expected to establish a counselling service, to set up separate departments (all staff members except those in the school had been reporting directly to the executive or his assistant), and to move toward a less regimented and more inmate-centered program.

Five years later another survey produced the charge that the institution had not changed in any meaningful way from its traditional repressiveness. The survey report stated that although a supervisor of cottage life had been appointed, many of the cottage parents continued to bypass him, rendering him impotent, flooding the top executives with specific problems, and thereby inhibiting the development and interpretation of an overall philosophy. The survey also claimed that, despite the fact that "rehabilitation not revenge" was the official motto, retribution was the true guiding principle.

After still another executive tried and failed, an executive known for reform was imported from another state in about 1950. He managed to accomplish many of the recommendations of the surveys: Departments were structured more formally, with cottage parents really made responsible to a director of cottage life; the counselling service was enlarged further, with each counselor responsible for seventy to eighty boys instead of a hundred and fifty; and a half-time psychiatrist was hired. After three years the reformer left. His successor, an educator, had served in the position for ten years at the start of our study. The organizational changes adopted around 1950 were still in operation in 1959.

At the time of our study Mixter still faced a great deal of community animosity centering on truancies. Community hostility had been a problem for several decades and led to what an early report called a "runaway psychosis" among staff members. Major organizational effort had been and continued to be devoted to the control of runaways. Partially spurred by the persistence of this concern with truancy, the parent organization increased its demands that rehabilitative programs be further implemented. Mixter, unlike Dick, showed the influence of the mental hygiene and child welfare movements, but it had remained bound by what staff members saw as the necessity to placate the surrounding community. Often the demands of the parent organization were complied with only in form—for example, the integration of all clinical services demanded in 1952 was accomplished by establishing a

single department of treatment, but personnel continued to perform their tasks independently. Near the end of our study, the parent organization, still critical of what it saw as custodial emphases, transferred the executive to another position in the state government.

*The Maxwell (Maximum Security)* unit of Mixter, established shortly before our second survey, was located in a semi-rural part of the state. It was relatively autonomous. Maxwell received all of its inmates from Mixter, where they had been defined as requiring a two or three month program of close supervision and maximum security, but the unit determined whether and when they would be returned to Mixter or released directly to their homes.

Maxwell was designed for 100 boys, housed in a single building with a small recreation area and surrounded by a high fence. To the extent possible the building was designed and decorated like a modern suburban school. The boys lived in four regular wings and a detention wing, each containing virtually indestructible single rooms. The regular wings were graded by openness of program, the boys first living in the closed reception wing and then being moved into another closed wing or a relatively open wing that they could leave for the dining hall, gym, or classes. Doors throughout the institution were always locked. A psychiatrist spent one day a week at the institution, and two trained social workers, one of them the executive, worked there full time.

*Regis (Religious and, in Latin, Rules)*

Regis was a private institution located in a working class area of a major city. Its purposes as well as location had changed since its founding in the 1900s. The original aim was to provide a proper moral atmosphere for youths working in the city. It was operated by a Catholic brotherhood in a large house. Regis allowed the boys to keep a small portion of their wages and banked the rest for them after deducting nominal fees for room and board. It served working boys until the 1930s, when it stopped attracting the kinds of boys it desired. The official historian of Regis had this to say in 1930:

> In these days such homes do not appeal to the young man whose wages render him independent. . . . Of necessity there must be rules and regulations regarding suitable hours at night [but] as amusements are now varied and cheap, anything that savors of the curtailment of so-called liberty is not

appealing to the thoughtless boy, who looks no further than the present hour of enjoyment. . . . There are not many to take advantage of the kindness of the Church in providing such a place for those who are homeless or come as strangers to the city for work. Thus, Regis has but a few working boys today; but it houses orphans of school age who attend a neighborhood or parochial school.

For a time Regis shifted to the care of dependent and neglected children. Then it was closed for several years. It went back into operation after World War II, when a Catholic lay group, which had been running a small home for dependent and neglected children since 1933, asked the order to take over and expand this facility. With the lay organization taking responsibility for financing, a new building, with a capacity of forty-eight boys and a staff of nine or ten, was erected a few years later.

In recent years Regis shifted its intake from dependent and neglected to delinquent boys, a shift sanctioned by the parent organization with some misgivings. This change reflected the executive's view that there was an increasing need for services to delinquents with few Catholic facilities to provide them. After the change in intake the population of Regis gradually doubled to a high of sixty, necessitating arrangements for some boys to sleep in homes in the neighborhood. Admission criteria excluded boys with serious psychiatric or homosexual problems, low intelligence, or apparent inability to adjust to a very open program. The program emphasized education and religion, although recently some professional social and psychological services as well as psychiatric consultation had become available. Boys stayed in the institution an average of eight and a half months.

Under the rules of the teaching order that staffed Regis, the executive and his assistant were rotated elsewhere at least every five years. The other brothers, students at a nearby university whose experiences in the institution were seen as training, stayed a shorter time. The parent organization was a lay board of citizens who sponsored and supervised a number of community programs for Catholic youth. It exercised rather close financial control over the institution, but allowed the executive a good deal of latitude in program, intake criteria, and so forth. Since the brothers were not paid for their work, per diem cost was small.

The boys attended twenty different schools, public and parochial, in the city. They walked or rode buses without supervision. In addition

they regularly attended entertainment and sporting events in the city in groups. Runaways were low despite this open program, in part because the truant probably would be sent back to court and then on to a state correctional institution. Most boys had private rooms, and a few lived in small dormitories. The rooms were well furnished, and the boys were allowed to personalize them with pictures, model airplanes, radios, and so forth.

## Bennett (Benign)

Bennett was the small private institution we erroneously thought would be repressive. In fact, it served moderately delinquent children and attempted to develop a homelike atmosphere. With its thirty-six boys and twelve staff members Bennett was the smallest institution studied. It also was the one institution that had no Negro inmates. The institution was located in the country, close to a middle class resort area. Most inmates came from a large industrial city nearby. Inmates were housed in two new cottages and a dormitory located in an old house that also contained the director's office and living quarters. Most of the boys in the new cottages had private, although doorless, rooms. The property was surrounded by woods and included a small lake, a stream, and a large playing field.

Bennett was founded in the middle 1940s to provide rehabilitation through farming. It was initially sponsored by a service club in the nearby city, which was concerned that the city's detention home had become overcrowded, with some boys staying there for months or even years. Bennett started as a complete farm for about seventeen boys, but the farm lost money and the boys were not interested in agriculture. When the present executive arrived about four years after the institution opened, he convinced the parent organization that the farm plan was unrealistic and argued for expansion. The farm was dropped and a few years later the two new cottages were built. The institution was controlled by a thirty-six-member board composed of representatives from the local county court and from the youth-serving organization that provided support.

The few boys who were in the ninth grade or higher attended a high school in the large city; the rest attended elementary school in a small community a few miles away. The inmates were carefully

selected. They tended to come from broken homes and to be "pre-delinquent," charged with minor offenses like truancy or minor steal-ing. They were younger than those at any of the other institutions. The mean stay at the time of our study was twenty months.

### Milton (Milieu Treatment)

With about 175 inmates, Milton was the smallest of the three large public institutions studied. It was located on the edge of a large city in a Midwestern farm state but separated from residential and com-mercial areas by farms and woods. The boys lived in six units, five age-graded and the sixth a small facility for boys thought to need isolation or restriction. The cottage for the youngest boys was new, but the rest were quite old, as were most other structures except for a vocational arts building.

Milton was founded before the turn of the century as part of a state department for eleemosynary institutions. Until 1946 the changes in its program were similar to those occurring generally. Thus it began with a large farm program, which it then almost totally eliminated. During World War I its military program was expanded and made com-pulsory for all boys, with the inmates organized into companies, march-ing and military decorum emphasized, and staff members referred to as officers. This program also made use of a merit system for inmates that had been put into operation by 1900. The system, in use at many in-stitutions at the time, was used to evaluate both the individual boy and the company in which he lived. If a company was rated well, everyone in it earned merit points and an earlier release. Boys with serious offenses needed extra points to obtain freedom.

The rigid paramilitary structure lasted until the 1940s, although there was increasing criticism of the institution for emphasizing con-tainment (major sanctions were reserved for truants) and for unauthor-ized use of corporal punishment by lower-level personnel. As early as 1920, annual reports referred to brutalizing behavior evidenced in earlier periods. Boys had been locked in collars for punishment and there had been a whipping post directly behind the chapel.

Change started in 1946 when a new superintendent was appointed. An educator by profession, he began to alter the program with mis-sionary zeal. He did not seem to have a clear-cut goal in mind but

strongly felt that the old system was inadequate. The result was movement toward modern treatment ideas and personnel. The changes preceded the rapid postwar growth of the mental health movement that occurred in this state, but this movement was crucial to Milton. Once it was started, the institution was able to base changes on the philosophy and resources it commanded. Professional personnel became more available, and the growth of the movement made the public and legislature relatively receptive to treatment concepts.

The transformation to a "milieu" institution came later with the development of a cottage-committee structure. Initially, the addition of social workers, psychologists, and psychiatrists did not curtail the power and traditional disciplinary measures of the cottage parents, and the professionals often could not agree on such matters as discipline and diagnosis. A clinical psychologist then initiated the cottage committees, in which cottage parents, social workers, and psychologists or psychiatrists met to discuss each boy for whom they were responsible. They interviewed boys individually and in groups and then formulated coherent treatment plans. After some difficulties with divided responsibility because committee members officially were equals, the professional with the highest status in each committee was given its chairmanship and chief administrative responsibility for the cottage. Under his supervision the social worker focused primarily upon attempting to manipulate the home environment of the boys, while the head cottage parent focused upon the training and supervision of the other cottage parents. Several psychiatric residents from a nearby training facility conducted group therapy sessions.

The characteristics of Milton's inmates were roughly similar to those in the other state institutions, the major exception being that the inmates of this institution tended to be younger. Average stay was fifteen months at the time of our study. Milton made little use of inmate labor, and had a rather elaborate vocational program.

### Inland (Individual Treatment)

Inland was a small private institution located on the suburban outskirts of a major city. Its plant was entirely new and consisted of several distinctive and modern buildings scattered over a rolling landscape of trees and lawns. Inland differed from the other institutions in the sample in

many respects, including not only its heavy allocation of resources to individual treatment but also in the facts that its inmates had relatively high intelligence and social class levels, and a sizable proportion were privately referred.

Founded in 1890 to help discharged prisoners, Inland became a temporary home for boys soon after the state took over its initial task. In 1907 the institution again shifted its services, this time to work with delinquent boys. The original institution was located in the downtown area of the metropolis. In the second decade of the century the institution, with the aid of several philanthropists, moved to buildings constructed on about 100 acres of what was then a rural area. The newest buildings were constructed about a mile from the old site three years before our study began.

The major change at Inland over the last three decades had been a shift from its use of a model of democratic rehabilitation to its present technology of individual treatment. Working with approximately seventy boys, the institution operated a system of self-government paralleling that of the better known George Junior Republic in New York State. The degree of implementation of the system seems to have varied from one executive to another. In principle, the boys meted out discipline and decided upon the program, but at least one executive appointed the boys' officers and did not allow them to pass any "laws" with which he in any way disagreed. At times the system seems to have worked well, but at others it appears to have degenerated into corruption and exploitation among the inmates.

The idea of operating a small democratic society extended to many phases of Inland life at the time. The boys earned money from the institution for going to school, doing the dishes, working on the farm or at other jobs, performing competently, and for making good adjustments. They paid for clothes, room, and board. A boy who became affluent could afford the "luxury" diet, which included an extra dessert; a boy who was in debt or had just arrived at Inland ate "economy." In 1935 the staff, feeling that criteria for release were too vague, added a monthly point-rating procedure to the system. Theoretically, a boy could accumulate sufficient points to be discharged in six months (with mean stay under this procedure running to eleven and a half months).

Two major changes occurred at the institution in the middle 1920s. First, the institution built an additional building, raising its capacity to

over 130 boys. The new building was used primarily for younger boys, who were not allowed to govern themselves but were put under "parental" supervision. The increased capacity of the institution led to an expansion of staff from twelve to twenty-one. The second change was the hiring of two men who were to work with the boys and their families after their release. These men served as probation officers, placing boys on farms, and as liaisons with various social and public agencies. Five years later the executive attributed a decline in recidivism from 34 per cent to 17 per cent to the efficiency of the after-care program.

Starting in the late 1920s psychiatric and clinical definitions began to take hold. At first a psychiatrist served as a part-time consultant to the institution. The first full-time social worker was hired in the early Thirties. By the time of a survey in 1941 a full-time psychotherapist had been added, and by 1950 there were three psychologists and social workers. These professionals apparently had little influence, however, on basic policies, intake, the discharge of boys, or discipline.

The advent of a new director in the mid-Fifties was the occasion for several significant changes—some initiated by him and others by the clinical staff. The institution was ripe for change: The buildings had become run down and condemned as firetraps, and several key staff members who had worked at the institution for over thirty years were about to retire. Change started when a large grant from the building fund of the central voluntary financing agency of the community was obtained in order to build a new plant. Further, upon the retirement of some of the older personnel the self-governing principle and merit ratings were abandoned, and work with boys after discharge largely disappeared. A clinical psychologist became assistant director and decisions about intake, discharge, and discipline became the responsibility of the clinical staff, with the primary focus shifted to the client-therapist relationship. In developing the new program the institution reduced its capacity to seventy-five boys, and began to refuse to accept boys who were not considered "workable" material. Delinquents with neurotic problems were seen as most amenable to treatment at Inland.

Inland was governed by a thirty-member board composed of influential upper-class members of the metropolitan area. The board met monthly and worked closely with the executive. It maintained close relations with the metropolitan community fund-raising agency, which

provided approximately 70 per cent of the budget, and had informal access to foundations that occasionally supported phases of the program. Inland had highly developed relations with the community and carried on a very active public relations program. During the study period it was publicized on state-wide television programs and, occasionally, on programs with national coverage.

Boys lived in three cottages, sleeping in private rooms or in rooms of two or three. The institution maintained an elaborate nature program, which included a small zoo. Average stay was eleven and a half months, but boys who "completed" the programs remained about eighteen months.

Shortly after our first field study the executive was replaced by the assistant director.

## NOTES

1. Max Weber, *The Theory of Social and Economic Organization* (New York: Free Press, 1947), pp. 329–341; *From Max Weber,* translated by Hans Gerth and C. Wright Mills (New York: Oxford University Press, 1946), pp. 196–244; and Talcott Parsons, "A Sociological Approach to the Theory of Organizations," *Structure and Process in Modern Societies* (New York: Free Press, 1960), p. 17.

2. An initial and very helpful analysis of goals and their substantive implications was performed by one of the project participants, Mayer Zald, and published in "Comparative Analysis and Measurement of Organizational Goals: The Case of Correctional Institutions for Delinquents," *Sociological Quarterly,* 4 (1963), 206–230. For a detailed classification of conceptions of goals partially consistent with the one given here, see Charles Perrow, "Organizational Goals," *International Encyclopedia of Social Sciences,* revised edition, forthcoming.

3. The study of scope, specificity, and effectiveness is the traditional public administration approach, while the sociological utility of study of official statements has been reasserted by Alvin Gouldner in "Organizational Analysis," in Robert Merton, Leonard Broom, and Leonard Cottrell, Jr., *Sociology Today* (New York: Basic Books, 1959), pp. 400–428.

4. Parsons, *op. cit.,* pp. 44–47; Amitai Etzioni, *A Comparative Analysis of Complex Organizations* (New York: Free Press, 1961), pp. 72–73.

5. See James Thompson and William McEwen, "Organizational Goals and Environment: Goal Setting as an Interaction Process," *American Sociological Review,* 23 (February, 1958), 23–31; also Peter Drucker's argument

summarized in his statement that "There is only one valid definition of business purpose: *to create a customer,*" in *The Practice of Management* (New York: Harper, 1954), p. 37.

6. See especially Philip Selznick, "An Approach to a Theory of Bureaucracy," *American Sociological Review,* 8 (February, 1943), 47–54; and Charles Perrow, "Goals in Complex Organizations," *American Sociological Review,* 26 (December, 1961), 854–866.

7. As in the military, where preparedness for hostilities is said to induce certain characteristics—see Morris Janowitz, *Sociology and the Military Establishment* (New York: Russell Sage Foundation, 1959); and Janowitz, *The Professional Soldier* (New York: Free Press, 1960). Or as in the required "combat" or "vanguard" character imputed to the Communist Party—see Selznick, *Organizational Weapon* (New York: McGraw-Hill, 1952).

8. Selznick, *Leadership in Administration* (Evanston: Row, Peterson, 1957). This part of Selznick's work is close to ours in its attention both to institutional analysis and executive goal-setting.

9. We are making the basic distinction between cultural and social systems found in Parsons and Edward Shils (eds.), *Toward a General Theory of Action* (Cambridge: Harvard University Press, 1951), in which, simply stated, the social system is the pattern of interaction common to a population and the culture is the pattern of beliefs and belief systems of that population.

10. Etzioni, *op. cit.;* also to the extent that goals are a part of the *cui bono* classification scheme given by Peter Blau and W. Richard Scott, *Formal Organizations: A Comparative Approach* (San Francisco: Chandler, 1962).

11. These are called "product goals" in Perrow, "Organizational Goals," *op. cit.*

12. In the people-changing organization, involving a "theory of human nature." See Erving Goffman, "On the Characteristics of Total Institutions: Staff-Inmate Relations," in Donald Cressey (ed.), *The Prison: Studies in Institutional Organization and Change* (New York: Holt, Rinehart and Winston, 1961), p. 78.

13. The custody-treatment ranking of institutions by their goals is straightforward for the three major institutional types. We shall see that within types it is straightforward too for the obedience/conformity pair, Mixter's goals having some treatment components while Dick's had none. Within the other two pairs, however, rankings by goals are not so clear cut. To obtain a complete ranking useful in presenting data we look also at the nature of staff orientations and practices toward the inmates—Regis's being more custodial than Bennett's, Milton's more than Inland's. On this basis we shall speak of an overall custody-to-treatment rank order of Dick, Mixter, Regis, Bennett, Milton, Inland.

14. The total numbers of questionnaires turned in by staff and inmates in the first and second surveys, respectively, were: Dick, staff, 62 and 57, inmates, 225 and 209; Mixter, staff, 155 and 170, inmates, 403 and 364; Regis, staff, 9 (first only), inmates, 56 and 57; Bennett, staff, 12 (first only), inmates, 36 and 35; Milton, staff, 108 and 105, inmates, 185 and 155; Inland, staff, 37 and 40, inmates, 60 and 65.

*PART TWO*

# Executive Strategies

*Chapter 3*

# THE EXECUTIVE:

# FORMULATIONS OF GOALS

## EXECUTIVESHIP

Executive leadership has a key influence on organizational achievement and adaptation. Above the chief administrator fans out the complex world of the parent organization, courts, official and unofficial regulatory or standard-setting groups, and publics. Below him is spread out the organization itself: chief subordinates who constitute the executive core, other personnel, and the inmates. The environment and the internal realities of the organization both exert pressures upon the executive; his behavior has crucial effects on staff performance and inmate response. Analysis of these modes of behavior is essential, therefore, to understanding operative patterns.

At least three crucial dimensions of executive leadership shape the organization. First, the executive formulates specific goals and basic policies that give meaning and direction to the enterprise. He must formulate operational aims and policies within the range of environmental mandates and constraints. Second, the executive is the key link between the organization and its environment. The most general and pervasive influences upon organizational behavior stem from external sources, and the executive has the task of mediating between these forces and organizational exigencies. He receives both mandates and resources from the environment, and external units hold him accountable for organizational performance. Third, the executive establishes the structure of roles and responsibilities within the organization that enables it to pursue its goals. He must define tasks, allocate personnel, and manage the interdependent relations that result. As part of this endeavor, the executive must delineate the competencies appropriate to staff roles and recruit persons to fill these positions.

Analysis of these three broad areas will provide a context for understanding the behavior of employees and inmates. We shall explore the executives' efforts in these areas in terms of *strategies,* emphasizing thereby the dilemmas, contradictory directives, and imperatives for action that are faced by the chief administrators. Attention to the nature and consequences of executive strategies must also take into account the sources or antecedents of administrative activity, including the mandates given executives, previous experience or training, career commitments brought to these situations, and so on.

Although anecdotal accounts and isolated studies have provided insights into limited aspects of executive performance, there is little systematic knowledge about executiveship or conceptualization of its major phases. There is perhaps least understanding of how executives can harmonize internal and external requirements or balance seemingly incompatible demands, for prior studies have tended to focus on limited aspects of executive behavior rather than upon how the executive confronts the full range of problems that face him.

*Executive Autonomy*

In performing his role the executive is neither wholly free nor completely a prisoner. Requirements, constraints, and opportunities are presented by both the environment and the internal situation. The environment sets severe bounds on the goals the executive may formulate and the means he may use, and it restricts his resources. At the same time, he is able to select from a set of alternative cultural definitions, a range of goals and means, and a variety of possibilities for resources. Within the institution he again encounters both freedom and constraint. Traditions and the perspectives of the staff set limits, as do the types of inmate the organization receives, the size and location of the institution, and so forth. Yet the executive may retrain, discharge, or promote staff members; violate traditions or create new ones; alter intake criteria to modify the types of delinquent received; and exploit the advantages of the physical setting.

Long-established patterns of conduct may be highly resistant to change, and drastic modifications may bring anarchy or organized opposition. Furthermore, some roles are set by the experiences or training that personnel receive elsewhere: A cottage parent cannot be transformed

into a psychiatrist or a psychiatrist into a classroom teacher. Others are required by law, as in legislation prescribing the provision of an academic school for the inmates. On the other hand, psychiatrists may be placed in direct charge of cottage parents or cottage parents trained to support the efforts of clinical personnel; the academic school may be integrated in a treatment program; and the support of staff may be developed for a program of planned change.

The selection of an executive presupposes that, on the basis of his background and his presentation of himself as a candidate, he will exercise his "freedom" in certain directions; he can be removed from office if he seems to exceed this expectation too far. Yet executives derive much of their autonomy from the uncertainties and contradictory pressures that play on the correctional institution and that make the expectations broad. This general condition, together with the multiplicity and segmentation of external groups that pose demands for institutional performance, offers further opportunities for executive initiative and discretion. Conflicting demands can be balanced, new coalitions of support can be nurtured, and ingenuity can be exercised in giving specific meaning and substance to ambiguous directives. Thus conditions that one executive perceives as constraining or fraught with risk may be seen by another as inviting manipulation and assertive action.

Emphasizing the freedom of action potentially available to the executive, however, does not imply that his action is highly potent or necessarily will achieve its intended purposes. A variety of forces attenuates the effects of administrative action, and a complex interplay of behaviors and difficulties surrounds and absorbs executive activity, generating unanticipated consequences. The concept of executive leadership, nevertheless, directs attention to the rational elements in organizational performance, to the relation between ends and means, and to the assessment of action strategies.[1]

## Sources of Data

The remainder of this chapter deals with findings on executive goal formulation. Chapter 4 deals with findings on external strategies and Chapter 5 with internal strategies and staff organization. Unless otherwise indicated, descriptions of executive strategies are based as far as possible on sources of data independent of those pertaining to the be-

havior of rank-and-file staff members or inmates. We conducted repeated and prolonged interviews with each executive and his chief subordinate or assistants. Executives were closely observed at work at their desks, at staff meetings, while talking with inmates or moving about the grounds and so on, and again in the feedback sessions when we gave them findings. We also examined such direct products of their activity as formal statements, manuals, annual reports, tables of organization, and some correspondence.

Analyzing executive behavior in Milton and Inland, the treatment institutions, we must consider two pairs of administrators. This is necessary because in each place the chief executive shared much of his authority with a top subordinate—and at Inland the latter person succeeded to the directorship midway in the research.

## GOAL DEFINITION

Definition and specification of the mission or essential productive task of the institution are primary tasks of the executive, necessary to give purpose and direction to staff activity and to earn support from external units. The executive must specify goals within the limits of the basic mandates and tasks shared by all juvenile institutions: to retain and contain committed youngsters, to provide care and sustenance, to educate those of a certain age, and to change the inmates in some respect. More important than variations in additional ends that may be asserted are the concrete definitions and relative weights accorded to these major purposes, given the lack of clarity and consensus on goals in the environment and among factions of personnel and the generality of official mandates coming from the parent organization. The primary elements of the goal definition refer to the kinds of change sought in the inmates and to the ways they should behave once such changes have been achieved.

The goal definitions actually selected have their sources in themes and models available from the general culture. When the executive chooses from among models—for example, by selecting from military, penal, religious, family, boarding-school, or residential-treatment models —he has committed himself to distinctive notions about the causes, nature, and cures of deviant behavior. He is committed as well to as-

sociated beliefs about the character of the delinquent and the nature of the delinquent population, to images of particular behavior or personality changes that are desirable and feasible, and to models of staff activity likely to induce these changes. Thus the executive's selection of one or another or combinations of these general models begins to specify major productive tasks and suggests a rationale that supports and extends the chosen alternatives. Of course, any general model requires specification, extension, and reformulation to fit the particular requirements and constraints and the press of events within and without the organization. These changes may give rise to a distinctly new institutional design.

We should expect the executive's choice to be partially conditioned by his background and personal commitments. Those chosen from professional ranks are likely to emphasize purposes and credos in keeping with their training and collegial reference groups. Others are likely to derive their orientations from more traditional sources or from experiences in other people-changing organizations like schools or adult prisons. Past traditions of the institution and the terms of succession should also have significant bearing on the executive's definition of goals. The promotion to an administrative position of a staff member who represents one faction within the organization or the appointment of a professional from another institution signifies expectations that press upon the new executive.[2]

Purposes must be communicated to various audiences inside and outside the organization. Within limits the executive may, to project the institution and its tasks to external publics, use terms different from those he employs to guide internal operations. Continuous surveillance from outside makes risky any attempt to treat the audiences as totally segregated, however. Therefore, one of the executive's continuing tasks is to formulate goals effective inside while legitimate outside.

## OBEDIENCE/CONFORMITY INSTITUTIONS

### General Perspectives

The executives at both Dick and Mixter defined relatively simple and limited objectives for change. These objectives centered on inducing

and requiring behavior compliant with formal requirements. Deference to adults, submission to authority, and overt conformity to stated rules were the primary expectations. Official statements of purpose, although evoking more positive themes than either executive otherwise appeared to assert, reflected these orientations. Jackson,[3] executive at Dick, prepared the following statement for the employees' handbook:

> The School exists to train delinquent boys so that they may become useful citizens. We may not succeed with all boys, but the training given at this School will determine the lives of many; and it is of the utmost importance, to the boys here, to their families, and to the communities to which they will return. Occasionally, an employee may lose hope of the reclamation of a boy, but he must remember that he will not succeed with all boys. *Fairness, firmness, and faith are very essential in reclamation.* Boys are quick to detect favoritism, laxness, and loss of confidence. Punishment is at times essential . . . but is never an end in itself and must be used with understanding.

An official publication issued by Mixter's parent organization stated the purpose of Mixter:

> . . . to provide a state school for the training of socially maladjusted boys. Its purpose is the beginning of a process of rehabilitation for boys who have shown themselves to be unable to make satisfactory adjustments in their home communities. In keeping with this philosophy, educational activities, work assignments, social training, and group living are planned for each boy as near as possible on an individual basis.

Hanna, the executive at Mixter, in the handbook for new employees added the concept of treatment:

> The training school should be looked upon as a place where a boy has the benefit of a number of training and treatment resources in learning how to live harmoniously with people. . . . Our job is not to punish boys, but to train and treat them.

Both executives maintained relatively simple conceptions of human nature, although Hanna's were somewhat more sophisticated, perhaps because of his greater exposure to mental-health philosophies. They believed delinquency to be a product of inadequacies in families or the

social order. Jackson stressed failure to implement the virtues of obedience and discipline, which induced willful misconduct. Hanna emphasized the corrupting effects of parental laxity and other improper influences.

Inmates at both institutions were to be worked upon and shaped up, with *conditioning* the essential theme of these regimes. Inmates' trust and loyalty could be sought, but complaisance rather than engagement was to be expected. The executives shared a pessimism about the malleability and potentials of the inmate's personality. In Hanna's words, it was "unrealistic to expect many cures when the cancer has progressed so far." The changes sought were justified as the maximum possible—in view both of available resources and of the nature of the "raw material"—and were premised on uncomplicated notions about the retraining of behavior. These administrators also argued that obedient conduct within the institution was desirable because it was most likely to insure submissive conformity to formal authority after return to the open community.

Apparently as a result of contacts and pressures from welfare and mental-health publics, Hanna, the executive at Mixter, evinced considerable ambivalence regarding his goal conceptions. Often his views about the character of the inmates were contradictory. He showed understanding of complex and differentiated conceptions of delinquents yet denigrated their validity. While avowing the need for treatment resources, Hanna defended the use of punitive measures as necessary "under the circumstances." In these respects he was a less able and consistent spokesman for his commitments than was Jackson, the executive at Dick, although Jackson also seemed to have some doubts about his conceptions.

Both men had obtained master's degrees in education, although here the similarity in background ended. Hanna had experience in both military and adult penal programs and in a decade at Mixter had served first as assistant director for a few years. Jackson initially had been a high-school teacher and athletic coach. Then, after operating his father's small business, he won election to the state legislature, where he had served on a committee concerned with Dick and other public institutions. He planned to make politics his career and hoped to become director of the state department that controlled Dick when the incumbent resigned to run for the governorship.

*Desired Staff-Inmate Relations*

In both institutions domination-submission was to be the guiding principle for interaction between the staff and inmates. Boys were to defer to all staff members and comply with all demands. The institutional program would be successful as it *acted upon* the boys. Status differences were to be emphasized, close or intimate relations and inmate voluntarism were not to be fostered, and many negative sanctions were to be available to enforce conformity.

At Dick, Jackson believed that inmates should be subjected to clear-cut and impersonal demands, with all infractions severely punished. Personnel should command respect by firmness while winning confidence by fairness and interested concern. Discipline was to be the watchword for the staff, respectful obedience for inmates. Harsh sanctions were to be liberally used for their instrumental value but not in a punitive spirit or for personal reasons. Responses that appeared positive —or at least deferential—in face-to-face contacts were for Jackson both a validation of his philosophy and an index of "reclamation." Jackson had increased the severity of Dick's sanctions upon becoming executive, although criticism from outside the institution gradually compelled him to modify some of these arrangements and may ultimately have weakened his position within the political party that had had him appointed. Hanna's approach was similar, although more tempered. He less frequently referred to the necessity for coercive controls and authorized fewer harsh measures. He distinguished among the inmates to a greater extent and arranged for cottage assignments that reflected differences in behavior patterns, as well as in age and size (the only factors used at Dick).

Both executives claimed credit for efforts to strengthen their educational programs, but both supported extensive use of inmate labor to maintain the institution. At Mixter, however, Hanna permitted less intrusion on classroom schedules to recruit able-bodied boys (the crop schedule on Dick's farm was given highest priority). Hanna also saw a need for some counseling personnel and techniques to induce conformity; Jackson believed these would be appropriate for only a small number of very disturbed boys.

Co-optation of informal inmate leaders was encouraged in both in-

stitutions, as well as the use of stronger or faster boys to control their peers. Special statuses and privileges were to be awarded to those who assisted the staff in handling others and, less often, to those who served as models of accommodation. Jackson otherwise ignored informal relations in the belief that they could not jeopardize staff dominance: "We have the dice loaded against them, and they can't do anything." In contrast, Hanna was constantly concerned about the emergence of inmate cliques, believing they had to be suppressed in order to avoid challenges to institutional order.

## RE-EDUCATION/DEVELOPMENT INSTITUTIONS

*General Perspectives*

The chief administrators of Regis and Bennett shared the beliefs that delinquent behavior is a product of social disorganization and deficient family patterns and that the consequences of these adverse conditions can be overcome by firm supervision of the youngsters' daily activities. Mitchell, executive at Regis, continued to present publicly an outdated statement of institutional purpose:

Regis is established for the care, guidance, and supervision of orphan, dependent, and neglected high school boys 14–18 years of age, regardless of race or creed, who are preferably attending school. Where placement is indicated boys presenting behavior problems will also be accepted. Regis does not offer services to (1) the mentally ill or emotionally disturbed boy who is in need of psychiatric care, or (2) the seriously delinquent boy.

Ramsey, executive at Bennett, used a goal statement with comparable terms but one that overstated his institution's concern with clinical services:

The broad purpose of Bennett is to provide small group care in a rural family home environment to boys who are having difficulty adjusting to their school, home, or community. Through personal counseling, psychiatric service, when advisable, and participation in a well-integrated program boys are given an opportunity to solve their problems and regain their place in society.

Although these goal statements did not show it, each of these executives had succeeded in transforming his institution from one primarily serving neglected or homeless youth to one including many delinquents and others manifesting behavior problems. These men retained, nevertheless, relatively uncomplicated conceptions of human behavior and the means for changing it. Both continued their institutions' quasi-boarding school traditions and emphasized the values of "constructive activities." Perhaps because both had been educators, they sought to develop new orientations through training and teaching.

Mitchell, the Regis executive, was a member of a religious teaching order who had taught in parochial schools. He expected to return to teaching after his current tour of duty and saw himself more as an educator than as an expert on delinquency (although he also had worked in another correctional institution). Despite this career, he had become convinced that there were not enough dependent and neglected youth to sustain the earlier Regis program and that services to delinquents should be augmented. His religious background and teaching experience influenced his attitude: He believed the basic cause of delinquency lay in home environments disorganized by divorce, separation, or working mothers. As a result, the delinquents had not learned to conform and had experienced rejection and chaos in their social and spiritual lives. He sought to "salvage" these youth by "educating them morally, spiritually, socially, physically, economically, and emotionally."

Mitchell was conversant with contemporary psychiatric theory but skeptical of much of it on doctrinal grounds. He was opposed to too much permissiveness in handling youth. He believed that what was needed instead was moral suasion, education, healthy activities to consume abundant physical energies, and firm guidance from concerned adults—although he saw that these remedies might not work for some delinquents who were seriously disturbed or hardened to deviant careers. He attempted to screen out such boys before admission to Regis. Those admitted had to express willingness to accept the institutional regimen, a criterion necessary partly because of the program's openness.

Ramsey's experience, beside teaching, had involved administering a large orphanage for many years before he came to Bennett. He was the oldest executive studied and was nearing retirement. In his decade

at Bennett he had expanded the institution, built new cottage facilities, and terminated the farm program, once the primary activity. Ramsey believed that there are many types of delinquent needing differentiated programs and that the task of his own institution was relatively simple. He viewed his inmates as primarily dependent and neglected youngsters whose deviant behavior was due to their inadequate and disorganized homes. The boys most needed a benign homelike environment with a "friendly arm around the shoulder," as well as constructive activities and firm adult supervision.

Ramsey asserted a goal of modest change for these inmates, feeling the institution would have achieved its objectives if boys "behaved," conforming to conventional standards of youth-adult relations. Several years earlier he had attempted to find out what had happened to former inmates and was reassured to discover that most were doing satisfactorily, though they were "not setting the world on fire." He believed an important deficit in Bennett's design was the lack of post-release services for inmates, as they generally returned to the adverse home situations that had produced the earlier problems. In keeping with these views, Ramsey also attempted to screen out boys presenting special difficulties. Nevertheless, he identified a minority of inmates present whom he saw as requiring more intensive individual services than Bennett had available.

The changes sought by both executives were somewhat more ambitious than were those of their counterparts at Dick and Mixter, with Mitchell's being the more extensive. The institution's task was to counteract the adverse effects of the inmates' prior experiences, and beyond this it was also necessary to facilitate development of their potentials. The focus was on adult-youth relations, with high valuation given to academic work (and also to moral training at Regis).

## Desired Staff-Inmate Relations

The dominant theme was *training*. These administrators emphasized the importance of their very similar routine programs, in which all boys spent most of the day in community schools, returning to the institutions to perform maintenance and housekeeping duties, to study, and to participate in recreational programs under the close supervision of staff personnel.

At Bennett Ramsey expected the cottage staff to provide the main impetus for change through interested response and engagement of inmates in communal tasks. Cottage parents were to use mild sanctions, but inmates who greatly transgressed standards or who persisted in uncooperative attitudes were to be referred to him for chastisement and, in extreme cases, to be returned to the court for another disposition. Ramsey regarded these practices as generally effective but worried about the proportion of inmates who did not seem to be trying to "make progress." Some did not apply themselves to their studies, engaged in stealing, destroyed property, or rebelled. With these boys the executive adhered to his basic practice of escalating sanctions but felt it necessary to convince them that the place was not really punitive.

In contrast, Mitchell advocated a more energetic confrontation. He required greater staff dominance and conducted a more strenuous activity program, with few leisure moments. Mitchell believed, in effect, that "idle hands are the devil's workplace" and insisted that staff members should "tire the boys out before they tire you out." He was more distrustful than Ramsey of what the inmates would do if left on their own. He also was concerned about their collective behavior; close informal relations were to be discouraged, and cliques were to be disrupted. In the executive's words, "We don't let personal friendships develop. The boys should get associated with all the people and boys here." Thus he preferred single dormitory rooms with doors always open, which other boys could not enter without staff observation. A controlled regimen was a necessary but not sufficient aspect of Mitchell's design. Staff members were to remain in close contact with the boys, setting clear expectations and models for conduct, showing concern for each inmate, and balancing disciplinary effort with helpful instruction and moral guidance. Boys were expected to work hard at their studies, and successful performance in this area was for Mitchell the chief index of rehabilitative progress. Here too, boys who did not adapt were to be subjected to intensive counseling and penalties and were eventually to be returned to the court.

Ramsey's prescriptions for staff activity at Bennett allowed greater freedom for inmates and emphasized the values of communal life. The model he chose was that of the parent-child rather than the teacher-pupil relationship. Although he also placed high value on schooling, study for classes was not stressed to the same extent.

## TREATMENT INSTITUTIONS

The chief administrators at both Milton and Inland were appointed to their offices at critical times and under expectations that they would achieve significant changes. Perkins had been brought in as Milton's executive four years earlier at a moment of near-crisis, when considerable staff unrest had accompanied a flareup of depredations by truanting boys and adverse newspaper publicity had led to the previous executive's dismissal. The change from a military-penal model toward clinical techniques had occurred within the preceding decade, but the clinical cadre had neither attained complete domination over internal operations nor produced leadership of sufficient caliber to win the executiveship. When selected as the new administrator Perkins was head of the unit of the parent organization that prepared reports on its operations and interpreted them to the legislature and public. A former newspaperman, Perkins was chosen as one whose "good sense" could be relied upon and who could improve Milton's adverse public relations. He was expected to resolve internal turbulence, end conflict among staff factions, and regain control over the inmates.

Perkins's lack of clinical training or credentials was not regarded as a handicap, as expertise in this area could be provided by other personnel. The chief subordinate's position, that of clinical director, was reserved for a trained psychiatrist and was soon occupied by Dr. Taylor, who had completed his residency some years earlier at Milton. Taylor was chosen for this post by a nearby psychiatric center which was very important for the institution. He remained closely affiliated with the center, which assigned trainees and consultants to Milton.

The position of executive director at Inland had long been vacant when Wright was persuaded to accept it. Inland was at low ebb in its fall from its early history of initiative and innovation—having become a custodial farm and vocational training program housed in unattractive dormitory buildings and considered a "last resort" among private institutions in its state. Major new building capital was believed to be available from the metropolitan community fund, and Wright's primary mandate was to obtain this money and transform the organization.

Burns, a clinical psychologist who became assistant director and succeeded to Wright's position during our study, had served as acting director during the interregnum. He headed a clinical triumvirate eager

to effect major changes at Inland but unable to obtain the necessary support. Burns had been considered for the executiveship but believed himself "not ready" for it, being neither interested in nor adept at fund-raising and preferring clinical duties within the program. It appears that the governing board perceived Wright as possessing a happy combination of professional and public relations competencies. He had been active in community and youth work, held a doctoral degree in social ethics, and, although he had never held a pastorate, was an ordained minister. Before appointment as Inland's executive, Wright was employed in community-relations work for a metropolitan church.

*General Perspectives*

The basic theme was *reconstitution*. Milton's executive, Perkins, accepted and absorbed the clinicians' perspectives and prescriptions for institutional design but made little effort to elaborate these notions. The following excerpt from one of Milton's biennial reports states the official goals avowed by Perkins:

> Our efforts . . . have been directed at understanding and treating the boys committed to our care rather than just holding them for a period of time and releasing them with the same problems facing them as when they had entered.
>
> The school conceives its purpose as one of diagnosis to discover the needs of its boys for treatment, treatment to create in each child positive feelings and social attitudes toward property and other people, and social planning for each boy aimed toward placement in an appropriate environment after treatment. The methods employed to fulfill this purpose involve clinical studies, positive management of boys in a relatively controlled environment, education, social psychological and psychiatric re-education through group and individual therapy, and whatever methods are indicated in individual cases. The school avoids the use of methods of management of boys which produce fear and insincere performance in children. There can be no successful treatment of children with problems without the use of the best possible methods of diagnosis, treatment, and social planning for placement and after care.

Wright, Inland's executive, succeeded in raising capital for a new million-dollar physical plant at Inland. As soon as these facilities were occupied the program was radically changed; most of the aggressive

gang-type delinquents who had been inmates were discharged, and intake became selective, emphasizing adolescents who manifested neurotic problems and might respond to individual treatment. The official goal statement reflected Inland's new remedial objectives:

> When a boy comes to us we are primarily interested, not in what he has done, but why he has done it. We are committed to demonstrate to our boys that the community is not hostile to the individual. We must symbolize to them the co-operative forces of our society which are interested, not in avenging aggressive acts, but in preventing them.
>
> We therefore inflict no punishment, either corporally or otherwise, in the handling of our boys. Treatment and education are the only tools we have. We are convinced that punishing teaches the child only how to punish; scolding teaches him how to scold. By showing him, by our own example, that we understand, he learns the meaning of understanding; by helping him, he learns the meaning of co-operation.

There were essential similarities in the two executives' conceptions of the delinquent personality and the institutional task. In both situations their chief clinical assistants held more extreme or professionalized views on these matters. At Milton, Perkins believed there were both environmental and psychological types of delinquent, perhaps more of the former, but that all had emotional problems that needed to be solved. He believed they were fundamentally "good kids" who had experienced deprivations and had been "failed" by adults. Damaging experiences had induced various degrees of psychological difficulty that required skilled attention if behavior was to be changed. These views were entirely compatible, on the one hand, with Perkins' warm and amiable approach to individuals and, on the other hand, with the tenets of dominant psychiatric conceptions.

As Perkins saw it, Milton's task was to provide a controlled living experience in which boys could be helped to overcome their distrust of adults, to resolve their emotional problems, and to develop internal controls. Vocational training was of importance because most of the boys were already academically retarded and, after more than a year at Milton, would enter the labor market rather than return to school. Perkins believed that Milton was both an educational and a treatment institution and stated: "We're still fighting to keep the distinction of being a training school rather than a hospital. There's a different ap-

proach here—the boy is supposed to use what he really has to care for himself. In a mental hospital you go into a closed ward and work your way out. You couldn't work that way with this age group. The more you lock up kids, the more they try to get out." The executive agreed with his clinical staff and the consultants from the psychiatric center that the inmates needed firm handling in a benign but controlled environment, on grounds that too much permissiveness invited trouble and did not help the boys to develop sufficient personal responsibility.

Perkins saw Milton's program as ineffective for certain inmates. Some were mentally retarded and belonged in other state institutions, to which they were sent as beds became available. Those who were assaultive in the institution or committed serious crimes while truanting (like car stealing) were to be remanded to courts and sent to the state reformatory, an institution for older offenders.[4] Although these practices were permitted under a statute that Perkins vigorously defended against external attack, they concerned him on grounds that "we're getting rid of our problems, we aren't working with these boys enough." At the same time, however, he and his clinicians were resisting pressures to add a maximum-security unit in order to accommodate difficult cases, for they believed it would jeopardize the permissiveness of their regular program.

At Inland, Wright also believed there were both environmental and psychologically disturbed delinquents, with an overlap between the two types. However, he and the assistant director, Burns, felt that Inland should concentrate on the latter. These boys were seen as rejected youths who had been exposed to damaging influences and who engaged in delinquent activity as a means of acting out internal conflicts. Their main difficulties were intrapsychic and could be resolved only through the development of insight. This required a permissive environment where the boys could act out their conflicts, but the environment was primarily an adjunct to the efforts of the clinical staff.

As executive, Wright was in sympathy with the major tenets of Inland's revised permissive and psychotherapeutic approach and claimed credit for its essential features, even though he did not and could not have formulated the more esoteric definitions and activities developed by the clinical staff under the leadership of Burns. Wright's major commitment was to the advancement and aggrandizement of the organization, however, and he concentrated primarily on a promotional

strategy in which fund-raising, publicity, and community relations were paramount. The executive's tasks of revitalizing the institution and building a new physical plant necessitated his developing or finding a novel program that would attract external interest and support. This was accomplished by use of the clinical model, which was then relatively new in the area. The rudiments of this model were already being espoused by Burns and his colleagues. Wright subscribed to the general outlines of this model although disagreeing with certain of its features. In particular, he believed that it gave insufficient attention to experiences other than therapeutic transactions and that it could not be conducted in disregard of community sentiments.

## Desired Staff-Inmate Relations

The perspectives of Taylor, Milton's second in command, appeared to be in transition from a conventional clinical point of view to one crystallizing conceptions of a milieu technology. Although a significant proportion of the inmates were assigned to psychiatrist-conducted individual or group therapy sessions, two-person clinical endeavors were not the major focus of Milton's treatment approach. Although Taylor doubted that emotional disturbances underlay most of the inmates' deviance, he asserted that emotions were of prime importance, that inmates should be engaged in self-conscious examination of their problems, and that change was both facilitated and manifested by talking about one's difficulties.

In the belief that cottage life was crucial and that boys' experiences within it should be structured therapeutically, Taylor forged a new design centering on sessions with cottage groups. These put all inmates living in the same unit in frequent confrontations with all staff members assigned to the cottage. The sessions were to provide opportunities for ventilating feelings, reviewing experiences in school and work areas, planning cottage affairs, and assessing the inmates' progress. They were distinguished from the group therapy meetings, in which attention was focused not on contemporary events but on more individual matters—family relations and the like. Taylor saw the cottage sessions as the most important means for effecting change and as the primary point of exchange between staff and inmates. The boys were expected to participate actively and to communicate freely in the sessions. Staff members

were expected to guide the discussions firmly and to handle individual encounters with inmates in the light of these sessions.

Harsh discipline was proscribed at Milton, and most sanctions authorized for staff were to involve only the reduction of privileges. As a large proportion of the inmates was not regarded as especially disturbed, the cottage group sessions were conceived as an efficient way to shape the inmates' conduct and maintain social control within the institution. Despite his reliance on this system, Taylor viewed the primary phenomena as *intra*personal, however, and the guiding conceptions of Milton's clinical personnel referred to psychological processes. Cottage and therapy meetings, therefore, did not particularly direct staff attention to interpersonal relations among the inmates or to the manipulation of these for treatment purposes.

Inland differed in two important respects from Milton. First, individual psychotherapeutic procedures were the core of the treatment technology at Inland, with group experiences only adjunctive. Second, Wright was less willing to grant his chief assistant, Burns, a relatively free hand within the program than was Perkins at Milton.

In collaboration with the other clinicians, Burns had formulated a distinctive psychotherapeutic approach. The primary measure of an inmate's improvement was to be his "emotional growth" (colloquially termed "EG"), manifested as responsive communication in therapeutic interviews, willingness to examine his inner life, and accommodation to the institution's modest norms for behavior. A wide range of inducements was to be offered the boys, with few and mild negative sanctions approved. Extensive recreational activities were to be provided in the new plant, and boys were to participate in off-grounds athletic events, dances, outings, and camping trips. Outsiders were to be encouraged to volunteer their services to work with the boys, and parents were to be allowed to visit weekly (some also participated in group therapy sessions). Some inmates were to be allowed weekend home visits.

Frequent private sessions with the clinicians were conceived as the major means for effecting change. Through these sessions inmates were to be encouraged to review their personal histories to discover the sources of their deviance, develop insight, and modify psychological forces. Other phases of the program were designed to support the clinical procedures. The school program was modified to emphasize

academic rather than vocational training, and cottage life was to provide a benign communal experience. In all phases of the Inland regimen inmates were to be allowed to act out their problems within reasonable limits, and staff members were expected to be relatively permissive and indulgent. Persistent or gross infractions of rules were to be reported to, and usually handled by, Burns and then referred back to the inmate's clinician for continuing attention.

Wright subscribed to the general outlines of this approach although disagreeing with certain of its features. He did not believe the clinicians were going to "save these boys in their offices"; he desired more "structure" in the boys' program and emphasized many aspects of conventional morality. For example, he proscribed the wearing of blue jeans and instituted a "spic-and-span" movement with special privileges for boys who kept themselves well dressed and well groomed. The highly individualized approach at Inland took almost no account of informal associations among inmates, although both Wright and Burns became aware that these might have significance. They created an inmate planning group to conduct certain campus-wide recreational activities and established a few other groups that combined recreation and therapy.

## CONTRASTS AMONG TYPES

The executives' formulations of goals provide the basis for classifying these institutions into the three basic goal types, obedience/conformity, re-education/development, and treatment. The types form a custody-treatment continuum based on the degree of complexity of beliefs about people-changing embodied in organizational goals. In the obedience/conformity institutions it was assumed that the orientations of the inmates could not be altered basically but that the inmates could be conditioned to behave properly (or would learn to conform out of fear of the consequences). In the re-education/development institutions there was greater concern for training the inmate—for developing his capabilities so he could pursue a gainful career after release. Executives in these places assumed that most inmates possessed resources that could be drawn upon and developed, thereby better equipping them for law-abiding lives, and that they were not irredeemably committed to

delinquent careers. In the treatment institutions the executives assumed that deviance could be corrected only by a thoroughgoing reorientation or reconstitution of the inmate; otherwise, his unconscious identifications and other intrapersonal forces would probably lead him toward continued delinquent behavior. The treatment executives believed the inmates to have significant potentialities, however.

Toward the treatment pole of the continuum the executives sought more extensive change and had greater optimism about the organization's capacity to effect significant change. Those in the obedience/conformity institutions demanded overt compliance and submission but were relatively indifferent to other phases of behavior or argued that these would follow from changes in manifest conduct. The treatment executives sought broad changes: altered personalities, enhanced cognitive and technical skills, and improved interpersonal relations. Executives in the re-education/development institutions sought change between these extremes, moderate both in the range of attributes to be altered and in the degree of change sought.

The patterns of staff performance designed by the executives were generally commensurate with their views of the delinquent personality and its malleability. Pessimistic and simplistic views shared by the obedience/conformity executives supported relatively standardized and even coercive methods, whereas the treatment executives' greater optimism and complex views supported more differentiated and voluntaristic methods. A core difference among the executives was in their views of whether staff members were supposed to *act upon* or to *engage* inmates in the processes of change. Within the obedience/conformity institutions inmates were to be forcibly molded, controlled, and otherwise dealt with as resistant objects. Inmates of the treatment institutions, in contrast, were to be worked with and to be won over and induced to adopt new behaviors and attitudes. They were presumably responsive and ready to be engaged in the change process. In the re-education/development institutions, the Regis executive appeared more inclined toward the former position, and the Bennett executive toward the latter.

All the executives encountered problems in specifying and assuring particular staff-inmate relations at the concrete level. None of the executives was satisfied with what he believed to be the actual patterns.

For example, Jackson at Dick was worried that his personnel did not balance their strictness with enough interested concern; Mitchell at Regis doubted that his staff members were able to respond with sufficient understanding; and Taylor at Milton believed that his subordinates tended to become overinvolved with the boys. There appeared to be deficiencies and inconsistencies in administrators' specifications for staff-inmate relations: The "message" seemed to be difficult to comprehend or did not appear to provide adequate guidelines. Further, at all institutions executives expected personnel to behave in ways that required unusual competencies and orientations, considering the quality of personnel available. Thus at Dick personnel were expected to employ frequent coercion in ways that generated confidence, whereas at Milton non-professional personnel were to assume a high degree of detached particularism. It is important to observe that these difficulties increased across the continuum: Executive prescriptions for staff activity became more esoteric, and specifications for behavior became more ambiguous and conditional nearer the treatment pole. Treatment institution executives, therefore, faced the greatest problems in developing arrangements to assure desired staff activity.

As we expected, there was an association between goal types and executive backgrounds. All but the treatment executives had backgrounds at least partly in education. Only Mitchell at Regis, however, as a member of a teaching order, had spent all his previous career in education. The others had also been in either business and politics (Jackson of Dick), military and adult corrections work (Hanna of Mixter), or orphanage administration (Ramsey of Bennett).

Careers of the treatment executives were sharply different. None had been an educator. Both the major subordinates had clinical degrees —Taylor of Milton being a psychiatrist and Burns of Inland a clinical psychologist. Furthermore, the chief executives of both institutions had rather unconventional careers—not in total institutions or clinical professions but in journalism and public relations (Perkins of Milton) or religious, youth, and community-relations work (Wright of Inland). Experience in schools or conventional total institutions appears not to have been compatible with leadership in treatment innovations, but experience likely to build facility in relating to the environment appeared to do so.

## NOTES

1. We do not assume the executive's behavior to be "rational" in any *total* sense; we accept Herbert Simon's notion of cognitive limits on rationality (*Administrative Behavior* [New York: Macmillan, 1957]) and Alvin Gouldner's assertion of the heuristic usefulness of a rational model of organization ("Organizational Analysis," in Robert Merton, Leonard Broom, and Leonard Cottrell, Jr. [eds.], *Sociology Today* [New York: Basic Books, 1959]). At the same time, starting with the concept of the organization as an institution made explicit by Selznick, we recognize the importance of non-rational, irrational, and unplanned-for elements and consequences. Much of the criticism of rationalistic theories is misdirected in that it assumes if an actor pays attention to such characteristics as system maintenance he is irrational; but the "rational" actor we see views such characteristics as constraints in undertaking calculative processes on the knowledge, albeit limited, available to him. His "true" rationality can be measured only *ex post facto* with indices of organizational effectiveness and is not assumed in our model of decision-making.

2. See Lloyd Ohlin, "Conflicting Interests in Correctional Objectives," in Richard A. Cloward, *et al., Theoretical Studies in Social Organization of the Prison* (New York: Social Science Research Council, 1960), pp. 111–129; and Richard McCleery, *Policy Change in Prison Management* (Lansing: Governmental Research Bureau, Michigan State University, 1957).

3. Names given executives are, of course, pseudonyms.

4. About twenty-five boys, some as young as thirteen, were thus forwarded each year.

# Chapter 4

# THE EXECUTIVE:
# EXTERNAL STRATEGIES

The second and perhaps most important major area of executiveship is that of linking organizational capabilities with external demands and resources. The adaptive and survival problems of an organization cannot be resolved primarily through management of internal operations. Publics that assess the organization and provide resources often lack means for evaluating its actual workings and may base critical judgments on events other than those occurring within the program. More important, these expectations for institutional achievement are themselves very much a focus for executive action. The institution's mandates and legitimation are neither given nor fixed, but are subject to continuous change and are at least partially accessible to executive manipulation. The specification of operational goals and principles not only has internal significance but also involves crucial relations with the environment. Commitment of the institution to a particular set of ends can become an important means for gaining support among like-minded groups in the environment while risking the antagonism of those who prefer other aims.

Interpretation and defense of selected goals are means to reap the benefits from key groups outside the institution or to neutralize their objections. Since none of these relations are static or self-maintaining, the executive must continually work to build and maintain legitimation and support. Although resources may be temporarily continued despite an erosion of support, the executive eventually must account for his regime. Modes of operation, the caliber of personnel, and occasional critical incidents must be explained and justified. Ohlin's observation that most publics of adult correctional institutions do not continuously

attend to organizational performance is probably true also for juvenile institutions.[1] But the executive cannot be certain who is watching when, or how events will be recalled long after they occur.

The primary resources necessary to sustain institutional activity are funds, personnel, inmates, and at least minimal cooperation from certain other organizations. Typically, each of these types of resources is obtained from a different source or from several external units, thereby requiring complex patterns of transaction. Both public and private institutions, for example, usually obtain inmates from a number of juvenile courts and from referrals made by schools, other institutions, and the like. Although the private institution may be faced with the problem of obtaining *enough* inmates to maintain desired levels of monetary support, it shares a concern with the public institution that it not receive *inappropriate* inmates. Both public and private institutions may attempt to control the *types* of youth referred or committed, since their operational modes are presumably better suited to boys who possess certain characteristics. Designs for the recruitment of inmates may also depend upon recruiting certain types of personnel, particularly when complex technologies are in use. Finally, all inmates must eventually be returned to their communities. In order to reduce delays in dispatching boys or to avoid discovering that there is nowhere to send them, the institution may need to mobilize action by such other organizations as local courts or child placement agencies.

Taken together, these boundary-spanning activities provide basic prerequisites for the institution's operation. The executive may himself undertake only some of these tasks, but he can ignore them only at his peril. External demands and transactions create the general conditions to which the internal program must be adjusted. We would suppose that executive attention, therefore, is more likely to be addressed to these events than to internal processes when both compete for time and effort. Executives may adopt more inward or more outward orientations or more passive or assertive postures toward the environment. Some may seek to mold these external forces and conditions, anticipating crises and opportunities, and perhaps energetically aggrandizing support and resources. Others may cope more reactively, responding cautiously to external exigencies and perhaps even seeking to insulate their institutions from the press of outside demands.

## OBEDIENCE/CONFORMITY INSTITUTIONS

*Interpreting Goals*

The parent organizations expected both Dick and Mixter executives to run their institutions efficiently, to avoid events that might invoke serious criticism, and to upgrade programs wherever possible. Here the similarities ended. All the evidence indicates that the primary expectation for Jackson was that he make Dick an asset rather than a liability in the record of his political party. His predecessor had been ousted some months before the first survey, and Jackson was given six months to "clean up the place" and, as he saw it, to improve the physical plant and institute a more coherent program. Shortly after he assumed office a new state-wide citizens' group concerned with correctional programs published a report criticizing most aspects of the institution. Because of the political implications, the charges enumerated in the report provided concrete themes around which Jackson developed his regime, planned innovations, and formulated a defensive rationale.

The report called for some liberalization of Dick's program and for greater emphasis on rehabilitation, but these recommendations were not strong enough to require a major shift in the types and level of changes sought. Jackson's conceptions of goals and technologies continued to be commensurate with prevailing orientations in his state, and the fortunes of his party could best be served by effecting visible improvements in the plant, demonstrating an efficient administration, and projecting an image of vigorous leadership. These became the guiding themes for Jackson's direction of internal affairs and for his energetic program of public interpretation, which was aimed primarily at newspapers, a state network of women's clubs, and the county judiciary.

Hanna's situation was different. He had been executive of Mixter for some years and in a state with a proud tradition of civil service and responsible administration of public agencies. Over the decade in which Mixter had become more centrally located within the parent organization and increasingly subject to its concern for gradual improvement of welfare services, expectations for the rehabilitation of delinquent youth had become more ambitiously defined. This was partly because of an expanding network of mental health and welfare groups and

partly because of the innovative examples set by several private institutions. The emergence of these pressures from external groups and through the parent organization had not signaled a diminution of custodial demands. With expansion of the population local courts and law enforcement agencies sought admission of ever larger numbers of youth and protested the reduction in length of stay necessitated when enlarged facilities were not constructed. Others within the local community continued to be critical of the threats to property and safety caused by runaways.

Hanna's response to these cross-pressures was essentially defensive and insulative. He argued that an improved program (both rehabilitative and custodial) was possible only if new security facilities were constructed to accommodate the more recalcitrant inmates. Even so, he asserted, the institution could do little with its boys, since the families and communities had failed and since for most boys it was too late. He engaged in minimal contacts with the public and discouraged his personnel from such contacts, in part by requiring advance clearance of statements to outsiders. In his view, a positive program of public relations was the responsibility of the parent organization. It was apparent that Hanna could not neutralize either of the sets of contradictory demands playing upon Mixter, nor could he harmonize these in a balanced statement of goals for external groups.

## Mobilizing Resources

Mixter already possessed many of the physical facilities that Jackson desired so much for Dick, yet Hanna too placed highest priority on securing additional capital funds. He particularly wanted a maximum security unit and hoped ultimately for a wholly new plant away from the city in which Mixter was located. Both men succeeded at least partially in these aims: the security unit (Maxwell) was built and opened toward the end of Hanna's tenure, and Jackson obtained a new school building and a swimming pool (although without the equipment essential for either facility). Hanna pursued his aims through the parent organization, whose director enjoyed very positive relations with the state legislature; Jackson worked through his superiors but also maintained direct contact with legislators, some of whom had been his colleagues. Mixter's operating budget was affluent in com-

parison to Dick's, and Jackson experienced much greater frustration in this area. At the same time, he did not give highest priority to enlarging the budget, perhaps because the benefits would not provide sufficiently visible evidence of his successful administration.

Both executives had special problems in staffing which were externally related. Teachers in the two institutions were the best educated and best paid personnel groups, principally because of the compulsory education laws and teacher certification regulations in both states. Neither executive experienced special difficulties in recruiting and retraining these professionals, despite their rather marginal situations in each organization. At Dick there was no other staff cadre for which specialized training was desired, and the adverse economic conditions in the region created a favorable labor market in which Jackson could recruit personnel. He appeared to have only two concerns with respect to hiring. First, he lacked enough positions to employ all the party faithful recommended by county political leaders. Some of those sent him were in his view unqualified, or they were adherents of the opposing faction within the party. He had to negotiate with county and state officials in order to reduce what he regarded as exorbitant demands for employment, and he increasingly voiced skepticism about the efficacy of the patronage system because of constraints it imposed on personnel selection. Jackson's second concern was to locate individuals who could assume special responsibilities within the executive core. Believing that professional training was a handicap, he emphasized qualities of personal loyalty and some success in other types of work. Selection by these criteria, however, did not always produce persons who could do the jobs to which they were assigned.

Hanna's main staffing problems were different. The parent organization expected that trained professionals, or at least college educated persons, would be employed and assigned to clinical duties. Such persons found Mixter's custodial emphases and constricted clinical roles frustrating, however, and either soon departed for other positions or remained as members of what Hanna believed to be a dissident cabal. The negative assessments of the clinicians were communicated to their counterparts in the parent organization and external welfare agencies, thereby increasing the frictions Hanna encountered with these units. Hanna saw his other major staffing problem as limitation on his freedom of action originating in the civil service regulations. He believed

he could neither discharge unsatisfactory employees without serious cause and considerable effort nor alter job assignments in accordance with individual abilities or changed staffing needs. He perceived no way to rid the program of inept and disaffected personnel who—in his view —tended to contaminate others and create serious morale problems. Despite these concerns he made no effort to train or upgrade personnel and was even reluctant to encourage staff meetings because he feared they would lead to collective opposition.

Both institutions were supplied with an ample flow of inmates, almost entirely through independent county juvenile courts. In neither state could these courts be dealt with collectively—except informally by using persuasion on the associations of judges or indirectly through stimulating modifications of the juvenile statutes. Each court adhered to its own patterns of committing certain numbers and types of youth, and each defined its own criteria for assessing the institution's performance. Because of the power of the judges in their communities and at the state level, they were significant figures for both executives. In fact, Hanna and Jackson seemed to be more consistently attentive to their relations with the courts than to any other external units besides the parent organizations. Hanna managed his exchanges with the courts largely through his social service staff, but kept a watchful eye on their activities. Jackson's approach was more active, with less delegation of responsibility to other staff members, and he more often supplemented individual contacts with appearances at judiciary conferences.

Mixter was under greater pressure to receive increasing numbers of committed youth. It was in growing conflict with metropolitan courts over the decreasing proportions of delinquents they could commit and the decreasing length of time those committed were incarcerated. This difference between the institutions reflected mainly the population and urbanization differences between the two states—although it was Jackson rather than Hanna who reported calculated efforts to cope with such problems by negotiations with the judges. Hanna was concerned about the types of youngsters committed by many courts, believing there were growing numbers of mentally retarded and disturbed boys who should have been sent to other institutions. He used Mixter's part-time psychiatrist and its psychologists to screen and certify boys so they might be transferred to other agencies. Although this effort absorbed much of Hanna's time and concern, it had little success because the

alternative agencies already had long waiting lists. He supported various stratagems, including a change in Mixter's classification system, to authenticate youngsters as meriting admission elsewhere, but did not initiate negotiations with courts to improve their own screening and commitment practices.

Jackson saw a small number of youngsters as inappropriate for Dick, but expressed little concern about the matter. Dick's simple program, particularly the farm work, made it relatively easy to handle boys with low intelligence, and the lack of serious admissions pressures induced no search for ways to transfer inmates. The same factors also induced relative indifference to the presence of mentally ill youngsters, although Jackson believed there were a few whose behavior was not wholly contained by the stringent sanctions system.

## Obtaining Cooperation

Both executives desired certain types of aid from outside units but, as we shall see, less so than the other types of institutions. Here the preferred forms of aid were limited to receiving gifts or privileges from community groups and getting agencies to make preparations to receive boys released to their local communities.

Individuals and groups in the immediate locale frequently wished to provide gifts or minor resources and receive boys as visitors or participants outside the institution. Because of the effort required to organize trips and concern that the inmates might run away or misbehave, neither executive encouraged attendance at outside affairs. Exceptions were trips by athletic teams—composed of trusted boys and carefully supervised—to compete with schools in adjacent communities, or trips to circuses or other entertainments, again providing the trips could be highly controlled. Visits by outsiders to the institutions and volunteer service on the grounds were discouraged except for those by church officials or observational tours. Women's groups and civic clubs were persuaded to purchase minor equipment or to provide holiday treats instead of serving on the grounds. Jackson permitted a women's organization to send birthday and Christmas cards to all boys unlikely to receive them from relatives. Both executives argued that relatively closed boundaries were necessary to custody and good order and that management of volunteer activities could excessively drain staff resources.

Although discouraging contact with the local community, Jackson undertook extensive efforts to inform groups throughout the state of the gains being made at Dick under his leadership. Newspapers and their editors were in his view particularly important—although he felt too many were identified with the opposition party. Women's clubs, PTAs, and various civic and religious groups he regarded as more amenable, and he spoke frequently at their meetings. His professed objective in these activities was to educate citizens about Dick and its programs, developing a base of interested support that would be useful in approaches to the legislature. Jackson freely acknowledged the political value of such activities both in publicizing his party's record and in extending his personal contacts.

Hanna believed the continual criticism Mixter received from the local community could be relieved only by construction of new facilities elsewhere. He believed contacts with local groups would not achieve this aim and that a more extensive effort beyond the community was the responsibility of the parent organization. Defense of Mixter and of his administration was attempted by reducing external relations and by justificatory explanations to those who succeeded in reaching Hanna directly.

As did all the executives, Jackson and Hanna sought assistance in discharging inmates. These were minors, and state laws required that each be accepted as a responsibility by an adult before release. Because of distance and statutory restrictions, the institutions had little direct access to the families—many broken—that would take them. County juvenile courts and local units of state welfare departments were the primary "marketing agents" to which released boys in both states were sent. A major problem for both executives, then, was to stimulate these agencies to be willing and able to receive boys as fast as they were released. Delays in processing release papers, in certifying home situations, or in making alternative arrangements meant that inmates had to remain in the institutions and occupy facilities needed for others. Because the courts could decide to send boys *to* the institutions, Jackson and Hanna had additional reason to deal cautiously with these relations. Local units of the state welfare departments could also help or hinder in arranging releases.

Jackson characteristically moved through the central state administration to obtain greater cooperation, insisting that he would not be

hampered by lower echelon state employees. Hanna's status with his parent organization was such that he could not expect to arouse its support. Further, this organization was reluctant to have its local units assume additional obligations for delinquent youth. Hanna was forced to deal directly with the county judges and chose to do so through his social service staff.

## RE-EDUCATION/DEVELOPMENT INSTITUTIONS

### *Interpreting Goals*

The Regis and Bennett executives did not find it difficult to interpret their relatively benign and simple goals to the general public. Bennett's executive, Ramsey, perhaps found it easier to do so because he relied on the analogy to the family, with occasional overtones also to the orphanage. The common difficulty of these executives arose with regard to types of boys they believed it had become necessary to serve: delinquent youths committed by juvenile courts. They were undoubtedly correct in arguing that there were no longer enough neglected or orphaned youths to maintain their earlier programs, but important supporting groups, including the two parent organizations, noted the shift in inmates with some regret. Neither institution had ever run a school, and both would have found it prohibitively expensive to do so, although the change in populations might eventually require it. The less conforming behavior of the newer types of inmates created new strains for the institutions. Bennett's rural setting and distance from highly populated areas reduced some of the hazards and allowed Ramsey to adopt a less rigorous design. Because Regis was located in an urban residential neighborhood its operations were much more visible, and misbehavior by its inmates was more likely to have serious consequences.

Mitchell, the Regis executive, felt exposed in still another way: his emphasis on training and spiritual guidance seemed outdated by contrast with clinical treatment philosophies stressed by certain other private institutions. He found it difficult to win support for his program from various child welfare and mental health interest groups even though he became an active participant in child welfare activities. More serious in his view than his disadvantages in recruiting clinicians was the skepticism with which his institution was regarded by the

professional staff of the metropolitan juvenile court which handled commitments. Without a steady flow of delinquents (for whom the court paid *per diem* expenses), Regis would have no reason to exist.

Ramsey was also dependent on a juvenile court for admissions but was in a county with fewer and less influential welfare and mental health organizations. Because there were fewer alternative programs, Bennett was still able to obtain referrals from a variety of sources.

## Mobilizing Resources

Although assuring a continuing supply of inmates was a greater problem for Regis than for Bennett, the two places were alike in needing to select boys who would present minimum demands for control and who would behave in ways positive enough to validate the institutional designs. Good relations with the juvenile courts were essential for these purposes, since the court's consent and payments were usually necessary even for referrals formally emanating from private welfare agencies, schools, or families. At worst, negative judgments by the courts would have jeopardized institutional legitimation and survival; at best, a lessening of good favor would have seriously complicated the screening process.

Two sides to the selection problem were faced by both executives. First, they could not precisely specify the types of youth who would best fit their programs and so had to resort to exclusionary criteria. Neither wanted delinquents who had already demonstrated they were hard to manage, likely to truant, or opposed to being committed. As the Regis statement on goals indicates, Mitchell was more emphatic about excluding such youths; in addition he did not want sexual offenders. Ramsey did not want Negro boys, saying they would not be accepted by the local schools and community. The second, corollary, problem was that their elusive and conservative selection criteria required them continually to negotiate with court representatives who gave priority to more serious offenders. Both institutions risked an erosion of good will from their courts. In both places the executives assigned their social workers to do the actual screening but closely monitored this activity.

Although Regis and Bennett were units of larger youth service organizations, nominally dependent on these organizations for support, each was compelled to participate in raising its own operating funds.

*Per diem* fees could not be set at the level of actual costs, and expansions in staff, program, or facilities required raising additional funds. Bennett was controlled by a semi-autonomous group of influential trustees affiliated with the parent organization's board. It received an allocation from the community fund, but Ramsey felt the fiscal situation was always troublesome. He solicited contributions from wealthy individuals and some months before the first survey had received a gift of $40,000 to build the newest cottage. He kept in close touch with his trustees, was active in a few civic clubs, and occasionally spoke about Bennett before community groups. These means of marshalling support increased the institution's dependence on local agencies and required Ramsey to be especially responsive to community pressures.

Mitchell employed other means to raise supplemental funds. An annual corned beef dinner produced most of the needed money, a ladies' auxiliary raised about $3000 annually, and the parent organization supplied the remainder. In these endeavors, as in some contacts with wealthy contributors, Mitchell moved within the boundaries of his religious denomination and its highly organized constituency. Regis was governed by a subunit of the parent organization's lay board of trustees. The executive appeared to have closer relations with the professional executive of the parent body than with the lay policy makers. He conferred frequently with this official and hoped to draw upon the resources and support of the larger unit to the extent he could without losing autonomy. He saw their relationship as an essential counterbalance to his dealings with the court, where opinion about Regis sometimes appeared precarious. In his customary forceful manner Mitchell also prepared a set of colored slides to use in talks before church and community groups, participated in a variety of welfare activities, and developed a program involving citizens in the neighborhood surrounding the institution.

## Obtaining Cooperation

Because both institutions sent their inmates out to schools, relations with these units constituted the next most critical area. Mitchell dispersed his boys among a large number of public and parochial schools. This reduced the visibility of problems of misbehavior or academic failure but increased the effort required of the social worker and, to a

lesser extent, of Mitchell to keep in touch with each school and to cope with individual situations. Such relationships with many schools and Mitchell's emphasis on academic criteria demanded considerable staff time but did not seem to be an area of tension.

Most of Bennett's inmates were sent to school in an adjacent small town, and so were a visible minority, especially because most of them were excluded from certain extracurricular activities and bussed back to the institution after classes. Ramsey reported continual complaints from school personnel and occasionally from citizens attending school board meetings. Some objected to the presence of inmates in conventional classrooms, and others objected to the fact that Bennett, as a tax exempt organization, did not pay its share of the costs. Ramsey was forthright in describing these tensions but ambiguous in explaining how serious they were and what he was doing about them. He reported occasional conferences with school officials, attendance at school board meetings, and the like. For some of these tasks he used the social worker, albeit with doubts about this staff member's abilities.

Both executives encouraged close relations with residents in the institution's immediate vicinity and invited them to attend certain programs or make occasional use of facilities. Ramsey allowed his inmates to visit nearby families and to seek part-time jobs in the locale. He regarded these neighbors as Bennett's warmest "boosters."

Mitchell had gone a few steps further, making arrangements for twelve of his inmates to live with neighboring families in order to increase Regis's capacity. These boys were subject to the same general rules and participated in most aspects of the institutional regimen but resided off grounds. Mitchell had also recently organized some nearby residents into a kind of "block committee." Initially this committee concentrated on relations with Regis, but it soon became involved with matters of more general interest in the neighborhood. Mitchell was especially proud that the committee provided a mechanism for bridging cleavages otherwise separating families in this racially mixed area of the city. Although only a small proportion of the Regis inmates were Negroes, he believed their presence contributed to favorable changes in neighborhood attitudes.

Unlike the two obedience/conformity institutions, neither Regis nor Bennett was subjected to heavy pressures to accept more boys. Consequently, they did not seek the same level of cooperation from external

units in releasing inmates. Ramsey expressed a desire for better post-discharge services to cope with the family situations to which boys had to return. Neither executive saw any need for work with inmates' families during the commitment period, however, despite their belief that such family situations were of prime importance in generating delinquent behavior.

## TREATMENT INSTITUTIONS

### Interpreting Goals

Both Milton and Inland had special interest mental health and child welfare groups to support their goals and confirm their effectiveness. Milton capitalized on but also faced the powerful influence of the nearby psychiatric center, although other mental health groups in the state were not particularly strong. Inland had to relate to a much more highly developed network of mental health organizations and to a metropolitan community fund agency that was very influential. For both places there also were other important outside units, such as juvenile courts, which were less concerned with treatment orientations but whose demands could not be ignored.

Milton's executive, Perkins, devoted a great deal of effort to building external support. He concentrated not on diffuse public activities but on positive relations with groups that controlled the institution's mandate and resources. He was especially sensitive to the psychiatric center. Because of the center's national prestige and its domination of the state mental health scene, its favorable assessment was crucial to Milton's stability and to Perkins's continuation as executive. The center's views could be—and were—expressed directly to legislators and state officials as well as to professionals who might contemplate employment at the institution. Means by which the center appraised events at the institution and maintained hegemony over it included the center's heavy representation on the parent organization's advisory commission on state institutions, its assignment of professional consultants at all levels of institutional operations, and its appointment of center-affiliated psychiatrists to the parent organization's division of institutions, as well as to Milton's clinical (assistant) directorship. Thus Milton was dependent on the center for legitimation of its clinical model, validation of its

performance, and recruitment of scarce professional manpower. Perkins maintained cordial relations with the center, welcomed the flow of personnel from it, and solidified this support by his partnership with Taylor, the clinical director.

Perkins also had frequent contact with officials of the state department of welfare and the chief of its division of institutions (also an appointee of the psychiatric center). The latter delegated considerable autonomy to Perkins and placed much trust in him, especially because he continued to fulfill his mandate. A primary concern about Milton's place in the state system was that growth in the child population would necessitate an enlargement of the institution's capacity. Both the executive and the clinical director feared this would jeopardize the institution's clinical design, particularly if it ultimately required the addition of a new security cottage. Perkins believed it difficult but imperative that Milton maintain a position midway between a residential mental health facility and a more custodial correctional program. The orientations of the psychiatric center pulled it in the first direction and pressures from the county courts, with which he negotiated in order to moderate these demands, pulled it in the second. Perkins also kept in active touch with local community groups and with the state's network of professional associations, welfare organizations, and public and private agencies. Milton's facilities were made available for meetings of such groups, and Perkins encouraged his staff to participate actively in their affairs.

The situation faced by Wright at Inland was more complex, and conflicting pressures were less easily reconciled. The many special-interest child welfare groups and agencies were little coalesced, and although the metropolitan community fund, which had provided capital to rebuild the institution, supported its adoption of more rehabilitative goals, it could not be counted upon to defend the clinical design, particularly since it required higher operating costs.

The striking new plant and the transformed program were the major features in Wright's effort to win support through a promotional strategy directed at diffuse audiences. Wright held to a demanding schedule of speaking engagements, participation in a variety of child welfare endeavors, and efforts to project the institution through the mass media. In order to reduce concern among residents adjacent to the new physical plant and to quiet local opposition to the more per-

missive program with its increased possibility of runaways and other incidents, Wright became active in affairs of the surrounding suburban community. He joined several civic organizations and even won election to the local board of education (but was later disqualified on a residency technicality). Community groups were invited to visit the new institution and occasionally to use facilities like the swimming pool and meeting rooms—in return for which Wright obtained tolerance for Inland and occasional contributions of money for athletic equipment or the like.

The crux of Wright's ultimate difficulty appeared to be an inability to adapt his methods to Inland's changed circumstances: approaches useful in raising capital funds and launching the new program were less appropriate in sustaining the operation. Wright never succeeded in harmonizing his promotional strategy with the requirements of the new clinical program. He had trouble maintaining a suitable inflow of inmates and winning approval from the groups and agencies that had boys to refer or that could validate Inland's claims to competence, for Wright's flair for publicity and his concern with diffuse audiences evoked suspicion among these specialized groups. An erosion of support for Wright among his own clinical personnel was both a contributing cause and a consequence of his inability to win sufficient recognition from professional elites in related organizations.

## Mobilizing Resources

Perkins and Wright faced common problems regarding resources in that both programs required high levels of support, special personnel competencies, and some selection of inmates having suitable characteristics. Differences in auspices and interdependencies demanded divergent solutions. Relations with the legislature were very difficult for Perkins because of its general conservatism and the competing demands made on it for expansion of state services. The executive believed there was a core of legislators sympathetic to Milton but that a major "dramatic event" would be necessary to obtain substantial enlargement of facilities or staff. He anticipated a serious dilemma, therefore, if commitment rates continued to increase. Failing to obtain an expansion of the institution, Perkins expected it would be necessary to risk conflict with judges by reducing proportionately each county's admissions or by establishing

long waiting periods. He did not consider reduction of the average length of stay—then fifteen months—as a real alternative. He was continuously apprehensive, furthermore, that his professional personnel would be attracted to more remunerative employment.

County juvenile courts were the primary sources of Milton's inmates, and the judges were influential in both state and local governmental affairs. Perkins assigned considerable priority to maintaining good relations with them. As commitments had risen he had been able to negotiate a "gentleman's agreement" with the judges to limit new admissions. This strategy had apparently worked satisfactorily. He had even succeeded in negotiating a procedure whereby judges confined commitments to Mondays in order to facilitate the processing of admissions. These arrangements were developed out of close contact between Perkins and the judiciary, by visits to the courts, attendance at state conferences (sometimes accompanied by Taylor), and by alert response to county inquiries by institutional personnel. Although he was apprehensive about the long run and wished that fewer mentally retarded or emotionally disturbed youths were knowingly committed, Perkins was satisfied with the existing level of cooperation. He contrasted the restraint exercised by judges with their power to inundate Milton by drastically increasing commitments, since state law required immediate acceptance of all youths who were committed. He was also concerned with the types of youths who were committed, but chose to emphasize the quantity issue in negotiations with county courts and to deal with the quality problem by winnowing out inappropriate inmates for transfer to other state institutions.

Wright's great problems in controlling Inland's inflow of inmates came with the transformation of the institution. Earlier it had served mainly as a convenient depository for the county court, operating at very modest *per diem* rates. The new treatment program required careful selection of inmates who could be responsive to therapeutic procedures, but these were more likely to be available from agencies other than the juvenile court. Referrals by clinics, schools, and private agencies also conferred more legitimation and prestige on Inland's new program than did those from a court, and inmate *per diem* payments from these new sources were often higher.

Support from the metropolitan community fund constituted about three quarters of Inland's operating budget and was contingent on

Inland's recruiting a preponderance of its inmates from sources in the fund's area. Strenuous efforts were made, principally by Wright, to increase referrals from local sources other than the court, but without immediate success. Boys were available and were accepted in growing numbers, however, from courts, agencies, and other sources outside the area that were willing to meet the more stringent intake criteria and to pay higher *per diem* charges. The number available was, nevertheless, below the institution's capacity, and the total income from *per diem* charges did not reduce dependence on the community fund. Relations with the metropolitan court steadily deteriorated after the shifts in program and in intake criteria.

Through these changes Inland ended its domination by the court but aroused the antagonism of the court's aggressive and influential judge. Tensions were escalated by the court's dissatisfaction with the elaborateness of Inland's intake procedures (then expanding to six weeks), and reached a climax when the court imposed a boycott on the institution. It made no further commitments to Inland until after Wright's discharge. Criticism from the community fund mounted with the decline in inmate population and was exacerbated by referrals from sources outside the area and confusions in fiscal management. Because of a worsening of the area's economic conditions the fund announced an anticipated reduction in its support for all agencies, coincidental with Inland's request for additional support for the institution's clinical program.

At the nadir of Inland's relations with the community fund and court, a metropolitan newspaper published a story strongly criticizing the institution for its lack of cooperation with the court and for taking so many inmates from outside the area. These events coincided with an offer made to Burns to take the directorship of another private institution. Inland's governing board quickly demanded Wright's resignation and asked Burns to become executive. Public announcement of the succession of executives was temporarily withheld to avoid an appearance of capitulation, and Wright was continued on a severance salary for some months.

On accepting the directorship, Burns moved to satisfy the community fund by reducing the proportion of referrals from outside the area and by re-establishing relations with the court. He was as concerned as Wright had been to preserve the institution's new autonomy while

effecting a stable flow of amenable inmates. In a conference with the judge he concentrated on negotiating reliable court referrral procedures. Insistence on higher *per diem* payments was temporarily abandoned, although within months these were raised approximately 12 per cent. This was far less than Wright had sought but was a satisfactory first step. Assurance was given that at least half the institution's capacity would be reserved for the court.

These moves did not resolve the problem of low *per diem* payments for court referrals, however, nor did they enhance Inland's prestige by expanding referrals from high status sources. Burns formulated a novel solution to these difficulties: he and the clinicians induced personnel at the court and other agencies to identify prospective inmates in the early stages of court processing, prior to their formal commitment as wards of the court. These boys could then be referred directly to Inland by agencies other than the court, and at higher *per diem* rates. When necessary because of family opposition or lack of agency funds, the same youths could be fully processed and formally committed by the court. This stratagem was seen as having many advantages: it demonstrated cooperation with the court and reduced that organization's caseload; it preserved Inland's selectivity of intake; it opened up direct channels to the institution from valued referral sources and assured these sources of a treatment-oriented commitment resource they preferred to the state correctional institution; and it provided the higher *per diem* payments that these agencies were willing to make. It was also useful in responding to the community fund's emphasis on "prevention," since Burns could argue that this was accomplished by accepting boys who had not yet been formally adjudicated by the court.

## Obtaining Cooperation

Linkages developed by the executives at Milton and Inland, indicated at numerous points in the foregoing discussion, were more often directed at objectives going beyond that of gaining cooperation than was the case in other institutions. These linkages involved complex interdependencies. They were most characteristic of Inland, but were best illustrated in our discussion of Milton's relationships with the psychiatric center.

At both places the executives used local resources to supplement their

programs and permitted inmates to cross the boundaries for trips, home visits, and athletic contests. Although boundary-spanning was smaller in volume than that at the open institutions, it was more varied. Executives at both institutions sought the recruitment of volunteers from the community, of interns and trainees from professional schools, and of consultants from outside agencies. Wright, encouraging the use of Inland's facilities by neighborhood groups, also worked to increase local good will by opening a small conservation exhibit (earning support from state conservation groups), by arranging for inmates to harvest and sell Christmas trees from the property, by sponsoring dances for inmates and church youth groups, and so forth. He believed these measures had the additional advantage of neutralizing local fears about Inland's relatively open program and neighbors' objections to occasional property damage by truanting inmates.

The executives at both Milton and Inland also made some effort to affect the situations of their inmates' families. At Inland direct therapeutic work with a few parents was begun and the new pattern of cooperation between institutional and court clinicians also resulted in a few mutual referrals for private "off hours" therapy when families could afford the fees. These activities were part of the general strategy pursued by Burns when he assumed the executiveship. He sought to resolve Inland's stressful environmental relations by projecting a thoroughly *professional* conception of the institution and by concentrating on certain crucial linkages. Besides strengthening contacts with mental health agencies and the courts, he also reactivated or created a number of committees on the governing board. These worked on major areas of institutional administration, harnessing board members' abilities and concerns to supplement his own endeavors.

A more extended effort at contact with families was required at Milton because of its role in the state system. Keeping in close touch with the network of welfare organizations and encouraging his staff to participate in their affairs, Perkins believed that assistance from the decentralized county-based field staff of the state department of social welfare was particularly important. The statutes required that inmates released by the institution be returned to their home communities under the parole supervision of the welfare staff. Failure to make adequate arrangements for these youths impeded the discharge process and kept needed bedspace occupied. Inadequate local supervision was also seen

as increasing the possibility of new inmate misconduct and raising the recidivism rate, thereby reflecting on Milton's effectiveness.

Perkins believed that rehabilitation required work with inmates' families and local situations concurrent with the period of institutional commitment, as well as careful follow-up service after the boys' return. He viewed the welfare staff—which had other statutory duties with other types of people—as the "field arm" of Milton and went to considerable effort to enhance the level of their activity and cooperation. Perkins and other Milton staff members visited welfare offices and attended all of their regional and state conferences. New welfare employees spent several days observing Milton's operations as part of their orientation training. Institutional social workers assigned to cottage committees were primarily responsible for continuing contact about their inmates with county welfare personnel, but Perkins hoped eventually to add a full-time professional whose sole assignment would be in this area.

## CONTRASTS AMONG TYPES

Because of the paucity of independent measurements for external events we cannot provide an adequate test of the proposition that external forces and how the executive handles them are the most important keys to organizational behavior. This notion is nevertheless consistent with available evidence. The executive himself is certain that these forces are potent: The chief administrators at half the places in the sample were discharged by the end of our study by the action of outside units (one, Jackson, at Dick, for uncontrollable political reasons).

The public or private nature of the institution defined a series of problems which transcended and interpenetrated those derived from the nature of its goals. The public institutions (Dick, Mixter, and Milton) enjoyed the "prime franchise" in their respective states for the care of court-committed delinquents. This meant that the institution was assured survival and monetary support at some level of sufficiency; that it was subject to commitment pressures from all jurisdictions of the state which could exceed the expansion of institutional facilities; and that, whatever its other claims or capabilities, it was required to

accept and retain delinquent youth whose behavior jeopardized local communities. The private institutions (Regis, Bennett, and Inland) functioned within smaller domains and were subject to commitment pressures only under special circumstances. Since they enjoyed neither "prime franchise" nor assured support, they faced serious problems in defining their missions and developing their "markets" in order to survive and avoid becoming satellites of other organizations.

The ways in which executives recognized and addressed these distinctive issues had fateful consequences for both the institutions and their personal careers. Executives of public institutions faced input and output difficulties that were the obverse of those pressed upon their counterparts at the private institutions. In the public institutions executives sought to work with courts to contain or reduce the volume of commitments they were legally required to accept and gave less attention to the issue of the quality of commitments (such as attempting to refer retarded or psychotic inmates to other state programs). They also worked with courts and local welfare agencies to enhance release arrangements so that limited bedspace was not filled with boys presumably ready to return to their communities. In contrast, executives of the private institutions sought to increase the volume of "desirable" commitments coming from the proper sources and with maximum *per diem* fees. Delicate and complex negotiations were necessary to obtain the desired balances of all three factors. In none of the private institutions did there appear to be special difficulties in arranging the inmate's release.

The risk for the executive of the public institution was that he would arouse the antagonism of influential judges or that his operational design would collapse under too great a volume of commitments. The risk for the executive of the private institution was that he would fail to maintain a sufficient flow of suitable inmates, or that his operational design would suffer from an influx of inappropriate types or lack of monetary support. Further, in all the institutions a great proportion or all of the funds were provided by external units other than those that referred inmates. These different and largely segmented dependencies created countervailing pressures on the institution and posed special problems for the executives. The description of Wright's troubles with the local court and community fund illustrated how obtaining one kind

of resource can become contingent upon serving another obligation and how miscalculations can hurt.

Our findings point to no overall generalization about the prerequisites or correlates of executive success in resolving external problems—except, perhaps, that a resolute and moderate level of effort was more effective than either avoidance (e.g., Hanna at Mixter) or over-striving (e.g., Wright at Inland). The evidence does suggest, however, some of the implications of executive goals and technologies for institutional adaptation. In all six organizations we saw indications of rising external support for rehabilitative goals and of diminishing toleration of punitive or merely custodial programs. The growing number and strength of child welfare and mental health interest groups were the most evident means by which these new demands were expressed. The different institutional designs can be viewed as alternative adaptations to this development, under varying situations and traditions.

The treatment institutions appeared to require more external support than the other organizations. In implementing treatment an institution is likely to become subjected to a double dependency on the professions: both the availability of skilled manpower and the validation of institutional competence become increasingly controlled by external professional groups. These are represented by an extensive and complex network of associations, university and related professional training programs, elites of other treatment organizations, and a cluster of welfare and mental health agencies. The structure of this network varies among the states (it is probably seldom dominated by a single unit, as in Milton's area), and its strength also varies relative to other coalitions of interest. Although unable to accomplish all their purposes, these groups can provide vigorous opposition to persons who profess the aims of treatment but of whom they disapprove. Neither Milton nor Inland could afford to antagonize this sector; to have done so would have evoked a challenge to the institution's competence and accomplishment, a conflict of loyalty among professional staff members, and a withholding of cooperation and other forms of resource exchange. All of these sanctions were threatened or employed against Wright prior to his removal from Inland. The patterns at both Milton and Inland suggest that if the executive does not himself possess the requisite professional credentials, he must develop a partnership with someone who does.

## NOTES

1. Lloyd Ohlin, "Conflicting Interests in Correctional Objectives," in Richard A. Cloward, *et al., Theoretical Studies in Social Organization of the Prison* (New York: Social Science Research Council, 1960), pp. 111–129.

# Executive and Organization

*Chapter 5*

# INTERNAL STRATEGIES
# AND STAFF ORGANIZATION

The third major area of executive leadership is that of defining and managing staff activity. This area of executive effort consists of prescribing work units and patterns to implement the productive goals set for the institution. The requirements of care and sustenance, academic schooling, and rehabilitation are sufficiently complex that multiple operational units must be established. The key issues then become how these major activities are to be assigned to work units and coordinated. The overall design of staff effort directed toward implementation of goals is referred to as the organization's *technology*.

In certain respects the executive is constrained by the general division of labor and definitions of competence prevailing in society. For example, state laws compel either the establishment of academic schools and employment of qualified teachers or the use of outside schools. Even in this area, however, the primary objectives of the educational program, as well as the terms of its integration with other phases of institutional regimen, remain for decision. The existing architecture and institutional plant and the requirements for congregate living also impose certain administrative patterns while leaving undecided the question of how much the inmates should be involved in providing for their own and the institution's maintenance. Similarly, established professional disciplines claim expertise with respect to treatment tasks and press for the employment of qualified representatives, but the executive has considerable discretion over the number to be recruited, the particular duties they will be assigned, and so on.

Of no less importance than the allocation of responsibilities and personnel are prescriptions for relations among units and for degrees of

93

power and autonomy officially given to each. The division of labor may be based on occupational roles recognized in the general culture (e.g., teachers, clinicians), on phases of the program (e.g., cottage, work, educational units), or on some combination of these. It seems inevitable that certain task units will be accorded greater power than others, commensurate with their perceived importance. The crucial operations are those designed to control and change the inmates, but any of several staff groups may be viewed as making the primary contribution to these aims.

Official plans for assuring collaboration among operating units are closely related to the executive's administrative style and definition of his own role. At one extreme he may attempt to supervise all major phases of the institutional program directly, becoming himself the chief instrument for coordination. At the other extreme he may delegate considerable authority to certain subordinates, encourage a decentralized pattern of operation, and establish other mechanisms for inter-unit coordination (e.g., staff committees or teams). Some combination of these approaches is to be expected in most instances, with the executive reserving certain tasks for closer control or investment of his own time while delegating other functions.

The scope and complexity of all but the smallest institutions provide a stimulus to both delegation of authority and specialization in the executive role. External demands and pressures can readily be distinguished from the flow of internal events, and the managerial implications of each appear to be of a different order. We would expect executive tasks to be frequently demarcated between external and internal processes. Further, we would think external relations so important that they would be less likely to be assigned to subordinates.

## OBEDIENCE/CONFORMITY INSTITUTIONS

Neither the Dick nor Mixter executives looked for training or expertise in staff selection except in filling positions of teachers and some clinicians. Both Jackson of Dick and Hanna of Mixter defined the basic competence desired as ability to maintain firm control in managing inmate work and leisure. Both were more likely to condone over-strictness than laxity or over-permissiveness, and both complained about

dissidence among employees who did not evidence proper loyalty, who wished to modify the organization, or (most offensively) who leaked information to those outside for use in criticizing or goading the current regime.

Jackson and Hanna used similar criteria for selecting personnel. They preferred middle-aged persons of working-class backgrounds who had already raised their own families, and were suspicious of younger college-trained men, especially those belonging to a clinical specialty. Teachers had to meet state-wide certification requirements in both places and were regarded by the executives as inclined to misunderstand the basic imperatives of the institutional situation. Hanna did not see as a real problem the fact that only a few of the members of his social service staff had requisite training, and Jackson was adamant in his distrust of professional clinicians and had no intention of employing any. (The Protestant chaplain, a long-time employee, together with the "social service director," a former used-car salesman and protegé of Jackson's, performed social service duties at Dick.) Hanna had less freedom than Jackson with respect to personnel selection, assignment, and dismissal because of the parent organization's requirements, the strong state civil service program, watchful external groups, and a vocal if weak chapter of a state employees' union. With political patronage powerful in Jackson's state, agency administrators were permitted to replace most employees with workers who supported the party in power.

Formally defined task and departmental units were roughly comparable in Dick and Mixter, but there were significant differences in the allocation of resources and authority among these units. In both organizations the major work units were cottage staff, academic school, work program (primarily farm work at Dick), social service, business office, and so on. At Dick the heads of these units—as well as many of their subordinates—reported directly to Jackson, and he exercised a controlling supervision over every aspect of the institution's operations. Tasks involved in the processing of boys and the conduct of the program were supervised by the assistant director, social service director, and chaplain under the executive's close direction. None of these subordinates had authority over any of the others, and even the assistant director functioned as Jackson's alter ego.

Department heads at Mixter enjoyed greater autonomy, although

here the assistant director's duties were restricted to scheduling the inmates' daily work programs. The head of the cottage staff was the most powerful subordinate; he conducted his own unit with little interference from Hanna while exercising considerable influence on the operations of other units. In both institutions the principals of the academic school were granted discretion within their educational programs but otherwise enjoyed little power.

At Dick, Jackson was both more directive in his administrative style and more involved in all phases of institutional operation. Further, he handled most external relations himself. Hanna employed a more "coordinating" style and was far less energetic in his management of internal affairs. He was also less active in handling Mixter's relations with outside units, delegating certain of these to subordinates.

The contrast between the two men was even greater with respect to their stances toward organizational change. Jackson expressed great pride in the innovations and advances he believed he had accomplished. He regarded Dick as very much subject to his influence and was optimistic about his plans for additional improvements in the physical plant. His self-assurance and confident assertiveness, in fact, were not markedly diminished until after the election that ended his party's control of state government. Hanna, however, was defensive about his regime and repetitively offered reasons why it was not possible to effect even those changes he valued. He insisted that most of his problems could be solved only by construction of new facilities, and adversely compared current conditions with those earlier in his decade at Mixter. His air of pessimism and defensive resignation was unmistakable. (His discharge shortly before the second survey came largely because he had failed both to implement the changes the parent organization expected and to quiet local community pressures.)

## RE-EDUCATION/DEVELOPMENT INSTITUTIONS

Both Regis and Bennett were small enough for the executives to assume direct charge of most activities, and neither delegated much administrative authority. Personnel units and arrangements were less complex in these institutions than elsewhere, and least so at Bennett. The major staff groups were personnel who supervised inmates' dormitory or

cottage life and personnel for kitchen and maintenance. Since all boys attended local schools, no teachers were employed. Several recreational workers were employed at Bennett but only one at Regis. Finally, there was one full-time social worker on each staff.

The Regis executive, Mitchell, was energetic and forceful, seemingly in active charge of every phase of institutional operations. His authority was buttressed by the staff's subordination to him within the religious order to which most of them belonged. Although urbane and witty with members of the research team, he was peremptory with his staff. One of the lay brothers served as the assistant director, but this position seemed to be defined mainly as that of an aide. Bennett's executive, Ramsey, was more permissive and less energetic; he delegated considerable autonomy to the cottage parents and others, and he appeared to busy himself with overall coordination or managerial affairs that did not intrude upon the staff.

Both men concerned themselves with critical inmate situations and assumed the role of chief disciplinarian or "court of last resort." Both also gave much attention to the selection of new inmates, although each delegated specific responsibilities in this area to the social worker. The latter person was used at Regis to help with difficult inmates and to maintain contacts with the community schools. Ramsey did not make similar use of the Bennett social worker.

Ability to handle youth was the staff qualification most valued by both executives. Each believed this was more likely to be a product of experience than of training. Personal qualities were also important. Ramsey sought married couples to live in the cottages and college students to conduct recreational activities. Mitchell depended upon a more restricted source: lay brothers of his religious order, some of whom were also attending college. This executive was more specific in the staff qualifications he desired and less satisfied with what he could obtain. He especially valued dedication to the institution and the welfare of the inmates as well as understanding that tempered the firm control staff members were required to exercise. He thought, as did Ramsey, that personnel were more likely to err by being too strict or authoritarian.

Both executives believed that their programs increasingly called for clinical expertise because of the kind of inmates they were getting, despite their efforts at selective intake. Ramsey believed his experienced

(though untrained) social worker lacked sufficient competence, but he had not succeeded in locating another. Mitchell observed that inmates were reluctant to confide in staff members who belonged to the order, and he said that additional skilled personnel were needed. He encountered difficulties in attracting or holding qualified clinicians, however. He thought this was because they preferred positions where they could associate with trained colleagues, and he also suspected that Regis's emphasis on training and control did not appeal to clinicians. Difficulties in this area appeared to be due as much to Mitchell's ambivalence about the utility of clinical expertise for Regis: apart from screening referrals and handling relations with the schools, clinical persons were desired only for coping with especially difficult inmates and supplementing counselling by the members of the religious order. Mitchell would have preferred to avoid the latter two tasks by enlarging the referral pool to get a better selection of boys and by inducing inmates to confide in staff.

## TREATMENT INSTITUTIONS

Internal strategies were much more complex and in flux at Milton and Inland. At Milton, Taylor, the clinical director, had instituted cottage committees as the major mechanism for organizing staff activity. Perkins, the chief executive, was sympathetic with this arrangement, believing it would reduce staff rivalry and conflict, which had been among the major sources of difficulty faced by his predecessor. The build-up of professionals and their assignment to specialty subunits (like psychology or social work) had underscored the necessity for devices to unify the staff and reduce tensions among clinical disciplines as well as between—in Perkins' terms—the "long hairs" (professionals) and the "short hairs" (non-professionals).

The cottage committee had additional values for Taylor: it permitted concentration of rehabilitative effort on the crucial living units, reduced the autonomy of custodially-oriented cottage parents, and facilitated more direct infusion of psychiatric perspectives among personnel whose activities had formerly been segmented from those of the mental health professionals. As the system was revised not long before our first survey,

each cottage had a team composed of a social worker, two cottage parents, several cottage supervisors, and a recreation worker, all under the immediate supervision of a clinical coordinator (a senior mental health professional). This team conferred daily and held weekly group sessions with all boys in the cottage. It was responsible for planning the inmates' programs, evaluating their behavior and progress, governing cottage life and leisure, and determining when boys could be released.

Under this system the clinical coordinators were granted most authority; they were responsible for the direction of their teams and for management of cottage life, as well as for exercise of clinical skills. These tasks required competencies in addition to those needed under the conventional department plan of organization. Taylor found that not every senior professional was either willing or able to assume these extended duties, and he was preoccupied with shifting them into and out of coordinators' positions in an effort to achieve the desired balance.

Perkins and Taylor recognized three other limitations to the cottage unit plan. The specialty departments had not been entirely abolished and their parallel existence with the cottage committees created confusing dual lines of authority. Heads of departments (e.g., of social services) were still needed to employ their respective clinicians, to perform certain cross-cottage tasks, and to provide "professional" supervision to members of their specialty groups. Second, academic and vocational teachers were excluded from the committees because the school structure could not be directly linked with that of the cottage. An attempt was made to involve the academic and vocational unit heads in all cottage committees, but the two men could not participate effectively in these decentralized operations. Finally, Taylor did not believe the cottage committee device had assured the degree of flexible problem-solving by the staff that he desired. He noted that the adaptiveness essential to the rehabilitative task was jeopardized by tendencies toward routinization. Therapeutic effects depended upon adjusting action to the particulars of time and person, but staff members were inclined to convert what were supposed to be discretionary actions into standard practices, and inmates came to expect as "rights" (such as passes to town) what were intended as special privileges. Taylor also expressed concern about achieving the desired balance of commitment among staff members. He regarded high interest in the task and willing-

ness to "work through problems" as essential staff qualities. Although he preferred over- to under-commitment, he saw some personnel as "neurotically involved."

Perkins and Taylor achieved an administrative partnership based on a well-articulated, highly complementary division of effort. Perkins retained general direction of the entire enterprise but concentrated on external affairs and certain internal managerial duties. Only Taylor and the business manager reported directly to him, but he kept in touch with other staff groups and their activities. As clinical director, Taylor was responsible for administration of Milton's operating personnel and daily program cycle. This arrangement suited their respective skills and interests and appeared to be remarkably viable and efficient, if not without occasional strain. They enjoyed mutual trust because of highly compatible conceptions about the nature of their inmates, the basic task of the institution, and the desirability of optimizing its achievements. Disagreements between them arose mainly from their different perspectives: Taylor retained his psychiatrist's dedication to the aims and technology of treatment, with distinctly administrative and external matters being of secondary concern; Perkins continued to be concerned about staff coordination and the external relevance of internal operations.

Taylor interpreted the scope of his responsibility as including administrative control over all personnel who worked with boys and over all areas affecting inmate-staff relations, however indirectly. He was anxious to avoid involvement in maintenance, fiscal, or public relations affairs, although he assisted Perkins in dealing with important external groups. While recognizing Perkins's ultimate authority within Milton, Taylor believed he himself could remain in his position only so long as he had a relatively free hand. Taylor was somewhat reserved but manifested an air of quiet competence; he employed a coordinative administrative style through which he attended to the flow of daily events and sought to modify staff performance through training and persuasive consultation. More than half his week was spent in regularly scheduled supervisory conferences with department heads and in routine meetings of the "consultation," division head, special cottage, and coordinators' committees.

The situation emerging at Inland differed in two critical respects from that at Milton. The chief executives did not develop a viable partnership, and the new operative design was not (at least initially)

adequately responsive to critical external pressures. The rough division of labor between Wright as executive and Burns as assistant, which was effective in rebuilding and transforming the institution, suited their preferences and was continued. Wright succinctly summarized this pattern as: "I'm Mr. Outside, and he's Mr. Inside." To Burns, however, being assistant director meant that he should have full authority for all internal matters other than business administration. He regarded himself as truly an associate of the executive, and believed that the executive's task was to provide the resources needed to operate a program the outlines of which should be determined by the professional elite.

The expanded clinical staff dominated the new program under the direction of a clinical director, a confidant of Burns who had been a colleague in the former regime. Personnel in this group were professionally trained and occupied private offices in the new main building. All other units—school, cottage life, recreation—were subordinated to the clinic. Staff members retained from the former regime were gradually replaced by younger and better educated persons who could be more permissive and flexible. All unit supervisors reported to the assistant director, who seemed to work around the clock and who maintained close contact with all staff and boys. Business affairs was the one area of internal management over which Wright retained exclusive responsibility. He discharged most of these tasks himself with the aid of a secretary, buying supplies, keeping account books, and preparing financial reports. Because of the pressure of other duties or Wright's lack of training in this area, however, his accounting procedures proved unreliable and eventually exposed the institution to criticism from the metropolitan community fund.

In managing the program there were two sources of strain between Wright and Burns. First, the executive was viewed as episodically intruding on internal matters, reversing a decision about a boy or dealing with a staff member directly rather than through the assistant director. For his part, Wright believed the clinicians were too little concerned with the "other twenty-three hours" (i.e., the non-clinical phases of the program); he was also concerned about the public's image of the program and did not believe events were handled with sufficient sensitivity to these implications. The mental health professionals became critical of Wright because he had done little to elaborate

or validate the psychotherapeutic approach, and they felt his appreciation of it was "superficial." They and the assistant director regarded Wright's involvement in program matters as capricious, opportunistic, and irrelevant to, if not disruptive of, the therapeutic effort. Second, Wright's approach to external affairs also created tensions with Burns and the clinicians. They believed that Wright was exploiting segments of the program for publicity and disrupting their handling of inmate selection. Conflicts over these matters not only eventually cost Wright the support of his professional cadre when the governing board moved to oust him, but also induced Burns to accept the directorship when it was offered.

The shift in executives occurred between the first and second surveys. Burns retained his basic inward or programmatic orientation and essentially reversed his predecessor's strategy: where Wright had emphasized external relations and the use of institutional program for organizational aggrandizement, Burns stressed internal achievement and sought to mobilize features of the environment in support of the rehabilitative program. The two men also differed in their administrative styles. Wright had many enthusiasms and gave an appearance of boundless energy; he was also outspoken and appeared to be somewhat arbitrary in dealings with his subordinates. Burns was more low-keyed, coordinative rather than directive of subordinates, and more concerned to involve them in problem-solving.

As a condition to accepting the directorship Burns obtained the governing board's agreement that he would not be expected to engage in public relations efforts and that business management would be handled by a competent subordinate. Thus freed, he addressed a series of external and internal problems that were sharply defined at the time of Wright's ouster. These tasks were sufficiently demanding that Burns could no longer serve the same role with inmates and staff that he had had as assistant director, and he moved to create a revised structure of authority and responsibility. This had to be one that assured the support and loyalty of the staff, particularly the clinicians. Thus internal dissension or troublesome incidents would not result in new pressures from outside. Burns was also concerned with enhancing Inland's treatment potential and with ameliorating tensions among staff subgroups.

Before the changeover, both Wright and Burns had wished to

reduce the relative isolation of teachers and to modify cottage counselor roles so that they could participate more significantly in treatment processes. As executive, Burns realized he could not guide internal processes through the clinical director, since he and his colleagues continued to restrict their interest and activity to more narrowly defined diagnostic and therapeutic procedures. They could not, therefore, be expected to resolve intra-program segmentation, formulate plans for greater participation by other staff groups in the treatment effort, or, as individually-oriented clinicians, enhance the potentials of the "therapeutic community" by utilizing inmates' informal relations. To accomplish these purposes and under stimulation from our "executive seminar" feedback sessions, Burns recruited a trained group worker with prior institutional experience. Had he appointed the new person to his former position of assistant director, however, Burns would have run several risks. The professional cadre, and particularly the clinical director, would have objected to being outranked by a newcomer, while the new person might have used the position as had Burns himself— to control the internal program and eventually to isolate the executive. Appointment of the new person as "program coordinator" assigned unified responsibility for all phases of the program, emphasized coordination without signalling a formal shift of power (i.e., downgrading the clinic), and assured Burns of continued access to inmates, staff, and internal processes.

Modifications of the clinical model were made to mesh staff groups, to gear school and cottage life more effectively into the treatment design, and to utilize the boys' informal relations. Unlike the pattern at Milton, these changes did not include integrated staff practices centered on the cottage, although staff employees in these units were now expected to mobilize boys in support of behavior norms rather than merely to curb excesses. A second group worker was subsequently employed as supervisor of the cottage units, and the two group workers began to meet regularly with clinical personnel.

## CONTRASTS AMONG TYPES

The central issue in the executive's internal strategies was the allocation of power or authority within the organization. Executives gave

structural support, especially power, to the subordinates, subunits, and operational patterns they believed to be most oriented to their major goals or most crucial in implementing them. To substantiate this conclusion we may examine the patterned differences among the three types of institutions—particularly in the investment of power in certain units, the composition of the executive core, and the executives' overall administrative style.

Personnel assigned to the cottages or living units were allocated most authority and autonomy in the obedience/conformity institutions, whereas clinicians were similarly favored in the treatment institutions. In each instance these groups could exercise greatest control over decisions about inmates, their views were deferred to most frequently by executives, and their activities were accorded primacy relative to those of other staff units (Milton put the clinicians in direct charge of other personnel). The situation was less clear in the re-education/development institutions because the academic programs were conducted by outside schools, but a more balanced distribution of authority seemed to be intended. Teachers' assessments of inmates were accepted as significant indices of progress, and the activities of living-unit personnel were regarded as crucial to inmates' social development. Further, clinicians were assigned to perform some important functions for which they were accorded independent authority.

In all organizations the tasks, authority, autonomy, and valuation assigned to staff subunits were roughly commensurate with the executive's major goals and program designs. Favored units were not necessarily those with the most personnel, those highest in the formal table of organization, or those best qualified under general criteria. Teachers, for example, constituted large cadres in both the obedience/conformity and treatment institutions and were relatively highly educated and well paid, but they were given relatively little authority anywhere.

Selective and unequal allocation of authority was also apparent in the executives' choice of chief assistants. At each institution the heads of major staff subunits constituted a kind of cabinet. It was accorded some recognition but actually exercised little real authority. There was, however, an executive core composed of those few subordinates with whom the chief administrator chose to work most closely and to whom he delegated most authority, regardless of formal patterns. Within this core executives at two of the institutions (Milton and Inland) formed

a particularly close association or an executive "partnership" with one other person. The executive at Mixter also yielded considerable autonomy to another person, the custodially-oriented director of cottage life, relegating the assistant director to minor duties. The composition of the executive core, the use of partnerships, and the allocation of power among these persons was systematically linked to the executives' major goal commitments. To some extent they also reflected personality and idiosyncratic differences among the executives.

In general, increasing organizational size and technological complexity are likely to give rise to greater specialization and delegation of executive power. The low levels of specialization and sharing of power found in Regis and Bennett seemed to result for precisely this reason. Size and complexity also seemed to underlie the contrasting patterns at Mixter and Dick. Mixter showed greater specialization and delegation of power, apparently because it was too large to be administered without it. Dick showed less, seemingly not only because it was smaller and its executive more energetic but also because of the institution's relatively simple and routinized design. Instead of sharing in administrative power members of Dick's executive core were assigned limited authority to implement Jackson's explicit directives. Two of the members of the core, further, were trusted lieutenants who assisted in advancing his political career, a concern for which executive-ship itself was largely instrumental.

Closely associated with the sharing of executive power was the administrative style by which leadership was exercised. The executives varied in their use of a directive or coordinative approach in the guidance of subordinates' activities. Those at the extremes showed the greatest contrast: Dick's executive exercised firm direction over all phases of staff performance, whereas the treatment executives tended toward the coordination of relatively autonomous subordinates. Again, the complexity of the technology appeared to have a major influence on administrative behavior, since the performance requirements at the treatment institutions were too intricate to be managed directly by the executives.[1] At such places, furthermore, the greater numbers of professional personnel probably required a coordinative administrative style because of their emphases on autonomy, rationality, and persuasion.

Perhaps most important in accounting for administrative style was

the incorporation of unified interaction principles for all persons within the institution. The model of the essential staff-inmate patterns of control desired by executives was exemplified in their own behavior vis-a-vis chief subordinates and other staff members. This definition of basically similar interaction patterns increased consistency within the organization and enhanced the clarity of executive philosophies and operational designs, thereby facilitating the chief administrator's infusion of preferred orientations throughout the organization. Reliance on unified and consistent human-relations principles may be of special importance for organizations whose primary task involves changing persons through interpersonal means.[2]

## FINDINGS ON ORGANIZATIONAL STRUCTURE

Other types of information beyond our observations confirm, qualify, or shed additional light on the executives' internal strategies, and allow us to test additional hypotheses about the implications of goals. These data include materials in institutional files, observations of staff activities, and questionnaire responses bearing on personnel characteristics, variations in role definitions, departmental structure, the distribution of power, and intergroup conflict.

*Staffing Patterns*

The data show, as we would expect, the existence of higher levels of education and professionalization among personnel in institutions having more complex goals and technologies. Table 5.1 presents the

### Table 5.1—Ratios of Inmates to Staff

|  | Closed Institutions | | | | Open Institutions | |
|  | OBEDIENCE/ CONFORMITY | | TREATMENT | | RE-EDUCATION/ DEVELOPMENT | |
|  | Dick | Mixter | Milton | Inland | Regis | Bennett |
|---|---|---|---|---|---|---|
| Inmate-Total Staff Ratio | 3.9 | 2.3 | 1.7 | 1.5 | 4.3 | 3.0 |
| Inmate-Cottage Parent Ratio | 22.7 | 10.0 | 5.7 | 8.6 | 9.3 | 7.2 |
| Inmate-Teacher Ratio* | 25.0 | 27.3 | 22.2 | 6.7 | — | — |
| Inmate-Social Service Ratio | 125.0† | 45.0 | 22.2 | 15.0 | 40.0 | 36.0 |

* No teachers in the open institutions.
† At Dick, the chaplain was classified as a social service worker because he did intake interviews and some counselling.

total inmate-staff ratios together with the inmate-cottage parent, inmate-teacher, and inmate-social service ratios. Setting aside ratios from Regis and Bennett because they did not have to staff schools and some other operations, we find that the total ratios of inmates to staff decrease in the following order: Dick, Mixter, Milton, Inland.[3] Although the pattern is especially striking for social service personnel, the same tendency holds for all positions.

The institutions varied markedly in their use of social service personnel. Dick had the services of a single untrained social service worker, augmented by the counselling activities of the chaplain. Mixter had six counselors, a psychologist, two psychometricians, and a part-time psychiatrist. Regis had a psychologist and a social worker, both part-time, while Bennett had a full-time but untrained social worker. Milton's social service staff had ten members, all with credentials in psychiatry, clinical psychology, or social work. (In addition, several psychiatric residents conducted group therapy sessions.) Inland's social service staff had four members, all trained clinical psychologists or social workers. In addition, there were a consulting psychiatrist and trainee in group work.

Table 5.2 presents data on age, length of employment, education, race, and previous professional employment for the total staff and for selected positions within each institution. The data reflect not only educational and professional differences but also the greater effort made by treatment executives to hire younger staff members, whom they thought more capable of forming close relationships with inmates and less likely to have personal histories of failure and ineptitude. Staffs at Inland and Milton had a higher median education and a lower median age than those at Mixter and Dick.

The pattern is complicated by data on Regis, where staff members tended to be both young and well educated. Because the brotherhood that ran it was a teaching order, all its members had gone or were going to college; moreover, the order staffed Regis with some younger brothers who could attend a nearby Catholic college during the day while the inmates were in school. Inland's very high educational level was based on its high ratio of professional and teaching staff to total staff and its policy of mainly hiring college students as cottage parents. At Mixter only one out of ten employees had had any previous experi-

## Table 5.2—Staff Background Characteristics

| Staff Characteristics | OBEDIENCE/ CONFORMITY | | RE-EDUCATION/ DEVELOPMENT | | TREATMENT | |
|---|---|---|---|---|---|---|
| | Dick | Mixter | Regis | Bennett | Milton | Inland |
| **Total Staff:** | | | | | | |
| Number* | 65 | 184 | 13† | 12 | 117 | 40 |
| Median age | 44 | 46 | 28 | 42 | 41.5 | 38 |
| Median years of service | 2.8 | 7 | 2 | 2.2 | 4.4 | 4.2 |
| Median education (years) | 10 | 11.6 | 16 | 13.3 | 12.2 | 14 |
| Per cent white | 100 | 88 | 85 | 100 | 78 | 72 |
| Per cent previous professional experience (social work, education, psychology, etc.) | 13 | 9 | 78 | 17 | 19 | 30 |
| **Cottage Parents:** | | | | | | |
| Number | 11 | 41 | 6 | 5 | 35 | 7 |
| Median age | 39 | 47 | 26.5 | 48.2 | 28.5 | 27 |
| Median years of service | 2 | 7 | 2 | 1.8 | 2.9 | 1.4 |
| Median education (years) | 12 | 12 | 15 | 14.2 | 13 | 16 |
| Per cent white | 100 | 93 | 100 | 100 | 70 | 56 |
| **Detail Supervisors:§** | | | | | | |
| Number | 18 | 26 | — | — | 9 | — |
| Median age | 54 | 42.5 | — | — | 54 | — |
| Median years of service | 2 | 6 | — | — | 4 | — |
| Median education (years) | 9 | 12 | — | — | 12 | — |
| Per cent white | 100 | 92 | — | — | 78 | — |
| **Teachers:** ** | | | | | | |
| Number | 10 | 15 | — | — | 10 | 9 |
| Median age | 44 | 50 | — | — | 39 | 40.5 |
| Median years of service | 3 | 11 | — | — | 2.5 | 6 |
| Median education (years) | 16 | 17 | — | — | 16.5 | 16 |
| Per cent white | 100 | 78 | — | — | 78 | 77 |
| **Social Service:** | | | | | | |
| Number | 2 | 9 | 2 | 1 | 10 | 4 |
| Median age | 32 | 37.5 | 30 | $>60$ | 37.5 | 36.5 |
| Median years of service | 4.5 | 6 | 2.5 | 6 | 4 | 4 |
| Median education (years) | 14 | 17 | 17 | 15 | 18 | 18 |
| Per cent white | 100 | 77 | 100 | 100 | 60 | 50 |

* Total staff includes part-time recreation personnel but excludes part-time consultants (e.g., doctors, dentists, psychiatrists). Total staff also excludes personnel paid by the institution but not connected with its integral operation.

† At Regis other information was not obtained on the four maintenance personnel. Since they did not work with boys, the data are not essential. All remaining tables are based upon the seven brothers and two social service personnel of the institution.

§ An individual was classified as a detail supervisor if his primary job was the supervision of boys in the production of work. Often it was difficult to distinguish a vocational instructor from a detail supervisor. In this case the education of the staff member was taken into consideration.

** Physical education instructors were classified with recreation personnel.

ence in social work, education, psychology, or the like; at Inland three out of ten employees had had such experience.

The hiring of more highly educated staff members may have negative consequences for organizational stability. College-trained staff personnel at Milton and Inland frequently moved on to better positions. Mixter, which had civil service job security and fairly high salaries and employed few college-trained personnel, had the staff with the highest median length of service. On the other hand, the use of educated and younger staff employees at Inland and Milton apparently facilitated the inculcation of a rehabilitative philosophy. The low median length of service of Dick's employees largely reflected political change.

Inland and Milton, the treatment institutions, had higher proportions of Negroes on their staffs. Part of the explanation probably lies in the fact that because Negroes are discriminated against in the labor market it is often possible, when educational level is used as a criterion, for treatment institutions to hire Negroes with better qualifications than those of available whites.

These differences in numbers and characteristics of staff personnel partially reflect constraints of finances and labor shortages, of course, but they also reflect executive strategies. All executives said they would like more and better personnel. As we have seen, however, most said they were satisfied with their programs and made little effort to raise the quality of present personnel through staff training or similar procedures. The strategies of the executives who had few trained personnel did not impel them to make forceful efforts to acquire the resources necessary to alter their staffing patterns.

## Variations in Task Definitions

Cottage parents, social service workers, and teachers are the personnel most directly involved in translating goals into actions affecting inmates. Descriptions based on direct observation indicate how their roles varied with differences in technologies and the allocation of power.

*Cottage Parents.* In all institutions cottage parents had general responsibility for supervising sustenance activities, eating, sleeping, and cleanliness. Beyond this, task definitions varied. In the obedience/conformity institutions definitions focused on rules and control through

the application of a wide range of negative sanctions. Within this framework cottage parents at Dick could define many other aspects of their roles as they liked, such as whether and what to advise the boys. At Mixter they were hemmed in by a series of regulations reflecting the prerogatives given the social service staff by the institution's partial efforts toward treatment. Dick allowed cottage parents much more freedom in disciplining. At both Dick and Mixter, however, whether the cottage parent encouraged boys to participate in activities or do extra schoolwork, and whether he planned a program of activities were matters of personal discretion. In both institutions the cottage parents played a major role in determining when inmates would be released.

Cottage parents at Milton and especially Inland were not to emphasize control and had little discretion over discipline. More important than supervision were their tasks of encouraging interaction and activities and establishing supportive and close relationships. There were vague injunctions to fit their supervisory techniques and encouragement to each inmate's needs. At Inland rewards and sanctions were only indirectly affected by cottage parents, their major sanction being to report misbehavior to a superior. Milton's cottage parents had many more short-range sanctions available to them, but in neither treatment institution did the cottage parents directly affect a boy's release date by grading, for release decisions were to be based on clinical judgment.

Cottage personnel in the re-education/development institutions stood between those in the obedience/conformity and the treatment institutions in terms of freedom to discipline and in the requirements to provide diffuse support. Regis's personnel apparently were given more latitude in immediate physical punishment than were Bennett's.

*Social Service.* Counselors, psychologists, psychiatrists, and social workers made up the social service staffs. The definitions of their tasks ranged from those of Dick, which were specific and routine, to those of the treatment institutions, which were broad and central to planning action toward the inmates.

Dick's social service director was responsible for receiving inmates, obtaining social and offense histories, and contacting courts and families to arrange release dates or home visits. He had no responsibility for decisions internal to the organization. In contrast, social service workers at Mixter, Regis, and Bennett were to do counselling as well. "Counsel-

ling" in these institutions meant discussing the behavior of boys when they had violated rules in some gross fashion; it was "adjustment counselling" aimed largely at reconciling the boy to the institution. At Mixter emotionally disturbed boys were seen occasionally in ten to twenty-minute interviews with the psychologist or psychiatrist, while at Regis they were referred for treatment to the child guidance clinic of the local court.

The outcome of the partial attempt to implement treatment at Mixter can be seen in the definition of social service responsibility for defending inmates against unfair usage by other staff members. If a boy committed a serious offense within the institution, such as fighting or "talking back," he was "written up" by the staff member responsible for the boy at the time of the incident. If the staff member's department head saw fit and the head of social service concurred, the case was presented at the "case conference" for decision on proper punishment. The social service counselor had the option of defending the boy if he felt the charge or the punishment was unfair. (A consequence of this task definition was that the interests of the counselors were seen as somewhat antagonistic to the interests of other staff members.)

At Inland and Milton social service workers were associated with prime organizational tasks. Between these treatment institutions role definitions varied on the basis of the commitment to individual or group treatment. Inland's social workers and psychologists aimed principally at promoting positive personality and value changes by use of individual counseling. Although the social worker occasionally interviewed the families of the boys, the primary focus was on individual treatment. The major focus of Milton's social service workers was on managing the institutional milieu and manipulating the inmate's home environment. In the division of labor among the social service staff, clinical coordinators directed cottage committees in working with the boys in the group while social workers were to work with the home. With psychiatric residents providing group therapy to between sixty and eighty boys, the other professional workers were free to focus to a large extent on the integration of organizational activities. A consequence of this role definition was that the professionals spent an increasing proportion of time working with other staff members rather than in direct contact with inmates.

The varying task definitions among institutions had important consequences for the relationships between cottage parents and the social service staff. The highest level of formal communication between the two groups occurred in the treatment institutions. Dick's role definitions required little discussion of individual cases. Cottage parents were to meet formally with the social service director and other members of the executive core once a month, and then only to evaluate boys for special privileges or discharge. In practice only a few of the cottage parents attended.

Regis's cottage parents had considerable informal contact with the social service workers but no formal meetings. Little internal communication was deemed necessary because cottage parents did not see social service skills as being very different from their own, and major decisions were made by the executive. The social worker at Bennett had little contact with the cottage parents, did not attempt to work with them, and was also rather isolated from the inmates.

The beginnings of an attempt to integrate the perspectives of cottage parents and social service personnel appeared at Mixter and Inland. At both institutions a counselor met with personnel from each cottage an hour a week to discuss problems. At Mixter the major consequence was an accommodation of social service to cottage parents. At Inland not all the social service workers took the responsibility seriously, nor did they have an agenda which consistently focused on cottage parent problems. Accommodation was in the opposite direction from that at Mixter.

In contrast, Milton's cottage parents met daily with the clinical co-ordinator and social worker to discuss problems of group management, activities, release dates, and treatment progress, and to conduct interviews with individuals or groups of inmates. Those cottage parents who were off duty at the time of the cottage meetings met with the head cottage parent once a week. Milton focused its professional resources on helping the cottage parent to a much larger extent than any of the other institutions.

*Teachers.* In all four of the institutions that had teachers on the staff, task definitions restricted teachers to classroom activity and extracurricular clubs or athletics, similar to school programs in the outside world. Because boys were behind their age level and academic potential, much of the teaching was remedial. But treatment institutions

tended to stress the necessity of coordinating educational and psycholog-ical programs, whereas obedience/conformity institutions minimized the necessity of teacher interaction with either cottage parents or social service staff.[4] In treatment institutions there was a greater attempt to plan education and vocational training in accordance with the inmate's future employment possibilities. Assignment to the school program at Dick was largely routine, depending on the inmate's age, while at Mixter the boy's interests and capabilities were given some attention in the boy's initial placement in the program—when the overcrowded facilities allowed room for choice. The lack of emphasis on career planning created little need for consultation between social service staff and teachers. Dick's teachers had no formal contact with either cottage parents or social service staff, whereas at Mixter the head psychologist was officially a consultant to the teachers on problem inmates, but only occasionally assumed this role.

The school programs at Inland and Milton differed in that there was much more contact between teachers and social service staff at Inland and much more educational and vocational planning at Milton. For several years clinicians and teachers at Inland had met in regular weekly case meetings, at which time the background and psychodynamics of cases were presented but little planning was done. On the other hand, the school and vocational coordinators at Milton met regularly with the cottage committees to attempt to develop long-range plans for each inmate.

Summarizing the consequences of these task definitions for opera-tions, we see that toward the custodial pole tasks were more routinized because they were more rule-oriented and universalistic and required little programming of non-repetitive activities. Toward the treatment pole, tasks required particularistic decisions, professional knowledge, non-routine programming, and greater voluntarism. The more treatment-oriented institutions, therefore, required more communication and co-ordination of activities. These differences in tasks created different and increased problems of executive control. First, treatment required greater knowledge of each inmate. Second, specifications for treatment tasks were more diffuse than for more custodial tasks. Simple injunctions like "keep the boys in line" or "keep the doors locked" did not provide a basis for role definitions in the treatment institutions. Third, control was required over a greater range of personnel and activities.

*Departmental Structure*

Internal strategies are also expressed in departmental patterns. We can hypothesize that as more complex goals, requiring greater organizational complexity and a breakdown of routine programs, are introduced, the executive's span of control will become overloaded and pressures to create departments will occur.[5] Further, to the extent that diverse functions or skills are seen as highly interdependent, the need for coordination will be seen and pressures for an integrated chain of command will be created.

The departmental patterns we observed can be classified into three types of structure on the basis of degree of departmentalization and extent of integration of departments, as follows:[6]

*Simple Structure.* In a simple structure there is little departmentalization and the executive remains in direct contact with the operatives. (Because the academic school is required by law and operates under standards independent of the institution, it will always be a separate department, resulting in some departmentalization.) Of the six institutions, Dick, Regis, and Bennett most closely approximated this model. Figures 5.1, 5.2, and 5.3 present the tables of organization of these institutions. Regis and Bennett were simply differentiated with no departments,[7] probably because of their small size and their relatively routine operations, while Dick was partially departmentalized. By comparing Dick's table of organization with that of Inland (Figure 5.5), however, it can be seen that Dick was considerably less departmentalized, even though it had over 50 per cent more staff personnel. Thus size alone does not account for the degree of departmentalization.

The departmentalization that *did* develop at Dick was not based on an attempt to control staff relations with inmates. The farm was made a separate department to improve efficiency after the institution was criticized publicly for growing a poor variety of vegetables. Even without supervising the teachers and farm supervisors, Dick's executive and assistant director had approximately fifty persons reporting directly to them. The executive did not find himself under pressure of time, however; he spent a leisurely hour every morning keeping up with political news from the state capital and was generally available to staff and inmates who wished to see him.

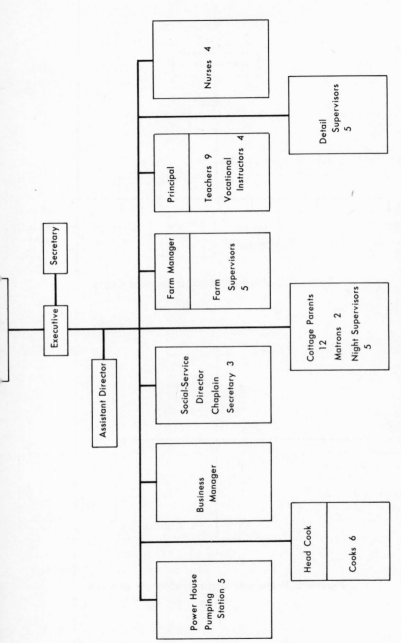

**Figure 5.1—Formal Organization at Dick**

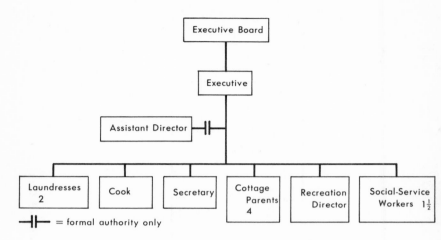

*Figure 5.2—Formal Organization at Regis*

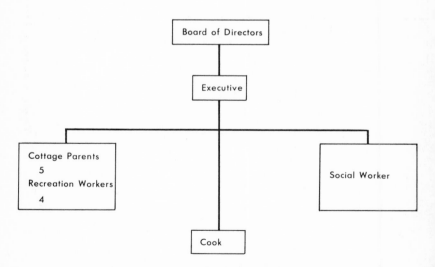

*Figure 5.3—Formal Organization at Bennett*

Institutions committed to straightforward obedience/conformity goals (that is unmixed, as in Dick but not Mixter) or re-education/development goals require little departmentalization. Operations can be routine and repetitive, for when containment and control, or hard work and study, are achieved, organizational goals are presumed to be implemented. Coordination is required primarily for movement of boys and rotation of shifts. Little departmentalization is needed because the executive can maintain a broad span of control over the basically simple problems that arise.

*Multiple Department Structure.* Each area of operation in a multiple department structure—school, social service, cottage life—is performed in a separate department, with little integration. This structure occurs when the diverse tasks of the institution are seen as relatively autonomous.

Mixter and Inland (Figures 5.4 and 5.5) showed this type of structure. In contrast with pure obedience/conformity and re-education/development institutions, those with mixed or treatment goals cannot operate so routinely. More complex combinations of personnel must be coordinated. Although the larger size of Mixter resulted in more divisions into subsystems than in Inland, the basic structure was the same. Mixter's, as contrasted with Dick's, reflected not only the difference in size but also the partial input of treatment (or efforts to make the institution more benign) in its otherwise obedience/conformity-oriented operations. Inland was, at least until the reorganization started when Burns succeeded to the directorship, an institution in which, because of the commitment to individual therapy, activities in the school or cottage were not perceived as important to rehabilitation.

The histories of Inland and Mixter show clearly the emergence of departments as solutions to problems of executive control. Until 1940, Mixter's structure, even with over a hundred employees, resembled Dick's. Departmentalization came in response to public criticism of lack of control over staff activities, especially in the cottages. Even after the change some cottage parents continued to bypass their official supervisor, so that it took several years to establish an operative department. Departmentalization of cottage life not only reduced the span of control of the chief executive but also allowed for effective control over cottage parents, consonant with the partial commitment to treatment expressed in the attempt to make custodialism benign. Departmentalization led to

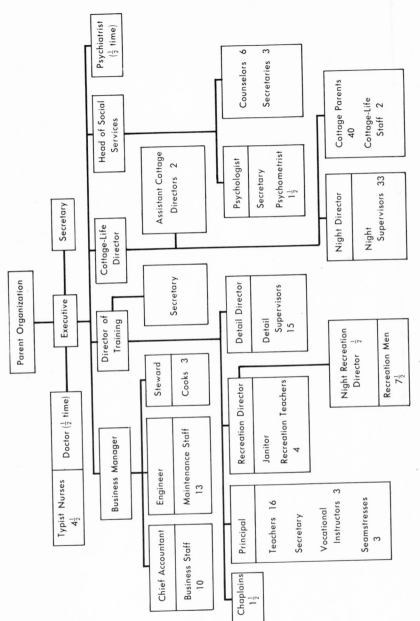

**Figure 5.4—Formal Organization at Mixter**

118

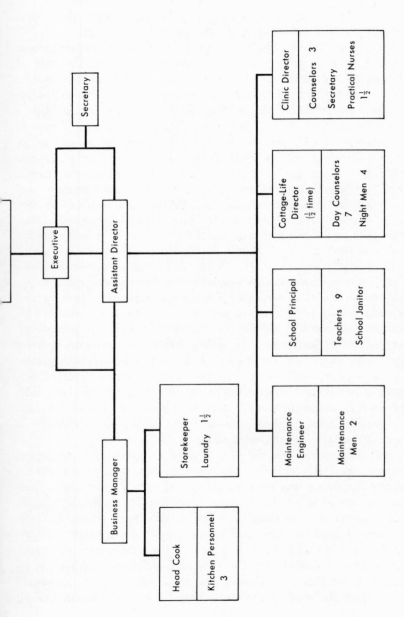

**Figure 5.5—Formal Organization at Inland**

more frequent handling of discipline problems through hierarchical referral rather than on-the-spot use of repressive techniques.

Inland's structure developed when the Wright and Burns administration took over six years earlier and attempted to formalize lines of authority through department heads. This was done in order to overcome a long-standing informal system of favoritism. The departmental structure had not permitted Burns, the assistant director, to establish a reasonable span of control, however. The institution's emphasis on particularism, voluntarism, and non-routinized programs, as well as the assistant director's role as chief disciplinarian (which required the weighing of many alternatives and consequences in a treatment institution), over-extended his efforts. Inland's clearly stated treatment goal minimized the possibility of the custodial-treatment bifurcation that could occur at Mixter, however, for even before the reorganization efforts the executives saw cottage life and the school as at least ancillary areas of treatment.

*Dual Department Structure.* A dual department structure integrates all activities with inmates in one inclusive division and gives supervisory responsibility to professional treatment personnel. Business and maintenance activities are grouped in a second department. This structure was found in Milton (see Figure 5.6). Like the pure obedience/conformity institution, the milieu treatment institution operates on relatively unitary criteria. It differs in its attempt to rationalize greater areas of organizational activity, in the complex combinations of personnel required, and in the substantive bases of its decisions. The centralization of control over all activities in which inmates are involved necessitates placing persons with treatment commitments directly in charge of the day-to-day operating staff.

Milton's structure was the outgrowth of an earlier multiple department structure, in which the clinicians were in a separate department and the institution was unstably bifurcated with high conflict. Even after the change to two major departments inmates continued to work under maintenance personnel in what basically were production jobs, with social service personnel still having only consultant responsibility. The real shift to a dual structure came with the cottage committees and, finally, the decision to give the clinical coordinators supervisory responsibility for these committees. The therapeutic role of the system was theoretically based on the relationship between the inmate and all

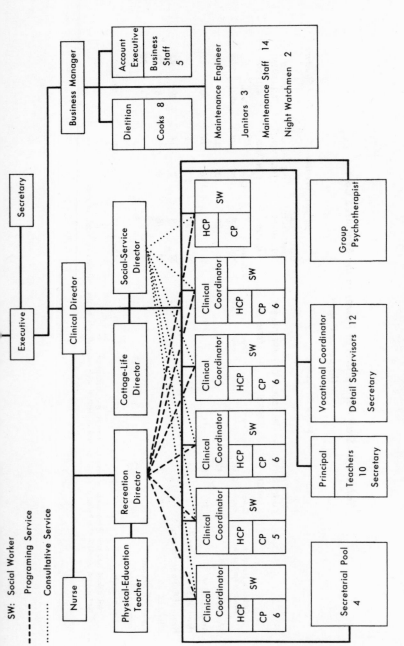

SW: Social Worker
▬ ▬ ▬ Programing Service
.......... Consultative Service

Figure 5.6—Formal Organization at Milton

121

# Table 5.3—Staff Perceptions of Power in the Executive Core
## (in percentages)

| | Simple Structure | | | | | | | | | | | Multiple Structure | | | | | | Dual Structure | | |
| | OBEDIENCE/CONFORMITY | | RE-EDUCATION/DEVELOPMENT | | | | | | OBEDIENCE/CONFORMITY BUT MIXED | | INDIVIDUAL TREATMENT | | | | MILIEU TREATMENT | | |
| Officials Listed as Having Influence | DICK | | REGIS | | BENNETT | | | | MIXTER | | INLAND | | | | MILTON | |
| | Great deal | Lot | Great deal | Lot | Great deal | Lot | | | Great deal | Lot | Great deal | Lot | | | Great deal | Lot |
|---|---|---|---|---|---|---|---|---|---|---|---|---|---|---|---|---|
| Executive | 86 | 12 | 100 | — | 100 | — | | | 64 | 26 | 70 | 27 | | | 56 | 30 |
| Asst. Director | 38 | 54 | 11 | 56 | * | | | | 26 | 43 | 86 | 14 | | | 70 | 22 |
| Head of Social Service | 13 | 24 | — | 11 | — | 22 | | | 20 | 34 | 20 | 40 | | | † | |
| Head of Cottage Parents | * | | * | | — | 22 | | | 57 | 29 | 3 | 14 | | | 29 | 43 |
| Principal | 17 | 32 | * | | * | | | | 9 | 16 | 6 | 23 | | | 8 | 30 |
| Business Manager | * | | * | | * | | | | * | | * | | | | 13 | 28 |
| Farm Manager | 11 | 26 | * | | * | | | | * | | * | | | | * | |
| No. of cases | (53–57) | | (9) | | (9) | | | | (136–143) | | (32–35) | | | | (97–100) | |

* Not asked because there was no such position in the institution.
† Not asked because the head of social service at Milton was subordinate to the assistant (clinical) director.

staff members with whom he had contact. Although Milton's school and vocational training areas were under the direction of the clinical director, they were not so fully incorporated into the unified authority structure as were the cottages, and the problem of integrating them continued to preoccupy the executive core. As a remedy, the vocational and school coordinators were required to meet with the cottage committees, and during the study Taylor, the clinical director, began a series of meetings between the teachers and the cottage committees and a series of discussions for the training staff led by the consulting psychiatrist.

*Perceptions of Power Distribution*

Findings on the staff questionnaire give general confirmation to our descriptions of the allocation of power by the executive and elaborate our understanding of how power is allocated within the context of departmentalization. Respondents were asked how much say or influence each of several officials had in the way the institution was run. They checked a five point scale, ranging from "a great deal of say" to "very little say" for each official listed.

The results (Table 5.3) help to document our observations of a monopoly of influence in the hands of the executives of Dick, Regis, and Bennett—the institutions with simple structures—and of a sharing of power by the executives of Mixter, Inland, and Milton—organizations with multiple and dual structures. At Dick, 86 per cent of the staff rated the executive as having a great deal of influence, with only 38 per cent giving this rating to his closest challenger, the assistant director. At Regis and Bennett all respondents chose the executive as having a great deal of influence; no real challengers emerged. In contrast, influence was divided between two men in each of the other institutions. At Mixter, the executive (rated as having a great deal of influence by 64 per cent) was challenged by the head of cottage parents (57 per cent). At both Inland and Milton the chief subordinates were named more frequently as having a great deal of say than were the executives themselves (86 per cent versus 70 per cent at Inland and 70 per cent versus 56 per cent at Milton). The results also indicate how members of the executive core whose tasks were marginal to the

central operating problems of the institution, such as the principals, were consistently seen as having little power.[8]

The findings on Milton and Inland were anticipated clearly in our descriptions of executive strategies for sharing power, but the results for Mixter are a little surprising. The power of Mixter's head of cottage parents, Johnson, was less a result of executive design and delegation than of default. Johnson, an elderly but forceful long-time employee, had gathered to himself a variety of informal powers. He unofficially controlled the assignment of inmates to cottages and would put a boy in an isolation cell at will, sometimes without informing anyone else. To an extent the findings on Mixter indicate a bifurcation of power, with the executive, Hanna, a professional educator, representing more rehabilitative goals, and Johnson representing more custodial ends. This bifurcation was not great, however. Although Hanna claimed to be committed to increasing modern rehabilitational programs, in practice he focused on attaining benign custodial aims; moreover, Johnson, while custodially oriented, was opposed to use of means he considered overly repressive. In fact there was little conflict between them. Hanna had reservations about Johnson and talked of removing him "if things were different," but he also felt that Johnson was doing a much better job than two social workers who had held the position previously and who "couldn't stand the pressure." Thus power went to Johnson rather than to the assistant director who, losing power also because he projected an image of vacillation and irrelevance, found his functions of coordinating the assignment of boys to school, work, and club programs impotent in an institution where programs were relatively routinized.

Patterns of power are also shown in responses to a question asking staff personnel to judge the amount of influence social service workers, cottage parents, and teachers have in making decisions about how inmates should be handled. The data (Table 5.4) indicate that the power of social service personnel was most often seen as great at the treatment institutions (with over 80 per cent calling it high at Milton and Inland). Fewest attributions of high social service influence (about 30 per cent) were made at Regis and Bennett, with Dick (45 per cent) and Mixter (53 per cent) intermediate. The frequency with which cottage parents were attributed high influence declined along the custody-treatment continuum from a high of 63 per cent at Dick to an

extreme low of 9 per cent at Inland. Milton was an exception. In this institution, where cottage parents participated through the cottage committees in making most decisions about the boys, they were most often seen as having high influence (by 77 per cent of the staff). Teachers were attributed relatively little influence at all institutions, and especially at Mixter.

**Table 5.4—Staff Perceptions of the Influence of Major Groups (in percentages)**

| Groups Having "A Good Deal of Influence" | OBEDIENCE/ CONFORMITY | | RE-EDUCATION/ DEVELOPMENT | | TREATMENT | |
|---|---|---|---|---|---|---|
| | Dick | Mixter | Regis | Bennett | Milton | Inland |
| Social Service | 45 | 53 | 25 | 33 | 82 | 88 |
| Cottage Parents | 63 | 37 | 33 | 29 | 77 | 9 |
| Teachers | 28 | 12 | * | * | 18 | 22 |
| No. of cases | (49–53) | (143–144) | (8–9) | (7–9) | (99–100) | (32) |

* No teachers.

In addition, we posed questions about "the importance . . . to the institution" of various staff groups and the "helpfulness" of social service advice in working with the boys. Differences between institutions were not very clear cut but were generally consistent with or elaborated our findings on influence. Social service staff were most often seen as having great importance at the treatment institutions, and cottage parents were most frequently seen as highly important at Dick and Milton. Social service advice was appreciated most often at Milton, especially by the cottage parents.

*Perceptions of Conflict*

Correctional institutions are frequently seen as ridden with intra-staff conflict—a result of division of responsibilities for containment and rehabilitation among subunits whose personnel have divergent perspectives. Because of our interest in departmental structure and because we correctly expected to find considerable disagreement over goals and means, we attempted to measure conflict, seeking especially to find how it might be expressed along departmental lines. We asked respondents to indicate the degrees of tension that seemed to exist between various pairs of groups. The "tension pairs" were cottage parents versus

social service, cottage parents versus teachers, teachers versus social service, and employees versus the administration. A large number of respondents did not answer, with the rate of non-response rising to a height of about 25 per cent at Mixter. Results for the four closed institutions are presented in Figure 5.7, which gives findings from both surveys because substantial differences were found between them.[9]

The findings are not clear cut, but tend to suggest that conflict is not so much a function of lack of concensus or of degree of departmentalization as of the *interdependence* of departments. Departmentalization may allow divergencies to flourish, but it appears that where there is little contact between departments there is little occasion for conflict. The importance of interdependence is suggested by findings from the first survey. Mean tension reported between all pairs was lowest at Dick, where there was least interdependence, and highest at Milton, where there was most.

Results from the second survey show a marked change, however: Mean level of tension at Inland has fallen below that at Dick. In Chapter 10, which discusses organizational change, we shall view this reduction of tension as the result of measures instituted between surveys to increase teachers' and cottage parents' understanding of the institution's clinical philosophy and to enlarge contacts between these groups. We shall see, further, that similar efforts at Milton did not bear fruit. This suggests that when interdependence is moderate but not high, tension may be reduced by promoting mutual understanding.

Detailed findings can best be understood in the context of both quantitative and observational findings in each institution.

*Dick.* Staff at Dick were in considerable agreement about goals. Communications between staff groups mainly involved only information on previous offenses and release plans. Tension was low, but rose for all pairs at the time of the second survey. Possibly this was due to an impending election, which was expected to result in victory for the party out of power. It was feared that virtually all staff members, except perhaps teachers, might be replaced.

*Mixter.* Interdependence was higher at Mixter—and so was the level of tension. Social service personnel and teachers were least interdependent, and tension between them lowest. Cottage parents and social service were most interdependent, tension between them highest.

Social service played a somewhat directive role in the initial assign-

ment of inmates and in formulating release plans. Cottage parents would write up instances of misbehavior, and social service personnel were expected to convince the inmates of the necessity for conformity and to report on their attitudes at disciplinary conferences. The social service workers had little control over the behavior of cottage parents, however. The latter frequently felt that social service sided with the boy and believed his account instead of theirs. There were thus many occasions for conflict, stemming from interdependence.

There was less interdependence between teachers and cottage parents. Teachers felt cottage parents were negligent in failing to encourage boys to bring books to cottages for study, but cottage parents felt it was too hard to keep track of the books. Cottage parents felt boys were not adequately supervised in school and were thus able to steal things, such as pencils, that could be used as weapons. These relatively minor occasions for conflict were augmented, however, by divergent perspectives regarding the goals of the institution and the way boys should be handled. The inmates used this divergence by telling "atrocity" stories to teachers regarding cottage parents' practices, and cottage parents in turn felt the teachers were too lax. Thus minor occasions for interdependence—books in the cottage, stealing pencils, and so forth—assumed more importance, and a moderate degree of tension was reported. This did not occur at Dick, where the competing perspectives of teachers and cottage parents were not subject to institutional debate (the teachers were more isolated and less powerful), and where inmates were not allowed to discuss or criticize the practices of staff groups.

Interdependence between teachers and social service was even lower than between teachers and cottage parents. Teachers made relatively few reports of misbehavior, and many of these were handled directly by the school principal. The teachers did request more information about how to handle recalcitrant inmates and eventually a psychologist began meeting with them, but the tasks of neither group were affected by it. The existence of similar educational levels and values may have furthered reduced tension between social service and teachers. Data from the second survey indicate little change in tensions.

*Milton.* At Milton, tension was high in all pairings of cottage parents, social service personnel, and teachers. The greatest interdependence existed between cottage parents and social service, since

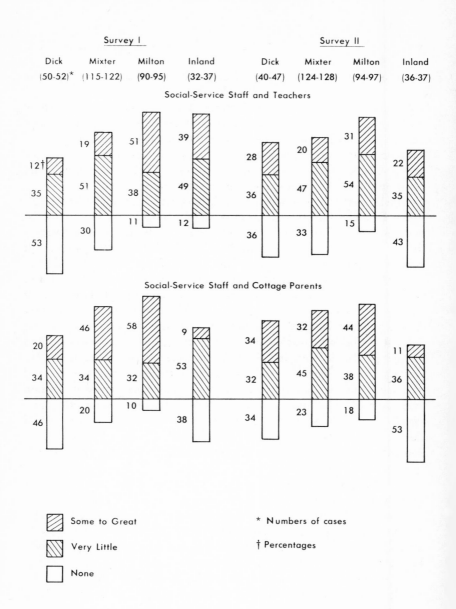

## Figure 5.7—Perceived Tension Between Staff Groups

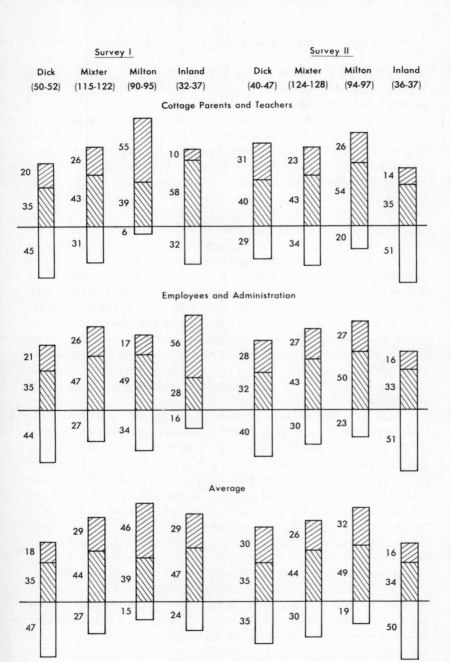

Survey I                                          Survey II

Dick      Mixter    Milton    Inland        Dick      Mixter    Milton    Inland
(50-52)   (115-122) (90-95)   (32-37)       (40-47)   (124-128) (94-97)   (36-37)

Cottage Parents and Teachers

Employees and Administration

Average

129

members of each of these groups worked together as a team in each cottage. Tension between these groups was only a trifle higher than tension between the other pairs, however.

Cottage parents on the afternoon and evening shifts had less direct contact with the clinical personnel, although they were responsible to them, and felt they were expected to deal with large groups of boys armed only with an injunction to "understand before you act." Resentment of the treatment program was highest among these staff members.

Staff members asserted that tension between cottage parents and clinicians had been much higher in the past. When the clinic staff was attempting to create a milieu program, it battled openly with the cottage parents. Older members of the staff referred to a past division between the "long hairs" and the cottage parents, and some of the cottage parents with long tenure still resented the incursion of the clinic staff. There is a direct relation between the tenure of cottage parents and their tendency to perceive tension. Only two of the eight with less than one year's service perceived high tension, while eight of the nineteen with one to six years' service did so. This suggests that while the integration of clinical and cottage personnel in each cottage may have promoted more understanding and reduced the very high level of tension, the continuing high level of interdependence insures that tensions will remain fairly high.

Teachers at Milton, as at all institutions, had little power and were relatively isolated. At Milton, however, institutional philosophy called for integration. This contradiction was apparent to some of the teachers. Further, while cottage parents were lower in education and social status, they were, under the integrated cottage plan, associated with treatment and had roles similar to social service. Contention frequently developed when teachers returned a boy to his cottage because of his disruptive behavior, or when a boy did not attend school because of a cottage committee meeting to discuss his program. Cottage parents felt that boys were sent back to the cottage too readily; teachers feared that cottage parents might not even discipline a boy who was sent back.

The least tension occurred between teachers and social service, though the level was still high. They tended to share similar conceptions of treatment means and similar social status, but some of the same issues that created tension between teachers and cottage parents were also present in the relations of these two groups.

Executive personnel at Milton were aware of the tension between teachers and the other groups and, prompted in part by our exploration of the issue, attempted to integrate teachers into the programs. A training program was instituted wherein teachers were better informed of the treatment philosophy of the institution and given more insight into the behavior of inmates as the clinicians interpreted it. In the second survey the proportion reporting high tension between teachers and both social service and cottage parents declined considerably. The overall tension level at the institution did not decline so much, since tension between employees and the administration was higher. This centered around a relatively specific issue—salaries—which was receiving considerable discussion at the time of the second survey.

*Inland.* A large part of the drop in total tension at Inland came in a decrease in tension between employees and administration involving the change in executives.

Considering the three role groups, tension was highest between teachers and social service during the first survey. The underlying basis for conflict was the incompatibility of psychotherapeutic and educational approaches to rehabilitation. Teachers felt they were not supported by clinicians in their attempt to exercise authority in the classroom. This was also true to some extent of Milton, but at Inland an even more permissive program had been established by the clinicians. Some of the "old guard" in the school were openly opposed to it. In addition, clinical definitions led to a minimization of educational and occupational planning for the boys. Some indoctrination of teachers in psychodynamic theory had occurred earlier, but in a form that stressed accommodation of teachers to the clinical program.

Tension between teachers and cottage parents was considerably lower. These two groups had little interdependence, and teachers did not hold cottage parents responsible for the clinical orientation. Tension was lowest between cottage parents and social service. The young cottage parents (often persons who had some college training and were acquiring more) recruited by the institution tended to be amenable to clinical definitions. Weekly meetings between them and the clinical staff increased acceptance of the program. While they found inmate management difficult because of the permissive character of the program, they did not have an opposed rehabilitative philosophy as did the teachers. Disciplinary problems were handled by the assistant director

or the head of cottage life, so that clinical staff were freed from decisions which might have led to conflict with them.

The overall reduction in tension seemed to reflect not only the change in executives but also conscious efforts to promote understanding. Shortly after the first survey teachers were brought into the clinical conferences that discussed boys' progress. Also, two cottage parents were assigned to work part-time in the school supervising study periods and working with boys who needed individual assistance, and weekly training programs dealing with group management were established. Tension between all pairs was down in the second survey.

It is possible, of course, that tension is cyclical. Perhaps it has risen again at Inland as groups have come to feel their interests threatened again or as issues have accumulated. It may even be possible that complex treatment organizations must experience cycles of tension if their programs are to undergo continual modification and experimentation. Our data do not indicate this, but it should be recognized that we measured tension at only two points in time, that not all groups are included in the measurements, and that the questions themselves are far from ideal.

## NOTES

1. Eugene Litwak, "Models of Bureaucracy Which Permit Conflict," *American Journal of Sociology*, LXVII (September, 1961), 177–84.

2. Jules Henry, "Types of Institutional Structure," in Milton Greenblatt, Daniel J. Levinson, and Richard H. Williams (eds.), *The Patient and the Mental Hospital* (New York: The Free Press, 1957), pp. 73–91.

3. This ranking parallels exactly the order of estimated annual expenditure per inmate: Dick, $1118; Mixter, $2533; Milton, $2600; Inland, $4500. For Regis the figure was $1425, for Bennett $1700.

4. The amount of emphasis on classroom discipline seemed to be a function of the general stress on discipline in the institution, to some extent deflected by conventional classroom norms and educational standards. At Mixter and Dick discipline tended to be looser in the school than in the rest of the institution. At Inland and Milton the converse tended to be true, and at Inland the institution's permissive emphasis led to classroom disruptions which were disturbing to some of the teachers.

5. We define a department as a relatively self-contained subsystem of an

organization. A group of workers are considered members of a department when authority is delegated to a supervisor of the group. Workers performing similar tasks but relating individually to the superintendent are not classified as members of a department.

6. Tables of formal organization were constructed from field observations for Dick, Regis, and Bennett because tables were not otherwise available. Tables were available at Mixter, Milton, and Inland, but had to be modified to bring them up to date.

7. Because Bennett's one social worker had considerable autonomy in counselling and arrangements for intake and discharge, she might be thought of as a separate department, thus making this a multiple department structure institution.

8. The second field survey produced one very notable change in power: At Inland, the assistant director, Burns, had succeeded the executive, and on this question 93 per cent of the staff placed Burns in the "great deal of say" category. The new assistant director at Inland had arrived just a few days before the second survey questionnaire was administered, so he was not yet able to share any of the influence of the executive, although we thought that in time this would happen.

9. No data are presented for Regis and Bennett because they had no teachers (thus cutting out two pairs), and the second survey was not made of staff in either institution. The perceptions reported are those of all respondents, but the picture changes little if tension is measured by the responses of only those staff involved in the tension pair.

*PART FOUR*

# The Staff

*Chapter 6*

# STAFF PERSPECTIVES

Findings from the staff questionnaire provided information about staff perspectives on organizational goals, delinquents, potentials for rehabilitating the inmates, and their own jobs and careers.

## PERSPECTIVES ON GOALS

To obtain our basic measure of employees' perspectives on institutional goals, we asked each staff member to select two statements from a list of six "which in your opinion best describe the purposes of the institution as seen by [the executive]." The statements included custodial conceptions (protecting the home community or punishment), traditional conceptions (teaching social habits and behavior or training and education), and treatment-oriented conceptions (changing attitudes and values or enlarging self-understanding). We also asked which two statements best described the way things actually were in the institution and which two best described the way things *should* be. There was little difference between the responses to these different phrasings.[1]

Findings on both choices made on all versions are adequately represented in Table 6.1, which presents the distributions of the first choices of executive purpose made by the staff respondents. Only very small proportions chose the custodial alternatives in any of the institutions, and in retrospect the wording of these alternatives seems to have been inadequate.[2] On the other alternatives differences among institutions are striking and generally consistent with executive strategies. Those choosing a treatment alternative ranged from 22 per cent or less at Dick, Mixter, and Regis, to 30 per cent at Bennett and highs of 42 per cent and 54 per cent respectively at Milton and Inland, the two treatment institutions.

**Table 6.1—Staff Perceptions of Institutional Purposes (in percentages)**

| Perceptions of Goals | OBEDIENCE/ CONFORMITY | | RE-EDUCATION/ DEVELOPMENT | | TREATMENT | |
|---|---|---|---|---|---|---|
| | Dick | Mixter | Regis | Bennett | Milton | Inland |
| **Custodial conceptions** | 2 | 8 | — | — | 2 | — |
| 1. Protect the home community for a period of time | 2 | 4 | — | — | — | — |
| 2. Punish delinquent behavior | — | 4 | — | — | 2 | — |
| **Traditional conceptions** | 85 | 72 | 88 | 70 | 57 | 46 |
| 3. Teach boys good social habits and behavior | 54 | 48 | 38 | 60 | 35 | 17 |
| 4. Train and educate these boys | 31 | 24 | 50 | 10 | 22 | 29 |
| **Treatment conceptions** | 11 | 22 | 12 | 30 | 21 | 54 |
| 5. Change a boy's social attitudes and values | 7 | 16 | 12 | 30 | 21 | 31 |
| 6. Help each boy gain an understanding of the kinds of things that got him into trouble | 4 | 6 | — | — | 21 | 23 |
| No. of cases | (55) | (139) | (8) | (10) | (99) | (35) |

The only exception to a perfect pattern of differences between institutional types was that the percentage choosing treatment conceptions at Regis (12 per cent) was almost identical to that at Dick (11 per cent) and less than that at Mixter (22 per cent). This may reflect the Regis executive's explicit rejection of psychotherapeutic techniques as well as custodial ends.

*Effects of Education*

It may be asked whether the differences in perspectives on goals are due to the higher educational levels of the staffs in the treatment institutions. Combining data on staff from all institutions, we found a direct association between education and selection of treatment goals. To assess the interaction between education, institution, and goals we may look at data on the goal choices of those with at least some college education and those with a high school diploma or less (Table 6.2).

It is clear that for those with some college, the institution had a considerable impact upon choices of goal statements. The following percentages of staff members with some college chose the two treatment

**Table 6.2—Staff Perceptions of Institutional Purposes, by Education (in percentages\*)**

| Perceptions of Goals | OBEDIENCE/ CONFORMITY | | RE-EDUCATION/ DEVELOPMENT | | TREATMENT | |
|---|---|---|---|---|---|---|
| | Dick | Mixter | Regis | Bennett | Milton | Inland |
| Staff with no college education | | | | | | |
| Custodial conceptions | 3 | 8 | — | — | 4 | — |
| Traditional conceptions | 87 | 82 | — | 100 | 66 | 83 |
| Treatment conceptions | 10 | 9 | — | — | 30 | 16 |
| No. of cases | (39) | (72) | (0) | (2) | (44) | (12) |
| Staff with some college education | | | | | | |
| Custodial conceptions | — | 6 | — | — | — | — |
| Traditional conceptions | 87 | 60 | 83 | 57 | 48 | 26 |
| Treatment conceptions | 13 | 34 | 17 | 43 | 52 | 74 |
| No. of cases | (15) | (67) | (8) | (7) | (54) | (23) |

\* Categories are identical to those in Table 6.1.

alternatives: Dick, 13; Mixter, 34; Regis, 17; Bennett, 43; Milton, 52; Inland, 74. Among those with less education, the impact was less pronounced. Comparing only the obedience/conformity and treatment institutions, since there are no cases in Regis and only two at Bennett, we find a clear difference, however. About 10 per cent chose a treatment alternative at Dick and Mixter, but at Inland and Milton 16 and 30 per cent did so. Thus although the recruitment of well-educated staff was necessary to implement complex treatment techniques, their educational level *per se* was not sufficient to account for institutional differences in goal perspectives. Whether highly educated or not, more of the staff in treatment institutions chose goals associated with complex treatment techniques. Similar conclusions come from an analysis by organization position; that is, although position (cottage parent, social service, and so forth) was associated with goal conceptions, it could not account for the organizational differences.

In assessing the impact of these findings it is also useful to take into account the size of the high education group and the extent of its contact with the inmates and other staff. At Dick the high education group comprised only 27 per cent of the staff, and ten of the fifteen persons in this group were teachers. They had contact with only about half the inmates and then only for a few hours a day, and were isolated from the rest of the staff. At Milton and Inland, however, the well educated

groups accounted for 52 per cent and 65 per cent respectively, and instead of being concentrated in the academic school, were in sustained and significant contact with inmates and less educated staff members throughout these institutions.

## Goal Consensus

Another look at Table 6.1, which presents data on perceptions of goals, indicates a considerable range of choices. At Milton and Inland the greatest concentration on any one alternative failed to exceed 35 per cent, and only in the two smallest institutions were less than four alternatives chosen. For a fuller understanding of goal consensus and disagreement we also analyzed goal choices in the four larger institutions by the respondent's level of authority in the organization to determine the degree of consensus among members of the executive core (department heads, assistant directors, school principals, and the like) and among the rest of the staff.

We found considerable disagreement among members of the executive core at each institution—only a little less, in fact, than among the other staff. Dick showed the least dispersion among the core members, as might be expected on the basis of the dominating role of the executive. Our assumption that there was some bifurcation of goals at Mixter received some support from the pattern of responses: only its executive core had a distribution of goal choices that was bimodal. The distributions at Milton and Inland indicated that a minority of department heads favored a more traditional philosophy.

In all four organizations members of the executive core indicated treatment conceptions more frequently than did other staff members. Perhaps the views of the lower level staff more accurately reflected the way the institions were run in daily practice. This discrepancy between core and other staff should not, however, obscure the major differences in goal choices between institutions.

## Attitudes Toward New Treatment Programs

In the findings on perceptions of institutional purpose we saw that few staff members chose the purely custodial alternatives. When the distinction between custody and treatment is taken out of the context of official institutional purpose and is posed as a matter of current policy, however,

we find greater support for custody and sharp differences between institutions.

Evidence on this point comes from a question asked in the four closed institutions that solicited opinions about "new treatment programs." Alternatives were that no new program should be started if it would jeopardize security, that treatment programs should be started even if a moderate number of escapes occurred, or that "custodial conditions are secondary." The findings (Table 6.3) show a heavy emphasis upon containment in the obedience/conformity institutions, Dick and

### Table 6.3—New Treatment Programs vs. Containment, in Closed Institutions* (in percentages)

| Staff Perceptions | OBEDIENCE/ CONFORMITY | | TREATMENT | |
|---|---|---|---|---|
| | Dick | Mixter | Milton | Inland |
| 1. No new treatment program should be started if custodial security precautions would have to be lowered | 50 | 50 | 14 | 18 |
| 2. Treatment programs can be started even though a moderate increase in number of escapes results | 38 | 25 | 46 | 32 |
| 3. Custodial considerations are secondary in setting up a treatment program (except for the clearly dangerous offender) | 12 | 27 | 39 | 50 |
| No. of cases | (52) | (135) | (99) | (34) |

* The question, adapted from one first used in a study of California prison personnel directed by Joseph Eaton, read, "If you were a member of a committee to advise the superintendent of the institution, which of the following statements about new treatment programs would you approve? (Check one only.)"

Mixter, in each of which 50 per cent of staff chose the most custodial alternative. This finding confirms numerous observations we made of a preoccupation with truancy in these organizations. This preoccupation was based on the assumption that running away is a sign of complete lack of rehabilitation—and at Mixter it was also based on staff accommodation to the surrounding community, which feared truants and saw them as a sign of institutional ineffectiveness. Custody was not *the* goal, but it was seen as a crucial means.[3] In the treatment institutions, Milton and Inland, where the number of truants was already very great and the staffs remarkably unconcerned, more than three fourths were willing to de-emphasize containment even further.[4]

In the two open institutions, Regis and Bennett, it was irrelevant

to ask the question in the same form because their inmates went unsupervised by institutional staff through most of the day while attending school. Therefore the question was altered to contrast a new treatment program with the nightly study program—school grades seeming to be a salient criterion of rehabilitation at both institutions. The responses indicate that the study program was, in fact, the important means of rehabilitation; none of the staff in either institution agreed that "educational considerations are secondary in setting up a treatment program."

*Perspectives on Volunteers*

Similar organizational differences emerge from data on staff perspectives toward the use of community volunteers. Modern treatment ideology suggests that volunteer aides should be welcomed into the institution as a way of mobilizing resources relating the inmates back to conventional life. When asked their opinion of volunteers, the staff in the obedience/conformity institutions and at Regis expressed very negative attitudes; more of the staff at Bennett and at the two treatment institutions had a positive attitude. The proportions who said volunteers could be "very helpful" were Dick, 13 per cent; Mixter, 24 per cent; Regis, 11 per cent; Bennett, 33 per cent; Milton, 52 per cent; Inland, 49 per cent.

## PERSPECTIVES ON DELINQUENTS

Our conception of the juvenile correctional institution assumes the significance of sets of beliefs about people-changing. The key hypothesis here is that variations in organizational goals are accompanied by variations in the staff's sets of beliefs about the inmates—what they are like and what must be done to change them. Our initial expectations were developed for the simple custodial-treatment contrast: we anticipated that in more custodial institutions the inmates would be seen as bizarre, dangerous, incompetent, untrustworthy persons, lacking in respect and obedience and needing strictness, firmness, and punishment, and that in more treatment-oriented institutions the inmates would tend to be seen as reasonable, trustworthy persons lacking the opportunity to express themselves and needing sympathetic understanding and permissive regulation. Later, as we elaborated our thinking about organizational types, we came to see that these beliefs might not reflect a single

dimension. For example, the perception of the inmate as trustworthy might be highest in the re-education/development institutions, in which the process of change is seen as relatively normal and attention is directed more toward academic performance than personality attributes.

As the major means for measuring beliefs we developed a series of seventeen statements on "delinquents in general" and asked for an expression of agreement or disagreement on each. From this initial pool a scale and two quasi-scales were derived.[5] Each measured attitudes related to staff perspectives on inmates, even though the items did not refer to concrete organizational practices.

Scale One, *Normal Relations,* measures the extent to which the staff believed it was possible to have normal, trusting relationships with delinquents. The scale was constructed out of the following three items:

Normal kids horse around some, but most delinquents are always horsing around.

Most delinquents can't even be friends among themselves, let alone with adults.

Most delinquents can't be trusted.

Scale Two, *Understanding,* measures the amount of emphasis on understanding believed necessary in working with delinquents. It was constructed out of the following items:

We can try, but it is difficult to understand the peculiar behavior of delinquents.

Understanding may be important in helping delinquents, but what is really needed is strictness and firmness. (Also in Scale 3.)

Sympathetic understanding is the key to helping delinquents.

Scale Three, *Discipline,* measures the degree to which staff believe that delinquency can be solved by authority and toughness on the one hand, or permissiveness on the other. The following five items comprise this scale:

The trouble with delinquents is that they haven't learned to treat adults with respect and obedience.

Society is going to have to be a lot tougher than it has been if it is going to cut down on delinquency.

Understanding may be important in helping delinquents, but what is really needed is strictness and firmness. (Also in Scale 2.)

Delinquents have to be punished if they're going to learn correct behavior.

One of the things a delinquent needs is a chance to express his feelings without being punished.

Table 6.4 presents the results. On the first scale, *Normal Relations*, no simple pattern of institutional differences appeared. The major findings were that staff members at Mixter more often fell toward the "no relationship possible" end of the scale (with 54 per cent in the two

### Table 6.4—Staff Attitudes Toward Delinquents (in percentages)

| Attitudes | Scale Type | OBEDIENCE/ CONFORMITY | | RE-EDUCATION/ DEVELOPMENT | | TREATMENT | |
|---|---|---|---|---|---|---|---|
| | | Dick | Mixter | Regis | Bennett | Milton | Inland |
| **Scale One—Normal Relations** | | | | | | | |
| No relationship possible | 1 | 24 | 26 | — | 8 | 18 | 16 |
| | 2 | 13 | 28 | 33 | 25 | 19 | 14 |
| | 3 | 28 | 19 | — | — | 23 | 14 |
| Friendship possible | 4 | 35 | 27 | 67 | 67 | 39 | 56 |
| No. of cases | | (61) | (149) | (9) | (12) | (107) | (36) |
| Coefficient of reproducibility: .94 | | | | | | | |
| | | | | | | | |
| **Scale Two—Understanding** | | | | | | | |
| Understanding difficult | 1 | 24 | 20 | 11 | — | 6 | 3 |
| | 2 | 52 | 38 | 33 | 25 | 31 | 22 |
| | 3 | 12 | 20 | 44 | 25 | 30 | 27 |
| Understanding the key | 4 | 12 | 22 | 11 | 50 | 35 | 49 |
| No. of cases | | (59) | (147) | (9) | (12) | (106) | (37) |
| Coefficient of reproducibility: .94 | | | | | | | |
| | | | | | | | |
| **Scale Three—Discipline** | | | | | | | |
| Permissiveness emphasized | 1 | 6 | 14 | 22 | — | 33 | 38 |
| | 2 | 9 | 11 | — | 33 | 10 | 22 |
| | 3 | 11 | 11 | 33 | 33 | 20 | 16 |
| | 4 | 11 | 15 | — | 23 | 15 | 14 |
| | 5 | 41 | 26 | — | — | 18 | 8 |
| Discipline emphasized | 6 | 24 | 21 | 44 | 11 | 5 | 3 |
| No. of cases | | (55) | (144) | (9) | (9) | (104) | (37) |
| Coefficient of reproducibility: .92 | | | | | | | |

low score categories) than did those at other institutions. Also, looking at the highest score category (friendship is possible), we find higher proportions in the two re-education/development institutions, Regis and Bennett (67 per cent each), than in any of the other organizations (including the treatment institutions).

Results on the second and third scales are straightforward and parallel almost perfectly the custody-treatment arrangement of these institutions. On Scale Two, *Understanding,* we find that the percentages in the two high score categories (emphasis on understanding) range from a low of 24 at Dick to a high of 76 at Inland, with Mixter having 42, Regis 55, Bennett 75, and Milton 65. The pattern repeats itself on Scale Three, *Discipline:* in the three lowest score categories (permissiveness) we find the following percentages of staff: Dick 26, Mixter 36, Regis 55, Bennett 66, Milton 63, Inland 76. (It should be noted, however, that four of the nine Regis respondents fell into the extreme high discipline category.)

Analysis of the effects of educational background on scale scores indicates that, again, variations in staff characteristics cannot explain differences between organizations. More highly educated staff members scored higher on understanding and lower on discipline than other staff members in every organizational setting, but the institutional differences held up within categories of educational level.

Altogether, these findings suggest a high consistency with executive strategies. Emphasis upon understanding and minimization of discipline are lowest in the obedience/conformity institutions, intermediate in one of the re-education/ development institutions (Regis), highest in the other re-education/development institution (Bennett) and the two treatment institutions. Further, the perception of the delinquent as capable of normal, trusting relationships was highest in the re-education/development institutions, which are open and which emphasize education as a "normal" route to rehabilitation.

Noting findings on Scale One, *Normal Relations,* one may ask why a larger proportion of the staff at Mixter (54 per cent) than at Dick (37 per cent) thought it difficult or impossible to have normal, trusting relationships with delinquents. Consideration of the conditions under which staff could feel they might trust inmates illuminates this problem. For staff members to trust inmates, they must be fairly sure the boys will not engage in prohibited activity when they are not being closely supervised.

The greater strength of sanctions at Dick (described in Chapter 7) apparently discouraged inmates from risking staff antagonism and the staff there could often trust the boys with tasks. In contrast, staff members at Mixter were not officially permitted to use strong negative sanctions. The additional fact that inmates were at Mixter for a shorter period of time than at any of the other institutions probably tended to limit inmates in forming close attachments to the staff. Moreover, task definitions at Mixter resulted in relatively specific staff-inmate relationships: boys were supervised in athletics by one staff member, taken to dinner by another, and put to bed by a third. Such specificity in relationships also is likely to discourage the development of ties.

Additional evidence on staff perspectives appears in Table 6.5, which presents results on three other items from this series on delinquents in

**Table 6.5—Additional Staff Attitudes Toward Delinquents (in percentages)**

| Staff Attitudes | OBEDIENCE/CONFORMITY | | RE-EDUCATION/DEVELOPMENT | | TREATMENT | |
|---|---|---|---|---|---|---|
| | Dick | Mixter | Regis | Bennett | Milton | Inland |
| Agree that unless you take precautions, a delinquent may attack you | 45 | 55 | 22 | 8 | 28 | 19 |
| Agree that most delinquents are in no condition to make decisions even about everyday living problems | 42 | 34 | 11 | 25 | 24 | 22 |
| Strongly agree that firmness will help delinquents learn right from wrong | 40 | 27 | 11 | — | 17 | 8 |
| No. of cases | (60–62) | (148–153) | (9) | (12) | (106–108) | (36–37) |

general. Higher proportions of staff members in the obedience/conformity institutions agreed that precautions must be taken to prevent attacks, that most delinquents are unable to make correct decisions, and that firmness will help delinquents tell right from wrong. These findings give additional confirmation to the hypothesis that staff beliefs about people-changing are correlated with executive goals and strategies.

## VIEWS OF REHABILITATIVE POTENTIAL

An important aspect of staff perspectives on the inmates is the extent to which the inmates are seen by staff as really having the capacity to

change. Relative pessimism about inmate potentialities for change should be more compatible with more custodial approaches.

Questionnaire data come from items asking the chances that a delinquent will straighten out (part of the series on delinquents in general), and how many of the inmates they realistically expected to change for the better, how many for the worse (Table 6.6). The finding is one

### Table 6.6—Staff Optimism About Inmate Change (in percentages)

| Staff Attitudes | OBEDIENCE/ CONFORMITY | | RE-EDUCATION/ DEVELOPMENT | | TREATMENT | |
|---|---|---|---|---|---|---|
| | Dick | Mixter | Regis | Bennett | Milton | Inland |
| Disagree with view that the chances a delinquent will straighten out are very slight | 81 | 66 | 89 | 100 | 90 | 89 |
| Believe a worker can realistically expect boys to change for the better | | | | | | |
| Few | 15 | 33 | — | — | 7 | 14 |
| About the same number as don't change | 28 | 26 | 11 | — | 19 | 8 |
| Most, but some won't | 57 | 40 | 89 | 100 | 74 | 78 |
| Believe boys will become worse | | | | | | |
| None | 5 | 5 | — | 25 | 3 | 14 |
| Few | 44 | 35 | 56 | 33 | 53 | 52 |
| Some, but most won't | 49 | 47 | 44 | 41 | 44 | 33 |
| Most, but some won't | 2 | 12 | — | — | 1 | — |
| No. of cases | (61) | (149–150) | (9) | (12) | (104–107) | (36–37) |

of higher levels of pessimism in the obedience/conformity institutions. On the item about delinquents in general, only 66 per cent disagreed with a pessimistic view at Mixter and 81 per cent at Dick, against 89 per cent or more in all of the other institutions. Similarly, to the question on how many inmates realistically can be expected to improve, only 40 per cent at Mixter and 57 per cent at Dick said most boys would improve, while 74 per cent and above said so in the other organizations. The pattern was similar, although the differences were less powerful, on the question about how many would get worse.

Our observations and interviews also pertain to this problem. In treatment institutions we frequently heard optimistic expressions of views about inmate potentialities for change. In obedience/conformity

institutions we frequently heard remarks—from cottage personnel, maintenance men, teachers, and even counselors—that the inmates were intellectually dull, unteachable, or imbued with a delinquent way of life—at least to the point where, as one Mixter counselor put it, "You can't undo years of experience in a few months' time with very limited facilities and resources." Results on questionnaires and observations suggest that despite the rehabilitative content of obedience/conformity goals, they may rather easily slip into pure custodial goals in the sense that the inmates are simply being "kept," with little prospect for change. In an archetypical statement of this attitude, Mixter's director of cottage life, talking about the institution's new maximum security unit, Maxwell, said:

If we send a boy down there it will do him some good, that is, it will take some of the aggression out of him. Of course, he'll come back the same boy. . . . You aren't going to change one of these boys.

## PERSPECTIVES ON JOBS AND CAREERS

Do differences in organizational goals also affect staff perspectives on their jobs and careers? Apparently not, at least not in any straightforward fashion. Questions about how long the respondent would like to stay with the organization, his views of chances for advancement, how he thinks the institution compares with other places in which to work, and how involved he feels in his work did not produce consistent differences among the institutions. We had expected staff commitment and involvement to be higher in the more treatment-oriented settings, but in retrospect it appears that such factors as longer tenure at Mixter, full-time living and relative isolation from the outside environment at Dick, and higher professionalization and employment of college students at Inland made the expectation unlikely and even impossible to put to a real test.

We did find a clear-cut pattern of institutional differences when the respondents were asked whether, if they did leave the institutions in which they worked at present, they would reject, accept, or favor jobs working with children and working in a correctional institution. Higher proportions of the staffs in Bennett, Milton, and Mixter indicated pref-

erence for a job working with children and rejection of a job in corrections.[6] When we asked the importance of "feelings for children" in working in the institutions, however, we did not find a parallel pattern. Feelings for youngsters were stressed in the two re-education/development institutions, in one treatment institution (Milton), and in one obedience/conformity institution (Dick), but not among personnel in Mixter or Inland.

## NOTES

1. In addition, we asked an open-ended question on goals ("In your own words . . .") which had a low response rate and drew many answers copied from the alternatives given in previous questions, thereby producing unusable results.

2. Somewhat larger—but still small—numbers of staff at Dick, Mixter, and Milton named one of the custodial conceptions as a second choice on this question or as an aim on the questions about the way things actually are or should be. This very low level of custodial response surprised us and seems to reflect the official goals statements of these institutions and the prevailing ideology in society about reforming delinquents even where actual practice sometimes departs from this. Had the first alternative read "remove delinquents from their community because they violated its laws" or "deprive them of their liberty," more staff might have chosen it, for the phrase we used, "protect the home community," was not equivalent to deprivation and its meaning was not clear.

3. The staff's perception of the community was oppressive at Mixter. When we asked its staff how, in general, the institution was viewed in the community, the proportion who said "most think it is bad for the community" was 49 per cent, compared to 8 per cent or less in the other institutions. Further, 70 per cent of the Mixter staff ranked truancy as the major complaint of the community against the institution, compared to 36 per cent at Dick, 43 per cent at Milton, 40 per cent at Inland, and none at Regis and Bennett.

4. Members of the executive core were more willing to risk truancy than the rest of the staff in each organization except, surprisingly, Milton, where lower level staff were more liberal than those at the top. Social service personnel and teachers were generally less concerned with containment than other staff groupings, and even less so in the treatment institutions; maintenance personnel and detail supervisors were generally the most committed to containment.

5. See Appendix B.

6. We were surprised to find the highest proportion of those who would not want to work with children in Regis. Speculatively, the reason may have been that the brothers, members of a teaching order, had been assigned to the institution without regard for their preferences.

# Chapter 7

# STAFF-INMATE RELATIONS

This chapter examines the consequences of variations in organizational goals and executive strategies for staff behavior toward inmates. The problem takes its significance from the fact that the basic productive task of the juvenile institution, like that of all people-changing organizations, lies in structuring social relations between staff and inmates. These relations bear directly on the goal of changing the inmate and indirectly on such conditions as organizational stability. We shall recount the major features and variations in staff-inmate relations and lay the groundwork for answering our major question about consequences: What is the impact of institutional goals and patterns upon the behavior of the inmates?

Some system of social control must be developed by the staff of all correctional institutions to rehabilitate and manage the inmates. The system must come to terms with the fact that the inmates are involuntary members of the organization who have a high potential for disrupting institutional activities. The system involves scheduling, monitoring, classifying, and differentiating among the inmates; defining authority and personal relations between staff and inmates; establishing rewards and sanctions over inmate behavior and the bases on which they are to be allocated; and dealing with the collective patterns that emerge among the inmates.

We come to the data with the general presupposition that the character of the staff's system of social control will vary systematically with variations in organizational goals. This expectation, when one contrasts it with much of the flow of literature on mental hospitals, is not so obvious as it may at first seem. That research suggests that no matter what attempt is made to change the organization, traditional practices will persist—on the basis of needs for system maintenance, latent social identities, situational pressures for management, and the like.[1]

It is our argument that precisely because these institutions are involved in people-changing, patterns of staff-inmate relations are not allowed to evolve in unthinking fashion or to become established simply on bases of efficiency or expedience. Value considerations and beliefs about the appropriate way to handle and change the inmates are omnipresent, and provide a basis for establishing and revising patterns of staff handling of the inmates.[2] A crucial aspect of all executive strategies is the specification of prescribed, proscribed, and preferred ways of relating to inmates. It is true that situational pressures and the requirements and exigencies of managing inmates on twenty-four-hour-a-day basis lead to wide departures from ideal practice. To a great extent, however, organizational technologies take account of and offer solutions to these problems.

Our data on staff systems of social control come largely from field observations, along with some results from the staff questionnaire. Our expectations about findings can be stated by recapitulating the major features of executive strategies which bear upon staff-inmate relations, ordered along the rough custody-treatment continuum:

*Obedience/Conformity Institutions.* The method of change is conditioning. Relatively limited change is sought, rather pessimistically, under simplistic notions of human behavior which assign to the inmates little voluntarism or variability and assume that they must be under constant surveillance. Social distance between staff and inmates is to be high, and rewards are to be given for compliance and deference. Rewards are to be scarce, limited mainly to release from the institution for stringent conformity to the institution's rules over an arbitrary period of time. Sanctions are to be harsh. Universalism in application of rules is to be high, and collective action among the inmates is to be suppressed or rigidly controlled through co-optation of informal leaders.

*Re-education/Development Institutions.* The method of change is training. Less modest change is sought, under somewhat less simplistic notions of human behavior, which involve ideas of learning and development but which continue to minimize voluntarism. Obedience is to be stressed here, too, but less to persons and commands and more to the precepts of hard work, academic improvement, and Christian and middle-class morality. Staff behavior toward the inmates is to be more nearly that of a parent, one who is "fair" and acts "with the best interests of the boy at heart." Social distance is to be high but authority relations

are to be tempered with personal and moral considerations. Sanctions are to be stern but not brutalizing, and a greater number of rewards, beyond gaining release, are to be given for showing progress academically, vocationally, and morally. Inmates are to be somewhat more differentiated, the stress on universalism in application of rules is not to be so great, and inmate collectivities are to be given freedom in some limited areas.

*Treatment Institutions.* The technology of change is reconstitution. The inmate is to give evidence that somehow he is changing himself into a different being, and staff members are to manipulate rather than dominate, giving the inmate enough freedom to develop his own controls. By definition, the treatment institution seeks a high degree of change with considerable optimism, and the staff applies relatively complex and sophisticated notions of human behavior. Treatment of inmates is to be highly individualized. The atmosphere is to be permissive: employees are observers rather than surveillants. Staff members are to develop close relationships with inmates and offer them a very wide range of rewards—first, to convince them that the legitimate order is better than the one they previously had accepted, and second, to encourage behavior that appears to indicate reconstitution. Staff members are to manipulate inmate social relations, incentives, the confirmation of affection and respect, and minor penalties, but are to refrain from using strong overt sanctions because these are defined as self-defeating. The major rewards, and these include release, are to be given when the inmate appears to have developed internal controls and to have learned to reward himself for proper behavior.

We now turn to the findings, on (1) the daily round of life—patterns of scheduling and monitoring the inmates; (2) differentiation in handling the inmates; (3) authority and personal relations between staff and inmates; (4) the character of rewards and sanctions and bases for allocating them; (5) ways of controlling the inmate group; (6) special problems of implementation.

## THE DAILY ROUND

At the institutions toward the custodial pole of the continuum, the daily round of life showed substantially greater emphasis on surveillance,

regimentation, mass handling, repetitive scheduling, and routinization of treatment. This was particularly true at Dick and Mixter, where daily routines were highly structured and the boys were policed more or less constantly. At Mixter, for example, the day's schedule for all boys except those confined to cottages or security cells was awakening; supervised dorm cleanup; lineup; counting and marching in silence to cafeteria; eating breakfast in silence or near silence; lineup, counting, and marching back to dorm; more supervised dorm cleanup, lineup and marching off to classrooms or job locations; and so on. At neither Mixter nor Dick (at least for the bigger boys) were the inmates supposed to talk during meals, and at Mixter the mealtime task of one staff member was to see that they did not take more than the allotted number of bread slices. Neither institution permitted inmates to move in unsupervised groups, except while on some special assignment or when granted special privileges like those of the "trustee" in the adult institution.

In the re-education/development institutions the round of life, though less harsh, was also highly scheduled and surveyed. This was especially true at Regis, where, as the director put it, "part of our philosophy is to tire the boys out before they tire us out." In this institution no time was to be "wasted"; each inmate was kept occupied nearly every minute of the day. For example, on return from school, he was required to take part in supervised athletics (which "drain off excess energy") until supper. After eating, he worked on institutional chores for about an hour and then attended religious services. These were followed by supervised study and a second period of organized recreation, again compulsory, until bedtime. Boys kept the institution scrupulously clean. During the study period they were required to be silent and to stay in their rooms with the doors open so the staff could either look in directly or view the hallway with mirrors. The staff at Regis were preoccupied with preventing homosexuality, and inmates were either to be alone or in supervised groups. At Bennett the boys were given considerably more leeway in participating in recreational programs and other activities, but were also watched almost all of the time.

The picture was considerably different in the two treatment institutions. Milton preserved some of the same forms as the obedience/conformity institutions—lining up and counting, for example—but the procedures were much less regimented and constituted only a portion of the program. Although the boys were required to line up to go to the

cafeteria, for example, formations were very informal, there were few check-off procedures, and in the cafeteria the boys could talk freely to one another and the staff. At certain times they were permitted to move freely around the grounds, and the outdoor recreational programs were little supervised and relatively spontaneous. Milton boys did not wear uniforms as did those at the other state institutions, Dick and Mixter (actually, the "uniforms" at the latter places were standard institutional fatigue clothing), and a much smaller proportion of their time was devoted to "vocational training"—laundry, food service, shoe repair, or farming tasks relevant to economical organizational functioning.

At Inland inmate handling was least regimented and routinized. To the outsider, in fact, it appeared confusing and erratic. The boys had periods of supervised study (at the school, because the cottage staff were unable to keep the boys quiet enough to study in their living units) but worked on institutional chores less than an hour a day. There was an extensive recreation and leisure-time program, but participation, although encouraged, was voluntary. Boys moved around the grounds freely. Roll call was taken only at classes and work programs, and the inmates were never lined up. In contrast to the typical activities of the obedience/conformity institutions, which often involved literally scores of boys in identical activities, groups at Inland were kept small. School classes were limited to eight students or less. Inmates were given a high degree of freedom, and even the rule that boys were supposed to be in their own cottages at night was loosely enforced.

That there were sharp contrasts in the rounds of life between institutions is shown emphatically in the following quotations—lengthy but worthwhile—from the field notes of observers who viewed the early evening activities in cottages at Dick and Inland. The observer at Dick wrote:

When boys leave the playing field, the commander [supervisor] just gives a signal to the outline boys [boys who help in supervision] and they shape them up. They call them in and get them lined up, the boys stretch out their arms so they can be counted, and then they walk over to the building. They stand outside the door until the commander gets there, he looks them over and nods to the outline boys, and the outline boys then take the kids in and upstairs. They march up a ramp—up three floors to the top floor . . . [to] a huge long room with no partitions, in the middle of which sits a platform on which there is a chair where the commander can watch the boys

at all times. The commander depended pretty much on the outline boys to keep order. Individual boys would come over to him raising their hands asking, "Please sir, may I go to the bathroom" or something like that, and he would nod and the boy would go off.

The boys filed into the room and broke up into two groups . . . both lined up until the commander gave the signal to dismiss. One group stayed there, took off their clothes, laid them on the bench, then lined up again along the bench naked and stood at attention until they were all ready. Then the outline boy gave them a signal and they marched into the shower room. The showers had already been turned on by K, one of the outline boys. They took a shower and then turned off the water and stood there till K told them to move on to the other side of the room; still in line, they filed past him or another outline boy and were handed small towels one by one. They dried themselves, hung their towels on a rack at the end of the shower room, made another formation, and stood in line till K gave them the word to come out. They marched out and back around the benches again and got their clothes.

Meanwhile, another group had lined up and the same procedure was followed. . . . One outline boy stood at the door of the bathroom to watch anything that went on in the bathroom. There was very little noise in the place, very little talking. [The commander] said that after they had gotten all cleaned up, etc., that he would allow them to sit around the tables and talk, play card games, or something like that, as long as they talked in low voices; then later on they would go to their bunks and watch television. . . . [The commander] told us that he had three boys who needed to be punished. They had been talking in the dining hall. He called out their names. The boys came up, stood at the platform, held on with their hands and bent over, and the commander took a paddle that was about a yard long and struck each of them three very hefty blows. All of the boys in the place stopped and watched rather sullenly, and I kind of flinched with each blow. The boy who was being punished, however, kept absolutely quiet and firm, and when the blow was over, he walked off as dignified as he could. . . . The commander in all this was a Mr. X., who . . . says you can't let the boys out of sight; the boys can't be trusted. You have to punish them . . . some of them have never been punished before and they have told him that.

Very different is this report from Inland:

We went to dinner soon, where the boys were unusually restless. First they griped about the leftovers from Sunday, chicken and roast beef, and then they started to jump up and run around trying to get something they

wanted. Joe Walton, the counselor, warned them about this, but some of them kept it up, so he told Paterson, Sawkins, and Kearns that they had lost their treats. . . . Paterson got real sore, blew up, and kept this up for quite a while. So did Kearns, but he didn't make it last so long. After supper I went back to Middle Cottage and wandered into Room No. 5, which is occupied by Dan Sawkins and Frank Dickson. Sawkins was playing records, of which he has quite a collection. Different boys wandered in and stayed for a while to listen. Greg Wilkins stayed the longest. . . . He and a couple of the others did a little solo dance now and then. . . . Barry Wink came in for a while too. He and Sawkins seemed to like each other pretty much. . . . Owen Dukes wandered in and out, usually doing a kind of solo dance and doing pretty well, too. First Sawkins, and then a few of the others, would light up a cigarette in their room. This is against the rules on the second floor, but they showed by this that they trusted me and didn't mind my seeing what they did. . . .

After listening to about a dozen records, O'Bannon asked me if I wanted to play poker or rummy, and he got ahold of Dukes and Sawkins and they said they would, too. We went down to the first floor to the rec room. . . . Sawkins and I lost the pinochle game we were in, so another pair sat in instead of us. Then Jack Corbett wanted to play rummy in his room. So I went in and played two-hand rummy with him. He said he liked to be alone from the noise of the other rooms. . . . While we were playing, a number of fellows came in off and on to ask for cigarettes, and usually he said O.K. Greg Wilkins came in too and sat on the floor reading one of Corbett's comic books. A boy from another cottage came to the window to get a suit-case from Corbett through the window. Evidently there's something wrong with giving or trading things to others on loan, because they didn't do it through the usual passage-way. The staff members in Middle Cottage seem to regard Corbett as a pain in the neck because he seldom does what he is told to do. Actually, he does a lot of smoking on the second floor and even in the staff room itself, in spite of what they say to him; and he feels he doesn't have much to worry about because he doesn't care much if he goes home or not. That seems to be the worst thing they can do to him—to take away a vacation leave. But once in a while they remind him that he could be sent back to court [which might send him to a harsher institution]. He's sure they wouldn't do that for the little things he's been doing, but it's the continual little things that get them down.

Before we finished the rummy game, Joe Walker came by and wanted me to play pinochle, so I went down shortly. . . . Before we finished this pinochle game, it was time for cleanup, as Walton [a counselor] called out; and Paterson was the one who was organizing it this time. . . . Paterson

had already blown up tonight, so I was surprised to see him getting things going. We stopped our card game in the middle of a hand to get going on the cleanup. Little Phil Daniels made an announcement while the treat was being passed out . . . that they were starting a new paper and that there was to be a big prize of a 25 cent candy bar to each boy in the cottage, whichever cottage came up with the best name for it.

By 9:30 they were almost ready to start to bed. Tonight Joe Walton was pretty worn out after an hour or two of trying to get them to go to bed. They would be in and out, start horsing around, come into the hall, talk to somebody in another room, play their radio too loud, their record player too loud. . . . Joe Walker got peeved at the two boys in his room and came out in the hall and sat on the floor until everything had quieted down, about an hour later. Since Brownell has moved, Owen Dukes is alone in his room. He has a morbid fear of the dark, so little Daniels went in with him to keep him company for the night. All of the boys are very friendly toward me now. They come up to me with their favorite stories, and they all said good night. . . . [All names are pseudonyms.]

The conclusion that such contrasts in modes of staff handling are related to staff beliefs about the inmates and definitions of appropriate behavior derived from executive strategies is supported by results from two staff questionnaire items. These items asked whether the respondent thought most boys would run away if they were not watched and whether he believed the executive wanted the staff to "keep all of the boys in sight" (Table 7.1). The results show that much higher proportions of the staff of the two obedience/conformity institutions thought the inmates would run if not watched closely and that much lower

### Table 7.1—Staff Beliefs About Running and Surveillance
#### (in percentages)

| Staff Beliefs | OBEDIENCE/ CONFORMITY | | RE-EDUCATION/ DEVELOPMENT | | TREATMENT | |
|---|---|---|---|---|---|---|
| | Dick | Mixter | Regis | Bennett | Milton | Inland |
| All or almost all of the boys would run away if we didn't keep a close watch over them | 68 | 70 | — | — | 49 | 19 |
| No. of cases | (59) | (154) | (9) | (12) | (103) | (37) |
| The executive expects them to "keep all of the boys in sight" (asked of cottage parents and boys' supervisors only) | 60 | 62 | 50 | 86 | 5 | — |
| No. of cases | (10) | (26) | (4) | (7) | (21) | (6) |

proportions of the cottage staff of the two treatment institutions thought they were expected to keep close surveillance.[3] Inland had particularly low proportions agreeing on both of these questions—only 19 per cent on the first and none on the second.

## DIFFERENTIATION

The institutions differed markedly in the degree to which they stressed universalistic modes of handling. The treatment institutions, especially Inland, stressed an individualizing, flexible, and particularistic approach. In the obedience/conformity organizations great energy was put into the promulgation and enforcement of rules (as, for example, at Mixter, where elaborate procedures were developed to insure that none of the boys who were permitted to smoke would have more than three cigarettes a day), with little separation of individuals except as they jeopardized rule enforcement. Similar approaches to rule enforcement were rather prevalent at Regis, a re-education/development institution. This can be seen in replies to the question, should all boys get the same discipline (Table 7.2). Eighty-five per cent of the staff at Dick, about

### Table 7.2—Staff Agreement that All Boys Should Get the Same Discipline for Breaking Rules

|  | OBEDIENCE/ CONFORMITY | | RE-EDUCATION/ DEVELOPMENT | | TREATMENT | |
|  | Dick | Mixter | Regis | Bennett | Milton | Inland |
|---|---|---|---|---|---|---|
| Per cent agreeing | 85 | 49 | 67 | 25 | 30 | 30 |
| No. of cases | (62) | (155) | (9) | (12) | (106) | (37) |

half the personnel at Mixter, and two thirds of the brothers at Regis agreed they should. In contrast, no more than 30 per cent agreed at Bennett, Milton, or Inland.

Universalism as well as rule enforcement pervaded almost all aspects of staff-inmate relations in the more custodial institutions. At Dick the executive and staff generally did not distinguish between types of boys except in such categories as "a pretty good boy," "a poor worker," "a liar," or in terms of outstanding behavioral problems, probable athletic success, or the boy's usefulness in keeping order among the other inmates. In this institution a boy's age, size, football prowess, academic

level, and record of good or bad behavior in the institution were about the only information necessary to place him and to make decisions about him. Dick received considerable background information about many of the boys from the courts that committed them, but used the data only at the time of making decisions to elevate certain inmates to the special status of "honor boy." This was done, if at all, shortly before release, when staff members examined the boy's background for anything that might lead him to misuse his privileges.

Dick's staff did collect some other "data" at the time each inmate arrived. Two staff members separately asked the boy the same questions about why he had gotten into trouble, then met to compare notes—to see if the boy was "honest." Also, the chaplain asked the boy about the church-going and drinking habits of each of his close relatives, about what he would like to have if he could have anything in the world, and about what animal he would like to be. Aside from providing the basis for informal negative judgments ("He said he'd like to be a snake and he does act pretty slimy"), this information had no apparent use.

On paper, Mixter presented a much more individualized system. Shortly after the inmate's entry the staff considered reports of his psychological test results, social history, behavioral problems and potential deviant behavior, observations made in the orientation cottage and, for some boys, psychiatric judgments. In usual practice this information was used only to establish whether the inmate fit into one or more gross types (serious and repeated offenders, truants, big city boys, colored boys, physically aggressive or acting-out boys), to decide what living unit to place him in (there were special cottages for emotionally disturbed, truant, and aggressive boys), and to channel him into some vocational slot that had an opening. Little else was done to distinguish among inmates except when disciplinary problems led to a need for punitive action.

At Regis and Bennett inmates were treated in a somewhat more individualized fashion, particularly since personal relationships between staff members and inmates were more likely to develop in these small and more homelike institutions. Both institutions made use of information on educational achievement and interest, intelligence, social background, personality disturbance, and delinquent behavior, but they did so principally as a way of screening out inmates before they entered the institution.

Extreme individualization of inmate treatment was seen at Inland and, to a lesser extent, Milton. In these organizations the staff collected and made use of a great amount of psychological and other data in an attempt to differentiate among and provide differential treatment to the inmates.

The organizations also differed in programming. At Inland and Bennett all boys attended school classes, while at Milton all but two boys and at Regis all but four did so. In contrast, at Mixter 24 per cent of the boys were not put into classes, and at Dick, 49 per cent had no classes (and classes were often called off when help was needed on the farm or the cannery). The boys who went to school at Mixter had only half-day sessions, and at both Dick and Mixter those not in school spent full-time on work details unless they were being kept in their cottages for disciplinary reasons.

## AUTHORITY RELATIONS

Authority relations varied markedly among institutions. The staffs at Dick and Mixter and, to a lesser degree, at Regis and Bennett, demanded obedience and immediate compliance, used domination as the principal technique of authority, maintained high social distance, and conducted rituals of deference and (in the most custodial settings) degradation. In contrast, personnel in the treatment institutions tended to take recalcitrance and minimal compliance for granted, to rely principally on persuasion and manipulation rather than domination, to allow and foster a breakdown of social distance, and to insist on few rituals that symbolized their superior position.

At Dick, Mixter, and Regis, boys were required to use formal modes of address (Mister, Mrs., Sir, Ma'am, Brother) for all staff members, and at Bennett they had to use such terms for all but recreation personnel.[4] In contrast, at Milton and Inland staff members were called by nicknames, often rather insulting ones. The inmates frequently ridiculed directives and often showed an attitude of jocular negativism toward staff commands and suggestions.

Institutional differences in the extent to which staff demanded immediate compliance are readily illustrated in the response to a questionnaire item asking staff members whether they agreed that "the inmate

would do best if he would do what he's told and do it quickly" (Table 7.3). More than 90 per cent of the staff at Dick and two thirds or more

**Table 7.3—Staff Agreement that Inmates Must Do What They Are Told and Do It Quickly**

|  | OBEDIENCE/ CONFORMITY | | RE-EDUCATION/ DEVELOPMENT | | TREATMENT | |
|---|---|---|---|---|---|---|
|  | Dick | Mixter | Regis | Bennett | Milton | Inland |
| Per cent agreeing | 95 | 76 | 67 | 45 | 46 | 17 |
| No. of cases | (60) | (153) | (9) | (11) | (105) | (36) |

at Mixter and Regis agreed with this statement, while only about 45 per cent at Bennett and Milton and 17 per cent at Inland did so.

In the two obedience/conformity institutions, Dick and Mixter, we found the development of strongly disciplinary and even punitive orientations among some personnel. One frequent theme was that the boys needed to be treated severely until their wills were beaten down and they became ready to conform. One cottage parent at Dick described how he had conditioned the boys not to deviate from the rules: during his first two weeks in charge of the cottage he had paddled the boys every time they violated a rule, no matter how minor the violation. Once the boys had learned that any violation was dangerous, he said, he could permit a wider range of behavior and did not have to watch them so closely. This same staff member described how he had cured an enuretic after the infirmary had failed to find a physical cause for the problem. He paddled him with a bed slat every time he wet his bed. "That stopped him—it just proved he was too lazy to get up and go to the can." A similar emphasis upon stern handling to "shape the boys up" is found in this statement by a supervisor in the reception cottage at Mixter:

This place just isn't run as tightly as it used to be, or should be. I came back after being absent for sickness a couple of weeks ago, and the place was really terrible. You could hardly hear yourself think for the din of the noise. But in two weeks' time, I've gotten the place back to where it's supposed to be. . . . I really like working here because this is the one place where you really have a chance to mold the boys. . . . It's like a shock treatment or like basic training. Most of the other cottages are too easy on the boys. We're

pretty rough with them here because we want them to see right away that they didn't come here for the fun of it.

A brutalizing exercise of authority was observed by a researcher in another cottage at Mixter:

I talked for a while with the cottage parent. He would stop every now and then and shout at the boys, "Stop talking so loud." There was one boy who was sitting in a corner with his back to the rest of the room, just sort of staring at the wall. The cottage parent turned to him and said, "Do you hear me?" And the boy said, "Yes." And the cottage parent said, "You'd better keep on hearing me. Do you hear that?" And the boy said "Yes" again. The boy had a hearing aid on. We stood there a few feet from the boy, and the cottage parent told me about him. He said that kid was "no good," that he had been bounced around from cottage to cottage and now he was stuck with him. He said he has to watch the kid all the time because he was always playing around with the other boys and trying to grab them. He said, always speaking in a loud voice, "This kid is really rotten and I don't know what to do with him, but I'm stuck with him for a while." I think the boy probably heard this, but I'm not sure because of his hearing aid problem.

In the re-education/development institutions the stress on obedience was less visible, although still strong. In these organizations the inmates were required to obey and to do so rather quickly; but it was expected that they might need to "ventilate their feelings," and staff members were ready to sit down and talk with them about their misbehavior. The director of Regis described institutional policy as follows: "We sit down and talk to them, talk the problems out. That's what they want; they want to be able to talk about things. If kids are wrong, they don't mind being punished." Discipline was seen as necessary and beneficial, but it needed to be accompanied by understanding, warmth, and trust. At Regis the authority system was reinforced by the numerous religious symbols. These appeared to constrain behavior and to provide a rationale for requiring respect, obedience, and socially acceptable behavior. Morning and evening religious services were almost compulsory for Catholic boys, who were in the great majority in the institution, and counselors reported they emphasized religion in individual counselling. "If we can just get a boy to have a good confession," the director said "his behavior is generally improved." Bennett's cot-

tage parents reported they had close relationships with most of the boys and that inmates came to them frequently to discuss problems. These staff members explicitly defined their role as that of parental surrogate.

At Inland almost universally and at Milton in several cottages, in contrast, staff-inmate relations were very informal, often involved close relationships, and showed the interaction of near-equals. We watched a teacher at Inland pat some boys on the back in camaraderie after they had jokingly lifted him off the floor and called him names, and we heard a cottage parent at Milton seriously tell a boy that he would give him some of his own tranquilizing pills since the inmate's bottle was empty. Most cottage employees at Milton consciously attempted to foster equalitarianism and informality; but when inmate behavior got "out of hand," they would reassert traditional disciplinary techniques: demanding silence, making everyone be seated, shouting accusations, singling out particular boys for blame, threatening or employing sanctions of temporary isolation or denial of privileges. The cottage staff at Inland did not have the authority to make any major disciplinary decisions, however. Their only real tool was persuasion.

We have proposed that these differences among organizations in staff systems of control reflect the executives' strategies. This hypothesis, applied to our observations of patterns of authority, is given further support in results from questionnaire items asking staff members what, in their view, the executive expected them to do with regard to controlling the inmates and establishing distant or close relationships (Table 7.4). On the first question, dealing with control, about half the respondents in the two obedience/conformity institutions and in Regis, a re-education/development institution, said they were expected to keep order at all times. About a fifth or fewer gave this view in the other three institutions. Moreover, we find that only in the two treatment organizations did sizable numbers select the third, very permissive alternative. Results on the second question, dealing with social distance, show a similar pattern. Less than a fourth of the respondents at Dick, Mixter, and Regis said they were expected to have close relationships, while about half gave this response in the other three institutions.

The nature of staff-inmate relations is also defined by the contacts inmates have with clinical or social service personnel. Even under conditions of domination and high discipline in the cottage, relations with

**Table 7.4—Staff Perception of Executive's Expectations in Handling and Relating to Inmates (in percentages)**

| | OBEDIENCE/ CONFORMITY | | RE-EDUCATION/ DEVELOPMENT | | TREATMENT | |
|---|---|---|---|---|---|---|
| | Dick | Mixter | Regis | Bennett | Milton | Inland |
| **Control.** Executive expects them to: | | | | | | |
| Maintain order at all times; otherwise the boys will get out of control | 60 | 48 | 56 | 22 | 14 | 14 |
| Let the boys have freedom to express themselves; but we have to keep a close watch over it | 37 | 47 | 44 | 67 | 66 | 58 |
| Let the boys set their own limits, except if it gets dangerous; otherwise the boys won't learn to control themselves | 3 | 3 | 2 | 11 | 19 | 28 |
| He's not concerned about whether staff let boys have freedom to express themselves or not | — | 3 | — | — | 1 | — |
| No. of cases | (60) | (147) | (9) | (9) | (104) | (36) |
| **Social Distance.** Executive expects them to: | | | | | | |
| Keep distance from the boys; otherwise we will both lose our objectivity and not be able to maintain our authority | 8 | 11 | — | — | — | — |
| Be close to the boys, but not so close that our status and authority will be questioned | 72 | 61 | 89 | 33 | 51 | 42 |
| Have close relationships with the boys, so that we can get to understand the boys | 20 | 24 | 11 | 58 | 48 | 56 |
| He doesn't care what kind of relationship we have | — | 3 | — | 8 | 1 | 3 |
| No. of cases | (61) | (149) | (9) | (12) | (105) | (37) |

these personnel could provide the opportunity for development of a close staff-inmate relationship. But data given by the inmates on frequency of contact indicate the existence of much higher contact toward the treatment end of the continuum. For example, proportions of inmates reporting two or more contacts with clinical or social service personnel in the previous month were Dick, 11 per cent; Mixter, 41 per cent; Regis, 38 per cent; Bennett, 40 per cent; Milton, 77 per cent; Inland, 85 per cent. Further, when we asked the inmates what they

talked most about with their counselors, boys in the treatment institutions more often reported higher levels of concern with personal matters ("Personal problems that bother me," "Why I got into trouble in the past," and "How I get along with my family") rather than with disciplinary or institution-oriented topics (like "Parole or release date").

## REWARDS AND SANCTIONS

Except as the inmate moved nearer to his release, life in the obedience/conformity institutions was generally unrewarding. These organizations had an elaborate array of techniques for discipline and punishment, and the allocation of rewards was almost always accompanied by explcit staff threats that they would be withdrawn for misbehavior. Even at an institution like Dick life was not always harsh, of course: there were movies once a week, sporting events with teams off grounds, a drum and bugle corps that occasionally would play elsewhere, occasional ice cream treats if there had been no truancies or other major infractions in the cottage, television, some card games and books, occasional moratoriums at sporting events when inmates could roughhouse with the staff, the somewhat privileged status of "honor boy," and semiannual home visits if behavior had been good. Each of these rewards was withdrawn for misbehavior, however—often on a basis of group punishment—and discipline and retribution pervaded institutional life. Sanctions included corporal punishment, which often was quite severe, numerous degradation devices such as isolation, head-shaving, benching (being required to sit in complete silence on a bench, hands tucked under one's seat, while others engaged in recreation or other activities), wearing special colored shirts, and, as the major sanction, longer stay in the institution. Officially only the executive could use corporal punishment, but all cottage staff members had paddles and used them. The boys lined up at night to receive their punishments, which were specified for various infractions (talking during a meal, for example, merited three or five hard blows on the buttocks, depending on the cottage). In the early part of our field work truancy brought paddling by the cottage parent or executive, head-shaving, a yellow shirt, two or more days in a solitary cell (the "dungeon") on bread and milk, benching for several days, and recommencement of the minimum period of stay.[5]

Rewards and sanctions were similar in Mixter, although because its executive was more serious about the official taboo on corporal punishment, physical means were used less frequently and more secretively. Sanctions included assignment to onerous work details, reduced smoking privileges, curtailment of recreation or membership in privileged groups, removal to a disciplinary cottage or isolation cell, and, of course, extension of stay. Cottage staff members usually punished a boy for major infractions with a "writeup," a memorandum about the violation which went to the "case conference committee" that decided on the appropriate discipline. Or they would lower the inmate's monthly grade, a practice that often substantially increased the inmate's length of stay. Sometimes they did both.

Rewards were more frequent and sanctions less stern in the re-education/development institutions. Boys were rather frequently taken away from the institution for movies, bowling, fishing, or other activities; they were allowed frequent home visits (especially at Regis, where boys on good behavior could get day passes every Saturday and Sunday); and they were allowed to participate in extracurricular activities at the schools they attended. Sanctions principally involved denial of minor privileges and activities, given for such infractions as tardy return to the institution from school. Corporal punishment was officially proscribed and relatively rarely used, although at Bennett cottage parents reported occasional paddling and at Regis the brothers sometimes slapped an inmate on the neck at the time of the infraction. At Bennett boys were sometimes confined to rooms, but at Regis isolation was never used as a disciplinary measure because of fear of masturbation. The major sanction, beyond denial of a home visit (or "jugging," as it was known at Regis) or denial of participation in such off-grounds activities as school events, was found in the threat to return the inmate to the court that committed him. Presumably the rejected boy would then be sent on to a more deprivational institution like Mixter.

In the treatment institutions the staffs saw the provision of a number of rewarding experiences and the minimization of negative experiences as part of their mission. Milton, for example, had a soda fountain and lounge, complete with jukebox, just like one in the outside world, and Inland had color television, a "zoo," and an old car for tinkering. Inmates were given frequent recreational, social, and entertainment activities as well as many off-grounds trips to plays, musicals, baseball games,

and cookouts. There were relatively frequent visits with family and friends.[6] Inland inmates sometimes were allowed to work in the community part-time to earn extra money, and although leaving the grounds without permission was officially tabooed, staff members often "winked" at the fact that boys went to town to walk, to shop, or to see a movie. More important, the tone of much of the staff-inmate interaction was rewarding: The boys frequently received compliments and honors for progress and, because of the relaxed atmosphere, appeared to feel that they were accepted as persons.

The staff at the treatment institutions did not, however, lack effective sanctions. Perhaps the major one was giving and withholding staff affection and respect. This was institutionalized at Milton in the cottage committee meetings, in which inmates who had "messed up" were confronted with intensive "rub-in" sessions to press on them a sense of deviation, guilt, personal responsibility, and, in front of their peers, shame. In addition, the treatment staff had numerous tangible sanctions, although their use was frequently cloaked in the rhetoric of treatment rather than of discipline. At Inland, although discipline officially was to be planned individually in relation to the boys' "needs," and it was policy that "counselling alone will continue to be used when boys are involved in negative behavior unless it is decided that the denial of a privilege is to be utilized," such denials were rather routinely used for some violations. Boys were denied home visits, removed from an activity (although never from trips or recreation), sent out of school classes to the library for an hour, transferred to another cottage or restricted to their cottage, taken to a juvenile detention home for an overnight or weekend stay, denied the nightly snack of dessert and milk, or infrequently, denied a weekend home visit. In addition, there was the major sanction of returning the boy to the court (which probably would send him to the state training school) on grounds that he had shown "inability to succeed in the treatment sequence." Since the institution had no maximum security facility, violent aggression could be handled in no other way.

Milton's staff had a larger number of sanctions at their disposal, including even some paddling (although officially proscribed) of younger boys. As at all the institutions we studied sanctions included denial of home visits and privileges, and the staff also utilized such

techniques as restricting boys to cottages, group denial of privileges, and extra cottage duty on such routine or useless tasks as using sandpaper to clean metal stair casings. Finally there were the major control mechanisms, sending the boys to a maximum security cottage, which included a few cells, and threatening to transfer them to the state reformatory or county jail. Even in using these sanctions the staff reflected a commitment to treatment ideology, however: unless the need to lock up the boy was extremely pressing, the staff tried first to induce the boy to ask voluntarily to be put in maximum security, "for my own good."

The application of rewards and sanctions at Milton and Inland differed greatly from those of the other organizations in a number of major respects. First, major sanctions in the other organizations were reserved for those inmates who went AWOL; in the treatment institutions truancy was considered unimportant unless repeated quite often. Truancy at Milton might draw restriction to the cottage, except during meals, school, or vocational training, for a few days up to four weeks, or no penalty at all—and at Inland truancies were not even recorded in any central file. Second, except for minor sanctions, decisions in fact were made on a highly individualized basis. For instance, if a previously passive boy got into a fight, staff usually reacted less strongly than if a boy who fought constantly was involved. They wished to encourage the boy to express his hostility appropriately, even though the institution officially proscribed fighting. Third, although the ends of control were not completely forgotten, clinical staff and treatment criteria were also usually involved in decision-making on rewards and sanctions. In addition, in common with the re-education/development institutions, the treatment organizations ordinarily penalized inmates only in limited aspects of their behavior and allowed them freedom of rewards in other realms. In contrast, in the obedience/conformity institutions punishment once rendered was generally extended throughout all activities.

Our observations of sanctions are corroborated by staff questionnaire data. A sanctions index, measuring staff readiness to use dominating disciplinary techniques for a variety of situations in which inmate behavior may be disruptive, was constructed out of responses to questions asked about the following vignettes:

1. A boy truants and is gone for a day. The police bring him back. He has broken a couple of windows to get into a garage, but he has not stolen anything. The boy truanted once before—he has made a fairly good adjustment to the institution, aside from his truancy.

2. A boy starts a fight with another boy and gives him a black eye. The boy who starts the fight has been very quiet before and has never gotten into a fight. The other boy has been teasing him.

3. A boy starts to complain about how he is being treated here. He gets very aggravated and swears at you. He has done this before and you had spoken to him about it.

4. A boy is talking too loudly, while playing a game. Several times before you have spoken to him about his loud talking. Usually he quiets down for a while but then starts talking too loudly again.

5. You have asked a boy to help another boy clean a room. He says he doesn't want to. You have gotten along well with him in the past.

6. A boy does not want to go to a meeting of a club group that he has joined. He has gone regularly before, but he refuses to go this time and begins to get upset and shout when he is told to go. He says that he just doesn't feel like it. (The wording of this supplementary item was changed at each institution.)

Closed-end alternative responses ranged from "Put the boy in a cell," "Slap him," or "Penalize him" as punitive responses to "Talk with him about it" as a non-punitive response. The vignettes, based on observations in some institutions and representing situations characteristic of all, portrayed a critical behavior problem which seemed to call for different solutions under obedience/conformity, re-education/development, or treatment philosophies. The issues involved in the stories were, in order: 1. Violation of containment; 2. Aggressive response to provocation; 3. Verbal aggression; 4. Lack of verbal control; 5. Refusal to cooperate; 6. Inmate voluntarism.

The results (Table 7.5) show that 50 per cent or more of the staff at Dick and Regis and 34 per cent at Mixter fell into the categories favoring high use of sanctions—indicating they would use negative sanctions for almost any disruptive behavior. Only six per cent at Milton and none at Inland and Bennett fell into these high-sanction categories.[7] These institutional differences remained when we controlled for educational background. Inspection of the questionnaires also indicated that because staff members in the more custodial institutions were more willing to use negative sanctions they probably were con-

fronted with less disruptive behavior, since the inmates recognized the cost of acting as they felt. Several respondents from Mixter, for example, wrote next to the vignettes that "it would never happen here."

The processes of allocating rewards and sanctions define the officially approved inmate role and confirm for each inmate a status in the legitimate order, denoting his progress, or lack thereof, in the institution. Our observations clearly confirmed that the major criterion for allocation in the obedience/conformity institutions was conformity to institutional rules, especially rules regarding truancy and obedience to

### Table 7.5—Staff Scores on Sanctions Index (in percentages)

| Score | OBEDIENCE/ CONFORMITY | | RE-EDUCATION/ DEVELOPMENT | | TREATMENT | |
|---|---|---|---|---|---|---|
| | Dick | Mixter | Regis | Bennett | Milton | Inland |
| High use of sanctions, including slapping or paddling | 19 | 6 | — | — | 2 | — |
| High use of sanctions, without slapping or paddling | 34 | 28 | 63 | — | 4 | — |
| Medium use of sanctions | 19 | 31 | 12 | — | 21 | 11 |
| Low use of sanctions | 14 | 20 | 12 | 55 | 25 | 19 |
| Reasoning only | 14 | 16 | 12 | 45 | 48 | 70 |
| No. of cases | (58) | (143) | (8) | (11) | (104) | (37) |

adults. Both Dick and Mixter had formal grading systems in which the ratings of cottage parents, work supervisors, teachers, and others were used as the basis for setting the release date. At Dick the final decision for release required a minimum performance on grades and the unanimous consent of a committee that included the cottage parents; at Mixter, an average grade of C was generally required and the grades of the cottage supervisors were given double weight. In both of these organizations the length of stay was increased for truancy and other violations.

The custodial emphasis upon conformity was shown clearly in the words of Mixter's psychologist, addressing an orientation session of inmates:

You are here, not for punishment, but to learn. You must earn your way out. You must learn to inhibit your impulses and cooperate. We only know what's bad about a boy; we don't know what's good about him. . . .

You are here to learn how to behave in a social situation whether it is right or wrong. You don't ask when you're driving whether a red light is right or wrong.

It was shown as well in the statement of the chairman of an assignment committee, speaking to an inmate:

If you go along with what we have planned for you, you will be successful.

It is also shown in the words of the orientation handbook, which says:

Set up a list of "don'ts," things which if you do will keep you at Mixter longer.

This booklet goes on to outline the counselor-inmate relationship, largely in terms of what will happen if the inmate fails to cooperate: He is threatened with longer stay or shipment to a reformatory. This emphasis upon conformity was shown not only by the cottage staff but also by the clinic staff. Mixter's director of social services explained his philosophy as follows:

If we are able to help them see the reason for conforming to the institutional setting here, they will be able to conform more successfully when they return to their own communities.

Similarly, this quotation from a counselor is typical of several made by Mixter social service personnel:

It is my feeling that the main job of the counselor is to see that the boy adjusts to the situation here . . . this is a bureaucratic structure and you've got to follow along with the way things are set up.

In this environment it was no surprise when a cottage parent reported that the Mixter clinic's case summaries were helpful "because they tell you what to watch for and whether the kid is a runaway problem or not."

The staffs of the re-education/development institutions looked not only for conformity but also for academic performance and moral

growth. At Regis, for example, grade reports from schools were received and checked by counselors every two weeks, and privileges sometimes were denied if the inmate did poorly. School records of academic performance and behavior along with knowledge of the boy's compliance in the institution were used to decide about release, while social service reports, officially required, usually were not even prepared.[8]

These patterns contrast sharply with those of the treatment institutions. Formal grading systems were not used or were considered unimportant. Release dates were based not only on behavior in the institution but also on attitudes expressed to treatment personnel during group or individual therapy sessions or cottage meetings, or, as at Inland, on completion of a "treatment cycle" of individual counselling. Inmates were expected to seek help voluntarily from the staff and to recognize their own problems and change themselves. Although behavioral patterns were taken into account—the boy who misbehaved frequently was unlikely to receive early release—conformity alone was insufficient. The boys were required to learn to verbalize their problems and to assure the clinicians that they had changed.

These variations in the bases of rewards and sanctions are also indicated in questionnaire data about staff views on "the best way for a boy to get along" (Table 7.6). (Unfortunately, this question was not

### Table 7.6—Staff Views on Best Way for an Inmate To Get Along (in percentages)

| Appropriate Inmate Behavior | OBEDIENCE/ CONFORMITY | | TREATMENT | |
|---|---|---|---|---|
| | Dick | Mixter | Milton | Inland |
| Keep out of the way of adults but get away with what he can* | — | 1 | — | — |
| Don't break rules and keep out of trouble | 60 | 49 | 8 | 3 |
| Show that he is really sorry | 7 | 6 | 3 | 3 |
| Get an understanding of himself | 33 | 44 | 89 | 95 |
| No. of cases | (55) | (162) | (104) | (40) |

* Although this alternative certainly was not one which would appeal to the staff, it was worded this way so the question would duplicate one asked the inmates.

asked in Regis and Bennett.) About half the staff members in the obedience/conformity institutions said the best way for the inmate to

get along was to avoid rule-breaking and trouble; under 10 per cent said this in the treatment institutions. Similarly, no more than 44 per cent of the staff members at either Dick or Mixter chose the self-understanding alternative; at least 89 per cent did so in Milton and Inland.

## CONTROL OVER INMATE ASSOCIATION

Staffs in all institutions put at least some effort into dealing with potential and actual inmate association and groupings. In the obedience/conformity institutions, personnel saw almost all informal inmate alliances as threatening to the organization because they assumed a natural tendency to polarize against the staff. In the re-education/development institutions, inmate association was viewed less as a challenge to staff authority than as a potential threat to the inmate's opportunities to establish "healthy" relationships with others. Therefore, great energy went into organizing group work and recreation activities at Regis and family-like activities at Bennett. In the treatment institutions, groups were seen as both potentially useful for rehabilitation and potentially inimical to therapeutic work with particular inmates.

Two simultaneous strategies for dealing with inmate groups were found in the obedience/conformity institutions: First, denying the existence of groups and energetically attempting to suppress group formation ("We don't have groups here, we don't allow anything like that!" said the Dick school principal); second, attempting to organize the groups to control inmates by co-opting their leaders or by imposing selected leaders. Dick had an officially prescribed "line boy" system in which larger and stronger boys, respected by other inmates and compliant to staff demands, were given the responsibility for lining up and supervising the others and reporting infractions of rules. In return, line boys were given such special privileges as later hours at night, more opportunities to smoke, and greater freedom of movement. The line boys were severely punished, however, if they were caught failing to report infractions. Although such a system was officially proscribed at Mixter, in the cottages with the most difficult boys individual boys functioned in the line boy role. They too received special privileges,

and in some cases physically punished the other boys. Mixter's director of cottage life described how an informal line boy system can develop:

> We had a boy in Cottage . . . who could really call the shots. Sometimes when things would get rough there, we'd threaten to lock him up—and then everything would change. . . . Locking him up wouldn't help the boy himself—he was flattered when he was locked up—but it would help us keep control. It's like a prison: you need a good deputy warden, a boy like this.

Through surveillance and command the staffs at Dick and Mixter attempted to break up groups that would not accept a co-opted leader; to this end the staff at Mixter also moved boys from cottage to cottage. The Mixter counselors periodically gave sociograms, ostensibly to "find out how each boy is fitting in." Actually, the results were used in an attempt to identify negative leaders and members of informal groups, usually to transfer them to separate cottages or to give them closer surveillance.

Because personnel in the treatment institutions did not define informal groupings as a threat *per se*, overt effort was not directed at breaking them up except in instances when, as happened at Milton, a group began to establish a kangaroo court, another became involved in distribution of weapons, and a third organized a large system of sodomy. At both Milton and Inland there was a considerable attempt, consciously or unconsciously involving a perception of inmate group structure, to manipulate inmate leaders by offering positive rewards for cooperation and involvement in positive programs. Further, at Inland, for reasons defined as individual treatment purposes, the staff very frequently moved individuals from cottage to cottage to prevent "contamination" of or by other inmates.

Inter-organizational differences in views of inmate group formation may be seen clearly in responses to two items asked on the staff questionnaire. The first read: "Sometimes boys hang around in cliques and informal groups in the institution. Are all of these groups bad—i.e., do all make your job harder and have a bad influence on the boys?" The second asked the staff member if he agreed with the statement that "The boys who get the most out of their stay here keep to themselves and don't get too close to the other boys" (Table 7.7). In response to the

### Table 7.7—Staff Views on Groups and on Inmates Keeping to Themselves (in percentages)

| Views | OBEDIENCE/ CONFORMITY | | RE-EDUCATION/ DEVELOPMENT | | TREATMENT | |
|---|---|---|---|---|---|---|
| | Dick | Mixter | Regis | Bennett | Milton | Inland |
| Say all or most groups of inmates are bad | 98 | 27 | 11 | 8 | 10 | 13 |
| Say boys should keep to themselves | 41 | 39 | 22 | — | 15 | 3 |
| No. of cases | (60–61) | (150–152) | (9) | (12) | (104–105) | (37) |

item about groups, an extraordinary 98 per cent of the staff at Dick said that all or most groups are bad; Mixter (27 per cent) had the second greatest proportion with that response. Results on the question about keeping to oneself show a similar picture: highest proportions of the staff in the obedience/conformity institutions agreed that the inmates should keep to themselves. Obviously many staff members at these institutions accepted what in adult corrections is the traditional injunction to "do your own time."

Parellels between the more custodial juvenile institutions and the adult prison are shown clearly in the distribution of scores on what we shall call the "prisonization" scale. This index measures a dimension of attitudes—the inmate is to keep to himself, obey, and be treated like all other inmates—that is believed to prevail in most adult penal institutions. The measure is a quasi-scale based on three questions, the individual response patterns to which we have already shown. The questions were the item on boys keeping to themselves (Table 7.7), the item on whether all boys should receive the same discipline (Table 7.2), and the item on whether boys should do what they are told and do it quickly

### Table 7.8—Staff Scores on Prisonization Scale (in percentages)

| Scale Type | | OBEDIENCE/ CONFORMITY | | RE-EDUCATION/ DEVELOPMENT | | TREATMENT | |
|---|---|---|---|---|---|---|---|
| | | Dick | Mixter | Regis | Bennett | Milton | Inland |
| High Prisonization | 1 | 41 | 38 | 25 | — | 10 | 3 |
| | 2 | 47 | 26 | 62 | 27 | 19 | 28 |
| | 3 | 10 | 19 | — | 46 | 21 | 3 |
| Low Prisonization | 4 | 2 | 17 | 13 | 27 | 51 | 67 |
| No. of cases | | (61) | (150) | (8) | (11) | (102) | (36) |

(Table 7.3). The findings (Table 7.8) show that roughly two thirds or more of the respondents in the three institutions closer to the custodial pole fell into the two high prisonization categories. In the three other institutions less than a third fell into this category. Under 20 per cent of the staff at Dick, Mixter, and Regis, moreover, scored in the extreme low prisonization category; at Milton and Inland half or more did so. These institutional differences held when we controlled for the respondents' education.

## PROBLEMS OF IMPLEMENTATION

At the operational level, staff-inmate relations tended to be more coercive and traditionalistic than staff goal orientations and perspectives would have implied. This was less true in the treatment institutions but strongly the case in the obedience/conformity institutions. This finding suggests that despite the increasing pervasiveness of "humanitarian" or treatment sentiments, traditional perspectives persist, especially at the level of concrete action. Further, there appears to be a general strain toward custodialism and the demand for conformity everywhere, posing serious problems in implementing benign executive goals except where these are forcefully stated in terms of treatment. The strain continues under the latter condition, but here lower level staff are given prescriptions for action which are sufficiently differentiated from those which flow from custodial orientations. Except at Milton and Inland, it was very difficult for executives to define concrete modes of staff-inmate relations other than in terms of conformity and domination.

Despite the general deviation between ideal and real, across institutions our findings show a high correlation between systems of social control and executive strategies. The obedience/conformity institutions showed a heavy emphasis upon universalism, constant surveillance, high social distance between staff and inmates, and obedience to rules and persons; a lack of close personal ties between staff and inmates; harsh sanctions; and an allocation of rewards—mainly release from the institution—based on conformity. The re-education/development institutions placed emphasis not only on obedience but also on hard work and academic and moral growth. High social distance seemed to be tempered by more paternalistic relations between staff and inmates, rewards were

greater, sanctions were less pervasive and strong, and institutional rewards were given for growth as well as conformity. Finally, treatment institutions gave the inmates much greater freedom, within which they were supposed to find their own psychological solutions—guided, persuaded, and manipulated by staff members but not so much dominated by them. Staff-inmate relations were much freer and often closer, there was a wide range of rewards, and sanctions were relatively weak except for withdrawal of staff affection and the decision to withhold the inmate's release.

This general statement oversimplifies the findings, however. There were some consistent and important divergencies within the organizational types:

1. Comparing Dick and Mixter, we see that Dick showed much stronger consistency with the obedience/conformity model. Mixter's patterns, although still basically congruent with this model, also seemed to reflect its injection of some notions and practices of treatment or benign care.

2. Patterns of staff control showed the sharpest divergencies between the two re-education/development institutions. Regis and Bennett were alike in their emphasis upon training and in the fact that their openness set one of the basic parameters for staff-inmate relations. On some dimensions, however—stress upon universalism, insistence upon keeping order at all times, social distance, and use of immediate, stern sanctions—patterns at Regis were like those at the obedience/conformity institutions. Speculatively, the Regis patterns may have flowed from the religious status of the brothers, which gave them claims for respect, bases for judging, and legitimation for acting which were supra-organizational in character.[9] In contrast, we found that patterns of staff control at Bennett often bore a great similarity to those of the treatment institutions.

3. Patterns expected under the treatment model were found to be more consistent and stronger at Inland than at Milton. At Milton, particularly, patterns of handling and punishing the inmates showed some similarities to those of the more custodial institutions. The strains of implementing treatment at Milton, a relatively large public institution, constitute one of the most intriguing phenomena observed in the study, and one to be examined in depth.

## Role Problems of Cottage Parents

Staff-inmate relationships create role strain for the personnel who supervise inmates. These role problems are similar to those of first-line supervisors in any organization: although under pressure from above to hold organizational standards, they must, in order to do their jobs, gain the cooperation of those they supervise. As basic modes of gaining inmate cooperation, both domination and manipulation (or persuasion) have limitations in terms of the situations in which they can be used effectively and the personal skills required for their use.[10] The role problems of cottage parents should be related to these limits. Observations bearing on this problem were made in the four closed institutions.

Cottage parent roles differed in the extent to which personnel were given autonomy and control over sanctions. Cottage parents in the more custodial institutions were likely to be "masters at home." At Dick the emphasis on control permitted the cottage parent to rule almost absolutely in his domain. The spatial and temporal separation of cottage parents' duties from other activities created a degree of autonomy and an absence of organizational control that were not found in the other institutions. Especially at treatment institutions, cottage parents and other staff members interacted simultaneously with the inmates.

Having the strongest sanctions, the cottage parent at Dick found his problem to be the maintenance of pre-eminent control. Failure to do this occurred most often in the dormitory used by the older boys. There, coercion required greater strength and firmness. During the evening few supporting staff members were available, and failure to dominate might have led to takeover by the inmates. When one Dick cottage parent attempted to "buy" control by giving the more difficult boys a party, the executive fired him on the grounds that he had given up his position of dominance. In another instance, the cottage parents at Dick criticized a supervisor of the older boys' dormitory because he had refused to fight when challenged by one of the boys. Dick kept a record of the truancies that had occurred under each staff member's supervision.

Personnel at Mixter, although similar in many respects to those at Dick, were to an extent "uneasy masters" with limited means. Official restrictions on the use of corporal punishment were sometimes en-

forced through dismissal or other punishment. The successful cottage parent in this situation found ways to use the few legitimate sanctions he had firmly and consistently. To gain an added degree of control he needed to create some kind of inmate-staff dependency relationship.

At both Mixter and Dick cottage parents found it more difficult to control the older boys. In general, Mixter cottage parents who supervised these boys were forced to give them much greater leeway in order to gain cooperation. Some cottage parents allowed the older boys to talk in the dining room, and some tended to be less firm with them in the monthly grading.[11] Because control was more tenuous at Mixter than at Dick, bargaining with inmates, resulting in the development of practices that subverted official rules, was more frequent. Although fighting was officially prohibited, some cottage parents and many night supervisors found they could gain the cooperation of the boys if they permitted it. It was therefore allowed as long as no physical marks showed, and the boys developed the practice of throwing a blanket or heavy coat over a boy before pummeling him. (The same practice was not allowed elsewhere in the institution; for example, when a boy was found beating another in the lavatory of the academic school, he was "written up.")

The tenuousness of control at Mixter existed in accentuated form at Inland. Inland's cottage parents might best be described as "tenants on trial." They were allowed no formal sanctions, were not given training in manipulative skills, and were not permitted to counsel the boys. Successful cottage parents at Inland found a basis of control through the appeal of their personal characteristics or through subtle encouragement or discouragement of inmate behavior, sometimes overreaching their authority to deny evening snacks or assign extra cleaning duties.

Some Inland cottage parents could not obtain even minimal compliance. Two were dismissed during the study, one for being inconsistent and "lazy" and meeting with purposeful non-compliance and teasing, and the other, liked but not respected by the inmates, for being unable to accomplish even such tasks as getting the inmates to clean up the cottage. Since coercive sanctions were lacking, the supervisors could obtain authority only by gaining respect. All the cottage parents who worked on the day shift, which had the responsibility for cleaning the cottage, found it more difficult to get cooperation. Persuasion alone was

inadequate to induce some of the boys to work. Persuasion without the backing of sanctions was unsuccessful when inmates did not feel the work was to their advantage.

Inland's cottage parents seemed to float in a structural vacuum. In contrast, Milton's were closely tied into the organization. The successful cottage parent seemed to be one who achieved stability by using a combination of firm control and positive gratifications. One informal index of stability was the runaway rate, and the head cottage parent with the lowest rate would jokingly point this out to those who had higher rates. Containment was not a major objective at Milton or even a basic criterion for judging cottage parent adequacy, however. Milton's cottage parents had their distinctive role problems. Clinical personnel applied pressure on cottage parents to handle the inmates in accordance with therapeutic criteria: compliant inmates were not to fade into the institutional shadows, repressive sanctions were not to be used, inmates were to be dealt with individually, and the cottage parent was to establish a supportive relationship with each inmate. Yet the cottage parents' distinctive role in the team effort—the one others on the team expected him to perform—was group management, a function which constrained him to avoid singling out any one inmate for special attention and to apply surveillance, controls, and discipline. How much of a relationship with the inmate he really could develop under this circumstance was unclear.

Some cottage parents at Milton found the emphasis on understanding to be meaningless, and institutional policy did not give them much guidance in working with the boys. In contrast with Inland, however, Milton's cottage parents had a greater number of tools with which to establish relationships; for they controlled more sanctions and participated in a wider range of activities.

### Difficulties in Implementing Milieu Treatment

Milton was in many ways the most fascinating institution to study, for the problems of tensions in goals, technologies, and staff groupings were highlighted here. In Mixter the "treatment program" was mainly a formality and the clinical staff employees were well adapted to more custodial functions and the basic obedience/conformity strategy. In Inland, the treatment goal was very strongly, if uneasily, implemented

through the processes of giving a monopoly of power to the clinicians and adapting the model of the relatively small, private, highly professionalized "residential treatment center." In Milton, however, we found a powerful thrust to implement treatment in the face of the usual problems of low pay, traditional orientations of staff, and so on, of the large public institution.

Milton's genius was to have developed the integrated cottage structure, which put the clinical coordinator (a psychiatrist or psychiatric social worker) right into the cottage and made him head of the cottage committee (which included the head cottage parent, or other supervisors, the cottage's social worker, and any chaplain and/or psychiatric resident attached to the unit). In this way it was possible to overcome much of the sharp bifurcation of custodial and treatment personnel, goals, and procedures which had shown itself when treatment first was introduced. Our data on staff patterns of control indicated substantial success in making treatment philosophies and practices operational; on the other hand, differences seen between this institution and Inland and various observations made at Milton indicate that certain basic problems of implementation continued to haunt the institution.

The first problem was the continuation of traditional orientations and practices among some employees. This was especially apparent among some of the personnel who were not tied into the integrated cottage structure. For example, one of the shop teachers, talking to the boys, referred to the clinical staff as "women" because they wouldn't use his brand of obscene language. He told us that most of the inmates could not be changed "for the same reason that a draft horse isn't going to win the Kentucky Derby."

Some cottage staff members also employed relatively custodial practices, especially in the maximum security cottage, where the boys spent many hours each day running floor buffers as a punishment employed on a very universalistic basis (one hour, for example, for a given obscenity). This was also true of one of the cottages for younger boys, where inmates reported a considerable amount of slapping and where the head cottage parent punished truants by restricting them to the cottage.

We have already indicated the dilemma of the Milton cottage staff: on the one hand, they were to be permissive, trusting, protective, and creative; on the other, they had to keep order and operate under long

lists of rules and regulations. One outcome was an omnipresent ebb and flow of crisis: their permissiveness invited smuggling in of weapons, the creation of kangaroo courts, and other developments that often ended in frightening staff members into taking strong and even frantic disciplinary action.[12] Attempting to carve out a position of authority, many cottage personnel felt anxious and unguided, and some found that only by resorting to strongly punitive actions now and then could they sustain themselves in the prescribed ways. For example, one supervisor told how he had been unable to manage the boys until the day he became angry and kicked an inmate; thereafter, he could control them in the approved manner.

Furthermore, faced with the constant difficulties of managing the cottages permissively, both cottage and clinical staffs tended to turn toward those notions abstracted from treatment philosophy, particularly that of the "need for strong external controls," which could provide a rationale for "clamping down" on a cottage. One clinical coordinator talked of the therapeutic values of keeping a very high level of "tension" in the cottage; and a head cottage parent, who agreed on most things with his clinical coordinator, gave the following interpretation to treatment philosophy:

The boy has to get along. It is his responsibility. If he isn't getting along it is because no adult is making him. You make it *their* problem; it is up to them. . . . [What if a boy calls you a S.O.B.?] One did that to me once. I asked him if he wanted to be treated like a boy or a man, and I told him if you want me to treat you like a boy I'll paddle you next time; if you want to be treated like a man, I'll knock your head off.

Both staff members and inmates expressed a great concern with "snagging," or telling on the other boys; much of the conversation between the staff and inmates at cottage meetings involved attempts by the staff to get the inmates to describe who had "messed up" and how. Cottage supervisory staff had an obvious interest in this question for reasons of control and frequently used group punishment to get an answer; the clinic staff, seeking "full clinical detail," provided a rationale for the frequent exhortation to inmates that "telling what happened isn't snagging."

A significant function of the integrated cottage structure was to provide for in-service training of supervisory personnel. This was especially

important because of the difficulty in recruiting and retaining competent cottage personnel in light of the low pay. The difficulties, and the partial success of this structure, are illustrated in this account of observations in one of the older cottages:

Head of the cottage is Smith, a retired army sergeant who has been here three years and head of this cottage for 15 months. He says his job is similar to the one he had in the Army, except the boys are a little sicker, but still it's getting them up in the morning, feeding them, etc. He's very angry about the pay here.

The clinical coordinator said he put Smith into the head cottage parent job after the previous head, who was old and had been around the institution for years, lost control and developed psychosomatic illnesses. He said he did this with real misgivings because Smith had been uninvolved with the kids and he told Smith so. The inmates say Smith used to be tough physically and would really hurt a boy, but he's changed. Smith himself says that he has changed a lot since he took the head's job; before, he generally sided with the kids, and would see things but not tell anybody because he felt it was nobody's business. Now, although he doesn't like being supervised by a clinical person, he says he sees what they're driving at and how what these kids do is important.

The cottage atmosphere is mostly informal. But there always seem to be some boys washing the red paint strip on the edges of the floor and using sandpaper on the stairways. This is their punishment, the activity they give to kids after running or some other infractions. Smith says you can't hit them and there aren't enough chairs to bench them.

Smith says he has had to fire a lot of supervisors for being tense and nervous; altogether, he's had about 12 different men working for him. He's happy to have hired a new man who really is concerned with the kids—he had set up a boy's club for delinquents in his home town before he came here. Today Smith was reassuring the new man that he shouldn't feel bad about the truancies, the man's first, which occurred during his shift last night. Smith must be working a 50 to 60 hour week, and last night, after the boys ran, he was up until 4 o'clock stomping around the railroad yards where he was sure they were. He said he knew they were somewhere in the woods nearby, and although he knew he wouldn't find them in the dark, he walked around just so they would know he cared what happened to them.

Smith definitely has made some transition from a military to a treatment philosophy, and the clinical coordinator professes to be moderately pleased with his progress. There's clearly some animosity, however, and it may have

to do with Smith's power: it appears that it is he, not the coordinator, who makes the decision when a boy sent to the maximum security unit is to return to the cottage.

The latter phenomenon, ambiguity and conflict in authority in the cottage, seems to be inherent in the integrated cottage structure. Clearly, the structure provides a way for changing the orientations of the cottage supervisory personnel, one imperative in an institution where the clinicians cannot manage everything. Speculatively, the structure may also provide a mechanism by which persons with clinical training can become more realistic and more control-oriented.[13]

The second problem was that of difficulty in developing elaborated notions of milieu treatment when the clinical personnel were dominantly schooled in and attuned to orientations appropriate to two-person therapy. Milton had explicitly given up individual counselling as the major mode of treatment and attempted to work mainly through cottage committee meetings with inmates and group therapy sessions. Yet many of the clinical staff members seemed insensitive to group phenomena. One of the clinical coordinators, for example, expressed real surprise when we mentioned observing that boys who monopolized the football field at certain times were all from the oldest cottage; in another instance, several staff members expressed enthusiasm over our telling them about "inmate informal organization," a concept they said they were eager to consider. Many of the professional personnel thought of most of the inmates as emotionally disturbed.[14]

The technology of two-person therapy led Milton staff members, furthermore, to make excessive demands upon the intelligence, verbal ability, and experience of many of the inmates.[15] The staff asked the inmates "to analyze themselves," "to let us know what's bothering you," "to work through these problems," and so forth. It was apparent that a substantial number of the inmates simply did not know what the adults were talking about, or at least were unable to verbalize replies. As a result the inmates often talked about how they had to "learn the lingo," and one staff member reported walking into a room where the inmates were rehearsing a cottage meeting—one boy playing the role of the clinical coordinator, asking the usual questions about problems, and another boy rehearsing his answers. An inmate put it this way: "If you

don't have problems, you'd better invent some, or you'll never get home."

The two-person technology seemed to assume a greater voluntarism than the correctional institution could under some circumstances realistically permit. When a boy who was acting in dangerous fashion had to be put in a cell in the maximum security unit to cool off for a period, a staff member might spend hours with him trying to get him to say he "needed" to be put there. Personnel sometimes went to what seemed to be ludicrous lengths to cast all decisions, no matter what their grounds, in a treatment rhetoric.

These difficulties relate also to the final problem of implementing treatment in Milton, that of defining and reconciling the system to the inmates. Not only were there problems because inmates became confused by the strains between treatment and control and, in some cases, by their inability to communicate meaningfully in the system, but there was also the fact that many of them *desired* to orient toward a more custodial definition of the institution. They wanted release, and they wanted to know in a straightforward way how they might conform in order to get it and how long it would take.

The problem was highlighted in cottage staff meetings with inmates.[16] There the boys usually tried to obtain passes to spend days or weeks with their families, to get information about parole dates, and to obtain changes in their programs. At the same time the clinical staff tried to elicit detailed accounts of feelings, to look for symptomatology, and to get boys to talk about their problems, while the cottage supervisory staff often seemed to be most concerned with information that would help in control. Usually several boys were brought in at once, and the staff's insistence that boys talk about cottage and personal problems turned the meeting into an uneasy group confessional with each boy eying the others fearfully because of the danger he would be thought of as a "snag." Clinical staff members generally refused to tell boys how well they were doing in the program—apparently because they were genuinely unsure, did not want to make promises that might lead the boys to feel they did not have to keep improving, and were committed to a non-directive approach in which they wanted the inmates to raise questions about themselves.[17] The conflict in expectations is illustrated in the following notes (near verbatim, since the clinical co-

ordinator and the boy both talked extremely slowly) taken by an observer at a cottage committee meeting. An inmate who had been in the institution about a year and a half requested the meeting in order to seek parole. Before he came in he was characterized by the staff as a boy with a low IQ (80) who was "doing well," who was a positive leader, who was having psychological difficulties because a heart ailment now prevented him from participating in sports (his major activity) and who had previously asked for therapy.

Clinic Coordinator (CC): What is the purpose of this meeting?

John: To see where I stand.

CC: Tell us where you are.

John: I'm doing pretty good.

CC: What have you thought about it? Don't you have some misgivings?

John: I want to get out to go to school.

CC: But when you came to see me you did not feel good about yourself. (John nods assent.) We want you to know we feel that you're doing well, but we also agree with you that you need more help. Tell us about your spells. You get mad.

John: I don't get mad.

CC: What happens when the other boys start to bother you?

John: I tell them to go away.

CC: Well, what would happen if they wouldn't go away? (The head cottage parent then told about an incident where the boy was harassed, and he asked him what had happened.)

John: I don't remember.

CC: So often you do not remember. (The CC then prodded him to answer what he would do if boys kept bothering him.) What if you went home? There'd be little brothers and sisters who would harass you, and it would be questionable what you would do then. (The meeting more or less came to a standstill then; nothing was said for a while.)

CC: So we can see what your problem is, how can we make you feel better about yourself?

John: What does that mean?

CC: Well, at my office you said you were happy over there but you would be sad when you went back to the cottage. What did you have in mind?

John: Nothing.

CC: Therapy will help you with these problems.

John: But I want to know how long before I get out.

CC: We're not thinking about that.

John: How can I tell when I can go?

CC: You'll have to be the one who tells us. When you feel better about yourself I think you'll know. When you talked with me last week, you said, "Sometimes I feel crazy." We certainly don't want to send you out until you work out these feelings. This is what we mean when we say you must be helped to feel better about yourself.

John: I don't see.

CC: I think that what's bothering you is not going home by September. (To the rest of committee) Can the others help me explain this?

John: I understand.

CC: Well, then what's bothering you?

John: Nothing. I knew it would be like this. (Looks out window.)

Social Worker: Did you *know* this or did you *fear* this?

John: I knew it.

CC: (The CC then asked the social worker to explain about the family, and the social worker said that she was worried about the boy's stepfather and that she had wanted to talk with the boy more often but hadn't seen him lately.) It's the problem with your family and your lack of comfort with yourself that holds you up. You need to be talking about these things here and in therapy.

John: So you took it serious when I said I sometimes felt crazy.

CC: I did, and you said you sometimes feel happy and sometimes sad.

John: (Delay) What's wrong with that?

CC: You're not happy with yourself. Why did you think I would take it as a joke? I take everything you say seriously. But the fact you said this isn't the only reason we can tell that you really need more help.

John: I don't need any more help.

CC: We think you do and you've been telling us this.

We have discussed the major difficulties in implementing treatment at Milton not to indicate that the milieu treatment strategy had failed but to show what still had to be overcome. Despite these drawbacks, to a considerable extent the Milton staff seemed to be making the treatment philosophy operational and creating a new moral order which most of the inmates recognized. In so doing the staff had made a major structural breakthrough and was beginning to forge a more reality-oriented treatment strategy than heretofore available, one addressed not only to intra-psychic problems but also to the realities of institutional life and control.

NOTES

1. This literature is summarized in Charles Perrow, "Hospitals, Technology, Structure, and Goals," in James March (ed.), *Handbook of Organizations* (Chicago: Rand McNally, 1965).

2. We do not assume that the flow in influence between values and beliefs about people-changing and practices is one-way. It is obvious that values and beliefs are frequently used simply to rationalize practices or procedures whose only virtue is convenience. We note the high ideological content of decisions about procedures in people-changing organizations, however, and assert that under many circumstances ideology (limited, of course, by other variables) is causal. This assumption makes more sense when applied to a bureaucracy, where performance is assessed by superordinates, than when applied to an individual's behavior.

3. The fact that none of the respondents at Regis and Bennett agreed that most would run if they had the chance probably reflects the fact that the open programs of these institutions gave no opportunity to think otherwise. Their lack of fear of truancy did not imply unconcern with surveillance (second item), however.

4. A supervisor at Dick described what happened when an inmate made the mistake of addressing him by his nickname. The supervisor said regretfully that he had had no choice but to paddle the boy, and the executive had then prohibited the nickname, even among staff, to prevent a recurrence of the incident. Dick's inmates also were compelled to stand in the presence of adults—a practice at first rather disconcerting to the researchers.

5. Political pressures, which eventually forced the closing of the cells (at least until after an impending election), penetrated so far into the organization that inmates occasionally argued and joked about whether Democrats or Republicans "beat you harder."

6. Number of home visits since arrival at the institution and other trips away from the institution in the previous two months were reported on the inmate questionnaire. Home visits were very frequent at Regis and Bennett, with almost half the inmates going home at least biweekly; median numbers of home visits at the other institutions were Dick and Mixter, 0; Milton, 1.5; Inland, 14. Median numbers of other trips were Dick and Mixter, 0; Regis, 8; Bennett, 4; Milton, 2; Inland, 5.

7. Regis's high score on this index results from the brothers' readiness to slap the boys on the back of the neck for an infraction at the moment of commitment.

8. At Bennett, where average length of stay was quite long, criteria for

discharge were difficult to discover. Boys usually were released in June or August so as not to interfere with the school year.

9. It should also be remembered that, in findings on the discipline scale constructed from responses to questions about delinquents in general, we found some extreme disciplinary scores at Regis. Further, we earlier found a low level of commitment to working with children.

10. For a suggestive study of some aspects of role problems of cottage parents in a juvenile institution changing toward treatment, see George H. Weber, "Emotional and Defensive Reactions of Cottage Parents," in Donald R. Cressey (ed.), *The Prison: Studies in Institutional Organization and Change* (New York: Holt, Rinehart and Winston, 1961), pp. 189–228.

11. Taking three months at random, we found that cottage parents gave A's and B's to 89 per cent of the older boys, 77 per cent of the "middle-aged" boys, and 72 per cent of the younger boys. This in effect allowed the older boys to be discharged in less time than the younger. A slight tendency also existed for detail supervisors and teachers to give better grades to older boys.

12. The ebb and flow of crisis was apparent at Inland too. A treatment program is much more difficult to run than a custodial one because the commitment to tolerate substantial aggressive behavior by the inmates frequently takes the staff to the brink of despair. For an analysis of this cyclical pattern in a highly therapeutic and permissive mental hospital, see R. N. Rapoport, R. Rapoport, and I. Rosow, *Community as Doctor: New Prespectives on a Therapeutic Community* (London: Tavistock, 1960).

13. It would be useful to study an institution like Milton intensively to establish the optimal balance of integration and segregation of the control and clinical roles. Personnel who are overly integrated might have difficulty performing either function because of their commitments to the other, and the inmates they deal with might have substantial anxiety over which role they were playing at a given time.

14. One of the clinical coordinators, pressed about whether the institution had any "social delinquents" whose trouble was not predominantly intra-psychic, finally said he had one himself—and read aloud the case of a Mexican-American boy whose delinquency seemed to stem from emotional problems with parents but whose ethnicity seemed to make him "social." The psychologizing of all events was not so great as at Inland, of course, where some staff personnel became highly enamored with classical and "deep" treatment, including the use of hypnosis.

15. Median IQ of inmates was below 91, with 34 per cent scoring below 81.

16. Because of the ambiguities and complications of running such a

program, Milton staff members spent a great amount of their time in meetings with the boys and with each other. Ordinarily, before he was assigned to school or other programs, the inmate spent the first nine weeks of his stay sitting around in the cottage waiting for the staff to write and consider the diagnostic reports.

17. In at least one case, one of the social workers had to keep trying to persuade a head cottage parent not to yield to the inmates' questioning and tell a boy a probable date of release. It must be realized that many of the boys lacked the interpersonal skills to pick up subtle cues on their progress. It would be intriguing to study the Milton system intensively in terms of Goffman's analysis of "The Moral Career of the Mental Patient" (in his *Asylums* [Garden City: Doubleday, 1961], pp. 125–169), in which he analyzes the difficulties of readapting one's self-image with the frequent movements from ward to ward. At Milton, except when the inmate was removed to the maximum security unit, there were few clearly demarked points of progress.

# The Inmates

*Chapter 8*

# INMATE PERSPECTIVES

Three basic questions structure the following discussion of the inmates. First, how do the perspectives of the inmates vary among institutions? Second, can variations in the inmates' perspectives be explained by variations in their background attributes, rather than by differences in organizational patterns? Third, what collective patterns develop among the inmates and what effects do they have upon perspectives? This chapter deals with the first two questions.

## ORGANIZATIONAL EFFECTIVENESS

In significant part our interest in the inmates reflects a concern with organizational effectiveness. As we have indicated, difficulties in assessing long-run success pervade the people-changing organization. Judgment of ultimate effectiveness is little more certain for the *student* of the people-changing organization. We can analyze data on the inmates with three major strategies in mind, however. First, we can evaluate our findings in terms of their congruence with the proximate goals and criteria used by institutional personnel—be they obedience and conformity or reconstitution and self-analysis. Second, we can make inferences about likely success in the long run on the basis of some fairly reasonable and straightforward assumptions. We can assume, for example, that most of the time inmate attitudes indicative of hostility, withdrawal, and alienation are likely to hinder attempts to change him, whatever the technology of change; and we can assume that attitudes indicating cooperativeness, openness, and trust will more frequently permit change, again whatever the technique.[1] Third, we can study the relationships among various dimensions of inmate behavior, which although unrelated to effectiveness in any straightforward way, are important sociologically or psychologically.

Our findings bear almost exclusively on inmate behavior and attitudes *within* the institution. We decided not to collect data on recidivism, for several reasons. First, neither the institutions nor any central record-

keeping agencies had data already collected that were adequate even to begin this task. Second, beyond the usual problems found in interpreting the meaning of recommitment to an adult correctional institution, juvenile populations and institutions present additional difficulties because of the ambiguity and multiplicity of alternative dispositions among different juvenile courts and states, the weakness and variations in record-keeping, the differences in parole and probation procedures, and the existence of variations in disposition by age, previous record, and so on. Third, an adequate study of recidivism would have required research efforts far beyond our resources, for it would have required us to go to widely scattered home communities and make long range studies intensive enough to control for home and community variables. Fourth, the important propositions could be tested adequately simply by observing behavior within the institutions.

We did collect some information bearing on success under one or another criterion, but we find it impossible to assert adequate validity or comparability. For example, institutional records of the number of boys returned after release might seem to provide a valid if only partial index of recidivism. Comparability is poor, however: Milton usually recorded as returnees only those returned after the completion of periods of parole, whereas the other institutions recorded those returned after any period of release. Further, the private institutions did not feel themselves under any obligation to take back boys the courts might want to return, and often would not take them.[2]

From a pure "efficiency" point of view one could conceivably use data on an average length of stay as a measure of effectiveness, thinking of stay as the time it takes before the institution is ready to say the inmate is ready for release. On this measure the institutions differed widely. Mean periods of stay were as follows:

> Dick — 10 to 11 months
> Mixter — 7.5 months
> Regis — 8.5 months
> Bennett—20 months
> Milton —15 months
> Inland —11.5 months (but many boys were screened out in the first 3 months; those who remained stayed about 18 months)

Differences among institutions in standards for release and the lack of information on the inmates' actual characteristics at release, however, make this criterion impossible to defend.[3]

Finally, records of disciplinary actions and runaways also might seem to provide objective indices of organizational effectiveness—from a custodial point of view. Only Dick and Mixter kept explicit records on discipline, however, and unreliability of recording and variations in criteria again were problems in regard to records on truancy. Official records gave the following proportions of inmates who had run away one or more times:

> Dick     —16 per cent
> Mixter  —20 per cent
> Regis    —10 per cent
> Bennett—16 per cent
> Milton  —50 per cent
> Inland  —29 per cent

These figures probably reflect a high degree of accuracy in recording at Dick and Mixter and unknown or lower accuracy at the other institutions. They also reflect great differences in defining the runaway. Dick classified as a runaway any inmate who made any movement to leave the grounds, whereas staff at Inland often paid no attention to boys sneaking away to go to the movies.

Despite ambiguities it is clear that Dick and Mixter, with strong internal sanctions, and Regis and Bennett, with periods away at school, frequent home visits to "let off steam," and threats to transfer runaways to harsher settings, did better under the containment criteria. Milton and Inland, however, considered truancy to be irrelevant, unfortunate, symptomatic, or even healthy. Further, effectiveness in containment may not have been compatible with survival for the organization or executive. Dick found it impossible to use its strongest sanction, the "dungeon," at election time for fear that mistreatment of inmates would again become a political issue; and Mixter's executive, stressing containment in order to reduce friction with the surrounding community, finally found himself moved out of his job by the social-welfare oriented department that controlled the institution.

## PROPOSITIONS

Our study of the inmates involved observation, unstructured interviewing, coding of data from institutional files, and administration of the inmate questionnaire. To find firm bases for comparison between organizations we relied most heavily on findings from the questionnaire. Appendix D presents results of a factor analysis, which confirmed the existence of a structure of attitudes among inmates in these institutions and provided a partial basis for the construction of indices.

Basic hypotheses that guide the analysis of data in this chapter are as follows:

1. Inmates of treatment institutions will have more positive and cooperative perspectives on the institution and staff than will inmates of the obedience/conformity institutions.

*Rationale:* The assumption is simply that the differences in the level of gratifications, severity of sanctions, and quality of relationships between the staff and inmates should "pay off" in inmate reactions. We would not expect holistic or linear patterns of findings on this hypothesis, however; inmate perspectives also should reflect difficulties in implementing various strategies and other limiting organizational conditions.

2. Inmates of obedience/conformity institutions will indicate adaptation to the institution through overt conformity, whereas inmates of treatment institutions will indicate adaptation through attempts to change their own attitudes.

*Rationale:* This proposition assumes that the basic moral order of the institution, as expressed through staff proscriptions, definitions of success, and rewards, will be internalized by the inmates.

3. Inmates of the treatment institutions will have more positive perspectives on self than those in the obedience/conformity institutions.

*Rationale:* We assume that the more custodial and degrading experiences at the obedience/conformity institutions will reinforce the feeling of rejection by society embodied in being sent there; the more positive practices of the treatment institutions should have some effects that counter this rejection.

4. Inmates of re-education/development institutions will be more like those of the treatment institutions than those of the obedience/conformity institutions in terms of perspectives on the institution and staff, adaptation to the institution, and self-image.

*Rationale:* Previous propositions say nothing about re-education/develop-

ment institutions. In terms of the impact of these organizations upon inmates, the fact that they were open, sending the boys out each day to ordinary schools, presents a serious problem in comparability. Although staff practices internal to these institutions generally were intermediate—between those of the obedience/conformity and treatment institutions—we had no adequate way of judging the effects of their openness upon the inmates' experience. This proposition is therefore more limited.

5. The differences hypothesized will hold regardless of the effects of inmate background variables, such as age or seriousness of delinquent offense.

*Rationale:* Validation of this assumption is necessary to our entire perspective.

In addition to these differences among organizational types, we would also expect variations *within* types on the basis of differences in staff behavior analyzed in Chapter 7. We would expect more positive outcomes at Mixter than at Dick, more positive patterns at Bennett than at Regis, and, in general, more positive outcomes at Inland than at Milton.

## FINDINGS ON INMATE PERSPECTIVES

Because, as we shall see, analysis of control data supports our assumption that variations in background attributes cannot explain inter-organizational variations in perspectives, we may present findings on perspectives unencumbered here by reference to control results.

### Perspectives on Institution and Staff

The inmate questionnaire asked a number of questions tapping general orientations toward the organization and its personnel. Responses on seven items that the factor analysis indicated were highly interrelated were combined into an arbitrary summary index of perspectives on institution and staff.

Results on this index (Table 8.1) show sharp differences among organizations. They support predictions that perspectives will be more positive in the treatment institutions than in the obedience/conformity institutions, and that responses in the open re-education/development institutions will resemble those of the treatment institutions more than those of the obedience/conformity institutions. High positive scores

### Table 8.1—Inmate Perspectives on Institution and Staff (in percentages)

| | Closed | | | | Open | |
|---|---|---|---|---|---|---|
| | OBEDIENCE/ CONFORMITY | | TREATMENT | | RE-EDUCATION/ DEVELOPMENT | |
| Inmate Perspectives | Dick | Mixter | Milton | Inland | Regis | Bennett |
| **Summary index** | | | | | | |
| Score high positive on index | 42 | 44 | 58 | 85 | 71 | 74 |
| **Individual items** | | | | | | |
| Would rather stay in present institution than in some other | 43 | 50 | 63 | 84 | 96 | 85 |
| Think this is a good place to be, relative to earlier expectation | 37 | 30 | 38 | 56 | 66 | 60 |
| Think this is a place that helps boys rather than a place to send or punish them | 33 | 44 | 62 | 86 | 63 | 78 |
| Think they have been helped by their stay a great deal or quite a bit | 72 | 71 | 65 | 80 | 73 | 82 |
| Say adults can be a lot of help on finding out why they got into trouble and how to change | 37 | 33 | 58 | 58 | 32 | 38 |
| Say the staff members are pretty fair | 59 | 66 | 65 | 75 | 79 | 60 |
| Disagree with the statement that staff don't care about the inmates | 42 | 45 | 53 | 81 | 73 | 54 |
| No. of cases | (196–209) | (358–364) | (149–155) | (63–65) | (56–57) | (32–35) |

were made by only 42 per cent and 44 per cent of the inmates at Dick and Mixter respectively, against 58 per cent at Milton and 85 per cent at Inland. Results at the open institutions were intermediate to those at Milton and Inland: at Regis 71 per cent had high positive scores, at Bennett 74 per cent.

There were clear-cut differences between the obedience/conformity and treatment institutions on five of the seven specific items. The exceptions were questions on whether the inmates felt they had been helped substantially and whether staff members were fair. On both questions

Inland had the highest percentage of positive response of any of the four closed institutions (as it did on all seven questions); but Milton's responses were not so positive, or no more positive, than those of one or both of the obedience/conformity institutions. Within institutional types the Inland-Milton difference was the only one to emerge consistently.

On the whole, these findings give clear evidence that perspectives were more positive in the treatment and open settings. Even in the more positive settings, however, there was substantial negativism. For example, on the item about whether the institution is a place to help, send, or punish boys, 11 per cent chose the category "punish" at Inland and fully 25 per cent chose it at Milton. Percentages at the other institutions choosing this category were 28 at Mixter, 50 at Dick, 13 at Regis, 10 at Bennett. Perhaps these attitudes flowed from the community outside the institution: when we asked the inmates how their family and friends saw the institution, results were similar. Percentages of inmates reporting it to be seen as a place for punishment were: Inland, 12; Milton, 31; Mixter, 36; Dick, 46; Regis, 11; and Bennett, 12.

*Perspectives on General Institutional Features*

Results on seven questions about opinions on food, smoking, activities, and help received in preparing for jobs in the future show further, largely predictable, differences among institutions (Table 8.2). Inmates of the two open institutions complained far less often than those of the other organizations about the amount and taste of food, "things like food and sports," and free time activities.

Between the obedience/conformity and treatment institutions there seemed to be no consistent differences in perceptions of the food (the researchers felt such a difference strongly), but there were consistent and expected differences—sometimes very small—on the other items. Thus inmates of Dick and Mixter complained more frequently than those at Milton or Inland about "things like food and sports," the amount of smoking permitted and the sufficiency of things to do in free time. Further, inmates of both obedience/conformity institutions were slightly less positive about the amount of help boys in general and they in particular had received in preparing for jobs than were inmates of either treatment organization.

### Table 8.2—Inmate Views on Food, Smoking, and Program
### (in percentages)

| | Closed | | | | Open | |
|---|---|---|---|---|---|---|
| | OBEDIENCE/ CONFORMITY | | TREATMENT | | RE-EDUCATION/ DEVELOPMENT | |
| Inmate Views | Dick | Mixter | Milton | Inland | Regis | Bennett |
| Disagree that "we get enough food at meals" | 21 | 40 | 31 | 65 | 1 | 3 |
| Agree that "the food does not taste as good as what I'm used to" | 61 | 68 | 60 | 75 | 21 | 14 |
| Say that "things like the food and sports here" are "worse for you here than they were at home" | 56 | 62 | 51 | 45 | 34 | 22 |
| Agree that "we are not allowed to smoke enough" | 44 | 70 | 30 | 15 | 18 | 57 |
| Agree that "there are not enough things to do during free time" | 55 | 53 | 46 | 52 | 16 | 29 |
| Agree that "boys here get enough help in preparing for jobs they want in the future" | 59 | 51 | 66 | 63 | * | 50 |
| Say they have received "a lot" or "some" help "to prepare for future jobs you would like to have" | 59 | 65 | 67 | 69 | * | 46 |
| No. of cases | (205–208) | (354–361) | (149–155) | (63–65) | (56–57) | (34–35) |

* Not asked at Regis.

## Perspectives on Staff Supervision

Although inmates of the treatment and open institutions did have more positive perspectives on the institution and staff in general, the same pattern need not hold for their perspectives on staff supervisory practices. As we have indicated, the movement toward permissiveness and the abandonment of universalism are likely to induce ambiguity, group machinations, and crisis. Findings on inmate perspectives on staff supervision are generally consistent with this notion.

One of the two items summarized in the index of perspectives on institution and staff (Table 8.1) that did not show a difference between the obedience/conformity and treatment organizations dealt with whether the inmates saw the adults as "pretty fair." On that question staff per-

### Table 8.3—Inmate Views on Staff Supervision
### (in percentages)

| Inmate Views | Closed | | | | Open | |
| --- | --- | --- | --- | --- | --- | --- |
| | OBEDIENCE/ CONFORMITY | | TREATMENT | | RE-EDUCATION/ DEVELOPMENT | |
| | Dick | Mixter | Milton | Inland | Regis | Bennett |
| Agree that "some adults here are too strict" | 67 | 69 | 69 | 53 | 51 | 86 |
| Agree that "there are too many boys here who push other boys around" | 65 | 69 | 71 | 58 | 51 | 74 |
| Agree that "adults here are not strict enough with certain boys" | 52 | 60 | 64 | 71 | 46 | 82 |
| Agree that "some boys can get away with too much" | 74 | 73 | 79 | 85 | 58 | 91 |
| No. of cases | (203–207) | (359–360) | (152–154) | (64–65) | (57) | (34–35) |

sonnel at one treatment institution, Milton, and at one open institution, Bennett, were not seen as fair any more often than personnel at one or both of the obedience/conformity institutions. Similar results emerge in findings on four items bearing on staff supervision (Table 8.3). On the first question, asking opinions on whether adults are too strict, Inland inmates are, again, relatively positive but inmates of Milton are no more positive than those in the obedience/conformity institutions. The same pattern is seen on the second item, on whether there are too many boys who push other inmates around (presumably reflecting staff permissiveness at least in part).

Findings on the other two items in this set indicate the existence of more negative perspectives on staff supervision in both treatment institutions than in either of the obedience/conformity institutions. The questions asked for opinions on statements that adults are not strict enough with certain boys and that some boys can get away with too much. Higher proportions agreed with both statements at Milton and Inland than at Dick and Mixter. Turning to the open institutions, we find that the more controlled institution, Regis, had the least negative response pattern of all institutions on all four questions. In contrast, the proportions of inmates negative toward staff supervision were higher at Bennett than at any other organization on all four items.

The data thus seem to confirm the notion that one cost of operating

a less disciplined and universalistic program is the creation of feelings that staff personnel play favorites and have lost control. These feelings, however, are not strong enough to jeopardize basic inmate perspectives on the institution and staff.

### Perspectives on Adaptation to the Institution

Our second guiding hypothesis was that inmates in the obedience/conformity institutions would show an orientation of overt behavioral conformity, whereas those in the treatment settings would often orient themselves to giving evidence of personality change and positive attitudes. Findings on the adaptations recommended by the inmates support this proposition.

These results come from a question asking about the "best way to get along," and from another on "what a boy has to do to get a parole or discharge" (Table 8.4). On the first item substantially higher proportions chose the "prisonized" responses of "stay out of the way of adults but get away with what you can" and "don't break any rules and keep out of trouble" at Dick (74 per cent) and Mixter (73 per cent) than at Milton (55 per cent) and Inland (45 per cent). Conversely, inmates of the treatment institutions selected "try to get an understanding of yourself" more often (50 per cent at Inland, 35 per cent at Milton) than did those of the obedience/conformity institutions (17 per cent at Mixter, 12 per cent at Dick). The rank-ordering of the inmates' response by institution is identical to that of the staff members of the closed institutions, who were asked the same question (Chapter 7); proportions naming the understanding category were much lower, however, among inmates than among the staff in each institution.

Results are parallel on the second question, concerning getting a discharge or parole. Seventy-one per cent of the inmates in the obedience/conformity institutions gave a "prisonized" response whereas 31 per cent did so at Milton and Inland. On both questions patterns differed in the re-education/development institutions. Regis inmates gave responses more like those found in the obedience/conformity institutions and Bennett's boys responded more like those in the treatment institutions, or even more positively.

The inmates' perceptions of what behavior is approved were presumably related to their views of which staff members held the power over

## Table 8.4—Inmate Views on Adaptation to the Institution
### (in percentages)

| | Closed | | | | Open | |
| | OBEDIENCE/ CONFORMITY | | TREATMENT | | RE-EDUCATION/ DEVELOPMENT | |
| Inmate Views | Dick | Mixter | Milton | Inland | Regis | Bennett |
|---|---|---|---|---|---|---|
| Perspectives on the best way to get along* | | | | | | |
| "Stay out of the way of the adults but get away with what you can" | 16 | 13 | 11 | 7 | 14 | 9 |
| "Don't break any rules and keep out of trouble" | 58 | 60 | 44 | 38 | 57 | 42 |
| "Show that you are really sorry for what you did" | 13 | 9 | 10 | 5 | 5 | — |
| "Try to get an understanding of yourself" | 12 | 17 | 35 | 50 | 23 | 48 |
| Inmates' "prisonized" response on open-ended question about ways to receive a discharge or parole† | 71 | 71 | 31 | 31 | 53 | 10 |
| No. of cases | (187–202) | (348–352) | (140–151) | (60–65) | (52–56) | (30–33) |

* The specific question: "Regardless of what the adults here say, the best way to get along is to: . . ."

† The question: "In your own words, write in what you think a boy has to do to get a parole or discharge from here." Responses of conformity to rules and expectations, avoidance of misbehavior, "doing time," and overt compliance were coded as "prisonized." "Treatment" responses (e.g., "gaining self-insight" or "working well with counselor"), responses indicating change in orientation or person (e.g., "prove you can be trusted"), and responses indicating conformity or positive behavior with reference unspecified or vague were coded as "non-prisonized."

them. Inmates were asked to write down "which adult here has the most to say about when you get out of here." The results were generally consistent with our observations in the institutions and with staff perceptions of power. Most of Dick's inmates (71 per cent) saw power over their release to be in the hands of the executive. Mixter boys split on whether it was in the hands of the superintendent (34 per cent said this) or members of the clinical staff (38 per cent), but a substantial number (22 per cent) assigned this power to cottage personnel. Milton's inmates most often saw the clinical staff as powerful (66 per cent), but also frequently said the superintendent had the most power (33 per

cent). At Regis nine out of ten said the director was most important, whereas at Bennett 60 per cent saw the social worker as most powerful, the rest naming the superintendent. We also asked the inmates to name the adult who "has the most to say about what happens to you while you're here." Results were very similar.

*Perspectives on Self and Self-change*

The third guiding proposition was that inmates of treatment institutions would have more positive perspectives on self than those in the obedience/conformity institutions. Findings on three measures of self-perception generally confirm the proposition (Table 8.5).

### Table 8.5—Inmate Views on Self (in percentages)

| | Closed | | | | Open | |
|---|---|---|---|---|---|---|
| | OBEDIENCE/ CONFORMITY | | TREATMENT | | RE-EDUCATION/ DEVELOPMENT | |
| | Dick | Mixter | Milton | Inland | Regis | Bennett |
| Characterizations of self | | | | | | |
| Someone who doesn't let anyone push him around | 10 | 7 | 8 | 5 | 7 | 9 |
| Someone who got a raw deal | 10 | 13 | 12 | 9 | 13 | 18 |
| Someone who knows what the score is and how to play it cool | 19 | 16 | 13 | 11 | 20 | 9 |
| Someone who is trying to straighten out | 50 | 54 | 48 | 53 | 43 | 58 |
| Someone with personal problems | 12 | 10 | 20 | 23 | 18 | 6 |
| *Scores on index of positive self-change** | | | | | | |
| Boys with positive score | 38 | 42 | 52 | 58 | 51 | 79 |
| *Expectations about making good after release* | | | | | | |
| Boys who say they have an excellent chance to make good | 38 | 39 | 48 | 65 | 40 | 59 |
| No. of cases | (188–207) | (325–358) | (143–153) | (57–65) | (46–57) | (31–35) |

* Based on two questions: "How much would you say that your stay here has helped you?"; and "If it has helped you, is it mostly because 'I have learned my lesson' [or] 'I have learned something about myself and why I get into trouble.' " Scored as positive were those who said both that they had been helped a great deal or quite a bit and that they were helped by learning something about themselves and why they got into trouble.

The first measure asked respondents to indicate which of several alternative types of persons they felt like: someone who doesn't let anyone push him around, someone who got a raw deal, someone who knows what the score is and how to play it cool, someone who is trying to straighten out, or someone with personal problems. Differences are relatively small, but treating the last two alternatives as the more positive responses, we find the proportions choosing these to be lower in the obedience/conformity institutions (62 per cent in Dick and 64 per cent in Mixter) than in the treatment institutions (68 per cent in Milton and 76 per cent in Inland). On this measure inmates of the open institutions (Regis, 61 per cent; Bennett, 64 per cent) looked more like those of the obedience/conformity institutions than those of the treatment institutions.

The second measure was an index scoring as positive those who indicated both that they had been helped considerably by the institution and that this help had come from learning about themselves rather than by learning a lesson. This provided a crude measure of "positive self-change." The expected differences emerge clearly between Dick and Mixter on the one hand and Milton and Inland on the other. On this measure Bennett's response was the most positive, and Regis's response was like that of the treatment institutions.

A query about how the inmate thought he would do after release was the third measure of perspectives on self. Higher proportions at Milton and especially Inland saw themselves as having an excellent chance to make good than at Dick and Mixter. The Regis response was close to those in the obedience/conformity institutions, and Bennett's was between those of Milton and Inland. Altogether, these findings consistently show more positive patterns in the treatment institutions than in the obedience/confromity organizations, with vacillating patterns found in the open institutions.

Data on what the inmates believed staff personnel thought of them are also pertinent. Inmates were asked about the extent to which they knew how the adults felt about how long they would have to stay in the institution, and about how long they actually expected to stay. We expected ambiguities to be greatest at Milton because of the staff's difficulties in communicating the intentions and criteria of the milieu treatment program.

The findings (Table 8.6) do show inmates at Milton to have had a

**Table 8.6—Inmates' Knowledge of Staff Judgments About Them and Expectations About Stay (in percentages)**

| | Closed | | | | Open | |
| | OBEDIENCE/ CONFORMITY | | TREATMENT | | RE-EDUCATION/ DEVELOPMENT | |
| | Dick | Mixter | Milton | Inland | Regis | Bennett |
|---|---|---|---|---|---|---|
| **Knowledge of staff judgments:** | | | | | | |
| I am sure how I stand with the adults (regarding how long I will have to stay here) | 14 | 15 | 16 | 31 | 26 | 35 |
| I think I know how I stand with the adults | 25 | 33 | 23 | 35 | 39 | 32 |
| It's hard to say how I stand with the adults | 25 | 33 | 30 | 26 | 18 | 24 |
| I have no idea how I stand with the adults | 36 | 19 | 31 | 8 | 18 | 9 |
| **Boys who think their stay will be:** | | | | | | |
| Shorter than most | 18 | 44 | 26 | 46 | 23 | 18 |
| About the same as most | 42 | 34 | 34 | 38 | 37 | 35 |
| Longer than most | 40 | 22 | 40 | 16 | 40 | 47 |
| No. of cases | (208–209) | (357) | (153–154) | (63–65) | (57) | (34) |

high level of uncertainty but, surprisingly, we see the same pattern at Dick and, to a lesser extent, at Mixter. Proportions in the two alternatives indicating greatest uncertainty on the question about staff views of release are 61 per cent at both Dick and Milton, about half at Mixter, and about a third at Inland, Regis, and Bennett. On the item about expectations for stay, we find a somewhat similar pattern among the closed institutions: relative pessimism about length of stay at Dick and Milton (with inmates of the open institutions also relatively pessimistic). The unanticipated findings on Dick and Mixter perhaps reflect the low levels of personal staff-inmate contact in these institutions. Even with relatively organized procedures for rating and making decisions about release, inmates there experienced considerable uncertainty.

Self-image was also explored as part of an analysis based on a series of projective measures developed by Rosemary Conzemius Sarri and reported in her "Organizational Patterns and Client Perspectives in Juvenile Institutions: A Comparative Study."[4] The measures differenti-

ated little among the inmate populations but results showed some greater tendency for inmates of the more treatment-oriented organizations to accept socially approved values and norms and to have less hostile conceptions of misconduct. Responses to the projective questions also were affected by institutional practices, as when 28 per cent of Dick's inmates, responding to the question "What is the worst thing a boy could do?", ignored such acts as murder and wrote in "run away."

## LENGTH OF STAY AND PERSPECTIVES

Although we lack longitudinal data on inmate perspectives, inferences may be made about the probable effects of the organizations over the course of time through a cross-sectional analysis by length of stay.

Figure 8.1 charts the proportions of inmates who were positive on the index of perspectives on the institution and staff by length of stay for the closed institutions. The diagram indicates that differences between types of institutions cannot be accounted for by the fact that treatment institutions usually keep their inmates longer; greater proportions of inmates of Milton and Inland expressed positive perspectives at almost every point in time. In both treatment institutions there was a rapid positive movement in perspectives, followed by a drop-off in the middle months and then a positive movement again in the later phase (note that Inland's initial sharp increase is based on a total of eleven cases, however). In contrast, in the two obedience/conformity institutions the overall trend was for the proportion of inmates with negative perspectives to increase with longer stay. Dick and Mixter differed somewhat in the direction of patterns during the early and middle months, but experienced rather similar patterns of movement toward negative orientations in the later months.

Figure 8.2 charts the same data for the open institutions. In Regis we find a steady pattern of increasing positiveness, with some drop-off (based on case bases of only eight and four) at the end. In Bennett the distribution of stay is so skewed that it is risky to draw any conclusions except about the longest two categories. Apparently there is a steady increase of positive response, followed by a drop-off, and finally followed by (this we can be more certain about) an increase in positiveness in the longest confinement category. The data do not allow us

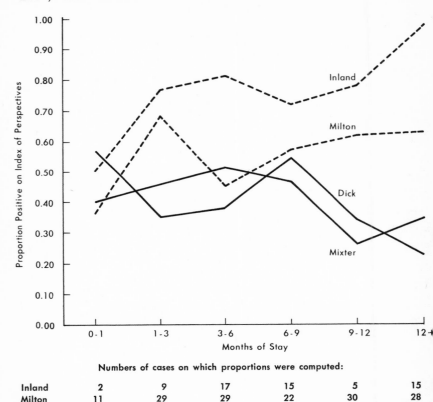

Numbers of cases on which proportions were computed:

| | 0-1 | 1-3 | 3-6 | 6-9 | 9-12 | 12+ |
|---|---|---|---|---|---|---|
| Inland | 2 | 9 | 17 | 15 | 5 | 15 |
| Milton | 11 | 29 | 29 | 22 | 30 | 28 |
| Mixter | 74 | 103 | 96 | 48 | 11 | 27 |
| Dick | 19 | 25 | 61 | 59 | 22 | 21 |

*Figure 8.1—Lengths of Stay and Proportions Positive on Index of Perspectives on Institution and Staff in Closed Institutions*

to draw conclusions about the effects of stay at Bennett, however, for twenty-eight of the institution's thirty-five inmates had been there at least nine months. It is conceivable that part of Bennett's relatively positive overall response derives from some distinctive effect of the long average stay found in this institution. Within almost every category of length of stay where some reasonable comparisons may be made—ruling out comparisons involving case bases of less than five—we see the Regis and Bennett inmates to have been more like the inmates of

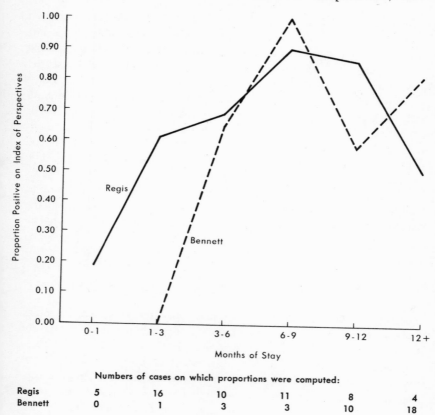

Numbers of cases on which proportions were computed:

| | 0-1 | 1-3 | 3-6 | 6-9 | 9-12 | 12+ |
|---|---|---|---|---|---|---|
| Regis | 5 | 16 | 10 | 11 | 8 | 4 |
| Bennett | 0 | 1 | 3 | 3 | 10 | 18 |

**Figure 8.2—Lengths of Stay and Proportions Positive on Index of Perspectives on Institution and Staff in Open Institutions**

the treatment institutions (or even more positive than the latter) than those of Dick and Mixter.

These findings may also be used to assess how well the prisonization model and its variants, developed from the study of adult correctional organizations, fit the juvenile institution. The prisonization model, derived from Clemmer's classic work,[5] posits a steady increase in negativism with longer stay, presumably as inmates became more fully socialized to a negative inmate culture. Against this, Wheeler has found evidence of a U-shaped pattern in which the tendency to negativism is

reversed as the inmate draws close to release.[6] Garabedian has replicated Wheeler's results, finding the U-shaped pattern to be predominant but also discovering that when he broke his sample down by role types some inmates showed little change in any direction, some exhibited the prisonization pattern, and some showed change in a positive direction.[7]

Our findings indicate that the fit of these models varies with organizational type. Net change in the obedience/conformity institutions is somewhat akin to that of the prisonization model; in the treatment institutions it is in the opposite, positive direction, with the U-shaped pattern seen to some extent when one looks at the middle phase. The overall change in the re-education/development institutions appears to be positive, with no U-shaped pattern emerging. These findings, together with Garabedian's results, suggest that future research on the development of inmate orientations must take into account both characteristics of inmates and attributes of the organization.

## THE IMPACT OF BACKGROUND ATTRIBUTES

Statement of our fifth hypothesis implied that it is plausible that older boys, more serious offenders, and boys from certain environments are predisposed to have particularly negative perspectives. Because of interorganizational variations in the recruitment of boys having such potentially predisposing background characteristics, we must inquire into the effects of these attributes to see whether organizational differences in perspectives can be explained by them. We shall analyze the impact of delinquency history, past institutional record, age, race, IQ, family disorganization, urban-rural background, social class, and the institution's psychological diagnosis.

### Variations in Backgrounds

Information coded from organizational files provides the basis for the following analysis. The accuracy and fullness of this information varied among organizations and for different types of data. On such attributes as age or race it seemed to be clearly valid and reliable. Such data as delinquency history and psychological diagnosis, however, were much more prone to error and to systematic biases differing among in-

stitutions. The latter data can be depended upon more for intra-organizational than inter-organizational analysis.

The distributions of various inmate background characteristics are shown in Table 8.7. The major organizational differences in these data are as follows: (1) Greater numbers of inmates whose records showed more serious offenses at the obedience/conformity institutions and to an extent at Milton, the other public institution. (2) Greater numbers of boys who were recorded as having committed large numbers of offenses at Milton and particularly Mixter. (3) Large numbers of repeaters at Dick, Mixter, and Regis, and very small numbers at Inland and Bennett. (4) Sizable numbers who previously had been institutionalized elsewhere at Mixter, Milton, Regis, and especially Inland. (5) Greater numbers of older boys at Dick and of younger boys at Milton and especially Bennett. (6) Substantial numbers of non-whites at Mixter and Milton and none at Bennett. (7) Large numbers of inmates with low IQ scores at Dick and Milton and small numbers at Inland and Regis. (8) Large numbers of boys from disorganized family situations at Milton. (9) A lack of inmates from urban environments at Dick and the near exclusiveness of urban backgrounds at Inland, Regis, and Bennett. (10) High social class levels at Regis, Bennett, and especially Inland. (11) Greater numbers classified as having more serious psychological problems (psychosis, physiological disorder, or personality disturbance) at Mixter and Milton, and substantial numbers classified as neurotic at Mixter, Milton, and Inland.[8]

Some patterns clearly reflect institutional biases in record keeping. The high proportion of inmates classified as coming from disorganized homes at Milton, for example, probably reflects the fact that its staff wrote more elaborate descriptions of the family and paid more continuing attention to it than did staff members at any of the other institutions. The high proportions with many offenses at Mixter may reflect the very detailed record-keeping procedures for offenses that existed in that institution.

The psychological diagnoses clearly indicated the tendency of clinic staffs to view behavior in terms of emotional disturbance. Substantial effort went into making diagnoses at Milton, Inland, and Mixter. At Mixter procedures were highly standardized. Classification and prognosis were made perfunctorily and reflected the staff's pessimistic view of inmate potentialities for change.[9] Except at Mixter,

### Table 8.7—Inmate Background Attributes, from Institutional Records (in percentages)

| | Closed | | | | Open | |
| | OBEDIENCE/ CONFORMITY | | TREATMENT | | RE-EDUCATION/ DEVELOPMENT | |
| Background Attributes | Dick | Mixter | Milton | Inland | Regis | Bennett |
|---|---|---|---|---|---|---|
| Have committed more serious offenses* | 67 (200) | 79 (361) | 55 (151) | 31 (65) | 39 (57) | 31 (32) |
| Have committed three or more offenses | 23 (209) | 89 (361) | 72 (155) | 16 (65) | 9 (57) | 25 (32) |
| Have been in this institution before | 25 (208) | 22 (361) | 12† (152) | 3 (65) | 27 (57) | 3 (32) |
| Have been in one or more other institutions of any type before | 8 (208) | 18 (361) | 22 (152) | 27§ (22) | 19 (57) | 9 (32) |
| Are under 14 years old | 13 | 6 | 22 | 7 | 4 | 37 |
| Are 14–16 years old | 64 | 87 | 73 | 86 | 79 | 60 |
| Are over 16 years old | 24 (208) | 7 (362) | 6 (155) | 8 (65) | 17 (56) | 3 (35) |
| Are not white | 12 (206) | 32 (361) | 32 (152) | 15 (65) | 12 (57) | — (35) |
| Have IQ's below normal (91 or below) | 68** (121) | 44 (361) | 61 (147) | 10 (61) | 18 (56) | 40 (22) |
| Come from homes that are broken or show serious problems | 54 (206) | 43 (361) | 72 (150) | 40 (65) | 51 (57) | 50 (32) |
| Are from counties with cities of: | | | | | | |
| Above 90,000 | — | 64 | 30 | 92 | 95 | 100 |
| 10,000–90,000 | 49 | 18 | 54 | 5 | 2 | — |
| Under 10,000 | 52 (208) | 17 (361) | 16 (152) | 2 (64) | 4 (57) | — (32) |
| Are from homes where head of household is: | | | | | | |
| White collar | 10 | 7 | 5 | 35 | 19 | 20 |
| Blue collar | 48 | 69 | 74 | 57 | 74 | 56 |
| Not in labor force | 42 (197) | 24 (349) | 21 (149) | 8 (52) | 7 (45) | 24 (25) |
| Are diagnosed psychologically as: | | | | | | |
| 1. Psychotic, defective, or physiological disorder†† | — | 1 | 9 | 1 | — | — |

**Table 8.7—Continued**

| | Closed | | | | Open | |
| | OBEDIENCE/ CONFORMITY | | TREATMENT | | RE-EDUCATION/ DEVELOPMENT | |
| Background Attributes | Dick | Mixter | Milton | Inland | Regis | Bennett |
|---|---|---|---|---|---|---|
| 2. Personality disorder | — | 54 | 40 | 34 | 12 | 29 |
| 3. Psychoneurotic | — | 40 | 24 | 32 | 7 | 9 |
| 4. Transient situational personality disturbance | — | §§ | 12 | 28 | 10 | 20 |
| 5. No serious psychological problem | — | — | 1 | 1 | 25 | 9 |
| 6. Not diagnosed | 100 | 5 | 13 | 3 | 46 | 34 |
| | (209) | (364) | (155) | (65) | (57) | (35) |

* Includes arson, forgery, sex offenses, breaking and entering, and crimes of violence. Excludes being dependent and neglected, truancy, "incorrigibility," "maladjustment," theft, and vandalism.

† Milton figures underestimate to an unknown degree the actual number of returnees. Usually only those who had completed several months of parole supervision and then were recommitted by a court were so recorded.

§ Information on a majority of cases at Inland is missing because of a coding error.

** The majority of inmates at Dick were not tested. Boys tested were mostly those who were enrolled in the school, and non-attenders included many dropouts; the figure given therefore probably over-estimates intelligence scores in this institution.

†† Except at Mixter, coded from diagnostic statements in files following the *Diagnostic and Statistical Manual* published by the American Psychiatric Association, 1952 edition. Mixter gave inmates formal classifications that we translated—with misgivings but after consultation with their staff—as follows: Category 1, "mentally defective"; 2, "character disorder"; 3, "disturbed"; 4, "environmental delinquent."

§§ One case.

where some inmates with certain psychological classifications were sent to certain cottages, we could find no relationship at any of the institutions between psychological diagnosis and assignment of inmates. Except in the treatment institutions, diagnoses seemed to be used mainly for screening out retarded or seriously disturbed inmates who perhaps could be sent elsewhere, and as an aid to intensive counselling.

Table 8.8 elaborates the findings on most serious offense. The information is only approximate. Often, detailed information was available only on the particular offense that precipitated the decision to commit the inmate. There were also sharp institutional variations in the attention given to and the salience of offense data. For example, staff members at Mixter were highly cognizant of this information, using it in classification and assignment, whereas the staffs at Milton and Inland were almost totally unaware of what their records said about manifest behavior.[10] We developed code categories and an arbitrary ordering of seriousness of offense on the bases of previous studies of delinquent

### Table 8.8—Specific Breakdowns of Most Serious Offense in Record (in percentages)

| Offense, in Order of Seriousness | Closed | | | | Open | |
| --- | --- | --- | --- | --- | --- | --- |
| | OBEDIENCE/ CONFORMITY | | TREATMENT | | RE-EDUCATION/ DEVELOPMENT | |
| | Dick | Mixter | Milton | Inland | Regis | Bennett |
| *Less Serious Offenses* | | | | | | |
| Dependent and neglected | * | — | 2 | — | 30 | 22 |
| Truancy from home or school | 6 | * | 2 | 6 | 2 | 16 |
| Probation violation | 1 | — | — | — | — | — |
| "Incorrigible," "disobedience," "delinquent," "poor home adjustment" | 2 | 4 | 3 | 9 | 18 | 16 |
| "Psychological maladjustment" | — | * | — | 23 | — | — |
| "Social maladjustment" | — | — | — | 6 | — | — |
| Parole violation | * | — | 1 | — | — | — |
| Theft, larceny (not auto) | 14 | 7 | 20 | 12 | 7 | 13 |
| Vandalism, malicious destruction of property | 2 | 1 | 3 | 2 | — | — |
| Auto theft | 7 | 8 | 13 | 11 | 5 | 3 |
| *More Serious Offenses* | | | | | | |
| Arson | * | 1 | 1 | — | — | 3 |
| Forgery | 3 | 1 | 5 | — | — | — |
| Drug addiction or alcoholism | — | — | — | — | — | — |
| Sex offense, unspecified | — | 1 | — | 2 | 5 | 6 |
| Exposure or indecent liberties | — | 1 | 1 | 6 | — | — |
| Homosexual | * | * | 1 | — | — | — |
| Statutory rape or other heterosexual offenses (not assaultive) | * | — | 2 | — | — | — |
| Breaking and entering or burglary | 55 | 49 | 31 | 15 | 18 | 16 |
| Assault, including sexual (not rape) | 6 | 13 | 8 | — | 16 | 6 |
| Robbery | 1 | 6 | 5 | — | — | — |
| Armed robbery | 1 | 6 | — | 8 | — | — |
| Rape | * | 1 | — | — | — | — |
| Murder or manslaughter | — | — | 1 | — | — | — |
| No. of cases | (200) | (361) | (151) | (65) | (57) | (32) |

* Some cases, but not enough to round to 1 per cent.

offenses[11] and interviews with the institutional personnel. We coded the most serious offense listed even when it had not precipitated commitment (thereby introducing a bias toward finding more serious offenders in institutions that collected more extensive delinquency histories).

These findings indicate that between a fifth and a third of the inmates of the open institutions had committed no offense more serious than being dependent and neglected, whereas almost none in the other institutions was in this category. The offense recorded most frequently in the three public institutions, Dick, Mixter, and Milton, was breaking and entering or burglary. Mixter had the largest proportion who had committed assaultive offenses and, in general, it had inmates with more serious offenses.

Altogether, the background data do indicate some significant variations among the organizations. Dick had older boys and many serious offenders. Mixter had the most serious offenders. Milton was more like Dick and Mixter than the private institutions, but did have a younger age distribution. Regis and Bennett had less serious offenders and, in the case of the latter, a very young population. Inland's inmates tended to be moderately serious offenders, and had higher levels of social class background, intelligence, and neurosis.

## Perspectives and Backgrounds

We performed a fairly elaborate analysis of the effects of backgrounds upon perspectives, controlling each of the background attributes in analyzing six different indices of perspectives by organization. We found that in most cases where a background variable seemed to have a direct association with an index of perspectives in one or more institutions, it would have an inverse association in one or more of the other institutions. Further, background attributes did not usually relate consistently from one index of perspectives to another within the same institution. Finally, we found that differences between obedience/conformity and treatment institutions held up, with only minor exceptions, within categories of background controls.

The findings are illustrated by those on the index of perspectives on the institution and staff (Table 8.9). There are consistent patterns of association across organizations on only two attributes—the number of times returned to the institution (ignoring data on Inland and Bennett,

## Table 8.9—Inmate Scores on Index of Perspectives on Institution and Staff, by Selected Background Characteristics (*in percentages*)

| | Closed | | | | Open | |
| | OBEDIENCE/ CONFORMITY | | TREATMENT | | RE-EDUCATION/ DEVELOPMENT | |
| Inmates Positive* | Dick | Mixter | Milton | Inland | Regis | Bennett |
|---|---|---|---|---|---|---|
| **Seriousness of major offense:** | | | | | | |
| Less serious | 38 | 52 | 57 | 82 | 71 | 70 |
| | (66) | (75) | (67) | (45) | (35) | (23) |
| More serious | 42 | 43 | 60 | 90 | 68 | 83 |
| | (140) | (286) | (84) | (20) | (22) | (12) |
| **Number of offenses:** | | | | | | |
| Less than three | 42 | 52 | 51 | 87 | 69 | 76 |
| | (161) | (40) | (43) | (54) | (52) | (25) |
| Three or more | 40 | 43 | 60 | 73 | 62 | 70 |
| | (48) | (307) | (112) | (11) | (5) | (10) |
| **Number of times returned to this institution:** | | | | | | |
| None | 44 | 47 | 62 | 84 | 79 | 74 |
| | (156) | (283) | (135) | (63) | (42) | (34) |
| One or more | 31 | 38 | 29 | 100 | 47 | 110 |
| | (52) | (78) | (17) | (2) | (15) | (1) |
| **Previous institutionalization elsewhere:** | | | | | | |
| None | 42 | 48 | 60 | 94 | 72 | 77 |
| | (191) | (295) | (118) | (16) | (46) | (30) |
| Some | 33 | 33 | 50 | 83 | 64 | 60 |
| | (15) | (66) | (34) | (6) | (11) | (5) |
| **Age†** | | | | | | |
| Younger | 34 | 50 | 56 | 85 | 77 | 58 |
| | (94) | (204) | (121) | (41) | (26) | (19) |
| Older | 47 | 40 | 62 | 83 | 63 | 94 |
| | (114) | (160) | (34) | (24) | (30) | (16) |
| **Race:** | | | | | | |
| White | 43 | 47 | 62 | 82 | 70 | 74 |
| | (181) | (245) | (104) | (55) | (50) | (35) |
| Non-white | 24 | 40 | 48 | 100 | 71 | — |
| | (25) | (116) | (48) | (10) | (7) | (0) |
| **IQ:** | | | | | | |
| 90 or below | 30 | 45 | 58 | 80 | 44 | 71 |
| | (44) | (120) | (41) | (5) | (9) | (7) |
| 91 or above | 37 | 43 | 64 | 85 | 76 | 77 |
| | (38) | (203) | (56) | (55) | (46) | (13) |
| **Family situation:** | | | | | | |
| Intact, no problems | 46 | 49 | 62 | 80 | 71 | 88 |
| | (95) | (204) | (42) | (39) | (28) | (16) |
| Not intact | 36 | 40 | 56 | 92 | 69 | 63 |
| | (111) | (157) | (108) | (26) | (29) | (19) |

### Table 8.9—Continued

| Inmates Positive* | Closed | | | | Open | |
| | OBEDIENCE/ CONFORMITY | | TREATMENT | | RE-EDUCATION/ DEVELOPMENT | |
| | Dick | Mixter | Milton | Inland | Regis | Bennett |
| Rural-urban origin§ | | | | | | |
| "Rural" | 41 (208) | 50 (126) | 55 (107) | 100 (3) | 100 (1) | 100 (1) |
| "Urban" | — (0) | 43 (235) | 64 (45) | 85 (60) | 71 (54) | 74 (34) |
| Occupation of father or other head of household: | | | | | | |
| White collar | 22 (18) | 71 (21) | 63 (8) | 78 (18) | 78 (9) | 80 (5) |
| Blue collar or not in labor force | 42 (179) | 44 (330) | 58 (141) | 85 (34) | 67 (36) | 93 (20) |
| Institution's psychological diagnosis:** | | | | | | |
| Less serious | | 48 (145) | 63 (59) | 88 (40) | 75 (24) | 85 (13) |
| More serious | | 42 (201) | 57 (76) | 78 (23) | 86 (7) | 70 (10) |

* See Table 8.7 for clarification of background categories.
† Younger boys are under 16, older boys are 16 and over except at Bennett, where younger boys are under 15, older boys are 15 and over.
§ "Urban" inmates come from counties with at least one city of 90,000 or more; "rural" inmates come from counties without such a city.
** Diagnosed inmates only; therefore none at Dick. The less serious category includes transient situational disturbance or psychoneurosis. Included in the more serious are personality disturbance, psychotic, and defective and other physiological disorders.

where there were case bases of two and one), and past institutionalization elsewhere.

Examining cross-organizational findings on the closed institutions, we see that within the categories of controls the inmates of both treatment institutions were more likely to have positive perspectives on the institution and staff than were the inmates of either obedience/conformity institution in nearly every instance. There were three exceptions to this pattern. Among those with fewer offenses, Mixter inmates (52 per cent positive) did not differ from those in Milton (51 per cent positive). Disproportionately few (29 per cent) of the Milton inmates who were classified as returnees had positive perspectives. A disproportionately large number of positive responses (71 per cent) came from Mixter inmates with white-collar backgrounds.

The first of these exceptions suggests that a portion of the relatively negative overall response at Mixter may have been a result of its heavy recruitment of inmates with many offenses. Such a pattern would not explain why those with three or more offenses were so negative compared with similar inmates at Milton and Inland, however. The second exception is probably a result of the fact that the Milton returnees, as indicated in a note to Table 8.7, were not directly comparable to the others, apparently constituting a specially "hard core." The last exception may simply reflect the small number of "white collar" inmates at both Mixter and Milton. Altogether, the exceptions do not challenge the conclusion that these background attributes cannot explain the differences in attitudes between these types of institutions.

The same conclusion emerges from data on the open institutions. Within every category of the control variables, inmates of both Regis and Bennett were more positive than those of Dick and Mixter, and were less like those of the latter institutions than those of the treatment institutions.

To the extent that background variables have any relationship with perspectives beyond random associations, they seem to do so mostly in interaction with the institutional environment. Background attributes apparently take on their primary significance through the emphases and interpretations staff personnel give to them, and the staff behavior toward the inmate that follows from these perceptions. Thus the data on inmate backgrounds do not upset our findings of predicted organizational differences on perspectives on the institution and staff, adaptation, and self.

## NOTES

1. Of course, these assumptions may be wrong, but within present knowledge about the processes of change, as it can be applied to masses of persons within large numbers of institutional settings, they are about the best we can find. To the extent that the institutional setting is irrelevant to what eventually happens to the inmate because of the primacy of his community, family relationships, or other variables, our assumptions become irrelevant.

2. The percentages of returnees according to institutional files and definitions were: Dick, 25 per cent; Mixter, 22 per cent; Regis, 27 per cent; Bennett, 3 per cent; Milton, 12 per cent; and Inland, 3 per cent.

3. We lost an opportunity to compare institutions on the proportions of their inmates who were staying longer than the institution's official expectations when we collected the data in code categories for length of stay that were too broad. Considerations in releasing an inmate include, besides his behavior, the suitability of the home situation and the population pressures within the institution. Mixter released some inmates under the explicit euphemism, "maximum benefit received," and Dick retained a star end, otherwise ready for release, until he could complete his participation in the institution's football season.

4. Unpublished doctoral dissertation (Ann Arbor: The University of Michigan, 1962).

5. Donald Clemmer, *The Prison Community* (New York: Rinehart, 1958).

6. Stanton Wheeler, "Socialization in Correctional Communities," *American Sociological Review,* 26 (October, 1961), 697–712.

7. Peter C. Garabedian, "Social Roles and Processes of Socialization in the Prison Community," *Social Problems,* 11 (Fall, 1963), 139–152.

8. We also coded religion. The percentages of Protestants, Catholics, Jews, and boys who were not affiliated were, respectively: Dick, 97, 3, 0, 0; Mixter, 77, 23, 0, 0; Milton, 85, 14, 1, 0; Inland, 66, 26, 8, 0; Regis, 4, 93, 0, 4; Bennett, 74, 20, 0, 6.

9. Clinic staff at Mixter asserted that their population was becoming increasingly disturbed. Observation of their classification procedures indicated that this assertion was based on changes in diagnostic categories. Although the data could easily be challenged, the executive used it with interest groups and with the parent organization to argue for additional resources.

10. At Milton one coder noted a case in which institutional records showed the staff assumed the boy to have had only minor problems of adjustment at home. At the back of his voluminous file, however, stapled together with other papers so that it was very difficult to read, was a record of the formal court commitment—which said the boy had attempted murder with a bow and arrow.

11. William McCord and Joan McCord, *Origins of Crime* (New York: Columbia University Press, 1959); and Herbert Block and F. T. Flynn, *Delinquency: the Juvenile Offender in America Today* (New York: Random House, 1956).

*Chapter 9*

# THE INMATE GROUP

Our interest in the collective patterns of inmate behavior stems, first, from the obvious salience of inmate social relations and groupings to staff, inmates, and observers, and second, from our reaction to the crucial and almost universally malignant role most previous students of correctional institutions have assigned to the inmate group. Accounts of these organizations generally have portrayed them as handicapped in attempts at rehabilitation by an informal inmate system invariably built around norms and values of solidary opposition to the official system and staff. The objectives of the inmate system, it is said, are to minimize interference and maximize accommodations from staff members, to enhance the inmates' access to both official and unofficial values, to exert vigorous control over communication between inmates and staff, and to sanction an ideal model of behavior in which the inmate becomes a master at "playing it cool." So far as the system succeeds, inmates released from the institution may leave more "prisonized" than rehabilitated. Such a description often has been treated as universally valid for adult institutions,[1] and the same account appears in generally accepted descriptions of juvenile institutions.[2]

Data presented in the previous chapter already bring this account into serious question as a general description and analysis, no matter to what degree it may be applicable to traditional adult prisons. Aside from our data, several general objections may be raised. Most conclusions on correctional institutions have come from case studies and unsystematic observations lacking adequate methods to assess similarities and differences among organizations, or even to make satisfactory estimates of variability in inmate orientations within the single population studied. Yet the notion of variation in inmate attachment to oppositional groups and culture has been at least implicit in much of this research,[3] and it is clearly explicit in such recent systematic research as the Wheeler and Garabedian studies of socialization in the prison.[4]

The "solidary opposition" account fails to give sufficient consideration to the consequences for the inmate social system of changes and variations in the larger organization, particularly through the introduction of modern treatment ideology and technology. The distinctive sociological character of the correctional institution and the deviant background predispositions of the inmates may indeed give rise to certain common patterns of group development in all correctional organizations, but it is equally probable that variations in the institutional context will generate changes in the inmate system. In addition, applied *a priori* to juvenile institutions, the generally accepted account ignores important differences between these organizations and those for adults, including the relatively short stay and presumed lesser criminality of the juveniles and the likelihood that many of the social forms that constitute severe deprivation and degradation in the adult correctional institution, where men are treated like children, are not so degrading in the juvenile institution.

Finally, many researchers in the correctional field, lacking comparative methods, have been insufficiently sensitive to the significant theoretical question: Under what organizational conditions do members collectively become committed to or alienated from the official objectives of the organization? By stressing the impact of deprivations and degradations on the inmates and the ways in which the inmates defend themselves, these researchers have developed a plausible hypothesis: that the inmate group serves the function of alleviating its members' deprivations and degradations.[5] Yet they have failed to go further to inquire into the effects of varying levels of deprivation or to analyze the conditions necessary to stimulate, permit, and sustain the successful *use* of such a group solution to the problems of deprivation. Such analysis would be consistent with the general proposition that the characteristics and functions of informal groups vary with the larger organizational context.

## A THEORETICAL SCHEME

Some kind of informal group structure arises out of primary relations among inmates in all institutions. It can be assumed that this structure has a significant role in socializing and relating the inmate to the

institution, in defining informal norms of inmate behavior and approved sets of values and beliefs, and in defining and allocating things that are valued (e.g., contraband) among the inmates. Accepting the conception of the inmate group as a system potentially oriented to the problem of ameliorating the deprivations of its members, we can conceive of two major environmental dimensions that could condition the response of this group: either variations in the nature of the problem itself—that is, in the balance of gratifications and deprivations, or variations in the conditions under which the group must attempt to find some solution to its problem—that is, in the patterns of control and authority that the staff exercises over inmate action and behavior.

## Variations in the Balance of Gratifications and Deprivations

It is assumed that the inmates will try to ease their lot to the extent that they need to and are able. A high ratio of deprivation to gratification sets the stage for the compensatory development of a system for obtaining the limited supply of rewards, both illicit (contraband) and licit (e.g., choice job assignments). If such a system comes into being, it will function to ameliorate the inmates' deprivations. Its development presupposes that some inmates are able to get access to things of value in short supply, that a system of allocating them comes into being, and that this system becomes stabilized in role expectations. Inmates must become interdependent if they are to obtain continuing access to the allocated rewards and to forms of mutual aid, and the system grows up around this interdependence.

Where such functions exist they will require some division of labor, which in turn is likely to lead to the development of leadership structures. Norms of reciprocity are likely to develop to provide some protection against the advantage and power of those who might monopolize scarce objects of value, but those in favorable positions in the system are likely to become organized in a leadership cadre with a relatively high centralization of power. To the extent that the system is deeply involved in secretive and illicit transactions of contraband allocation, the leaders recruited by such a structure may be highly negative, at least covertly, toward the staff and institution. Such leadership cadres might react back upon the group and make it more oppositional to the official system than it otherwise would be. (It should be clear that in

analyzing the inmate group we are more interested in deprivations as *shortages* inspiring collective actions than as perceived deprivations.)

## Variations in Staff Patterns of Control and Authority

Variations in control and authority are likely to operate in two different ways. First, rigid and categorical practices are likely to facilitate the recognition of a common fate and the potentialities for collective problem-solving among the inmates. Differences in authority, general status, age, and often social class between staff and inmates in all institutions generally lead the inmate to see the other inmates as fellow travelers, but the authority structure and its impact are subject to some variation among institutions. Frequent scheduling of mass activities, techniques of group punishment, and administration of physical punishment before groups of inmates would further the probability that inmates would identify strongly with one another against the staff. When in addition staff personnel maintain domineering authority relationships and considerable social distance, inmates would further perceive themselves to be members of a group with interests divergent from theirs.

Second, staff patterns of control and authority exert a limiting influence upon inmate association and group elaboration. Thus at the same time that rigorous practices of control and authority would provide greater stimulus to the recognition and use of group solutions, they also would make such solutions more difficult to achieve. Although only such extreme techniques as keeping the inmates locked in separate rooms might effectively prevent the emergence of any level of social relationship among the inmates,[6] rigorous control could severely limit opportunities for interaction and group formation—particularly the formation of groups over the whole of the institution. In this situation group activities would have to be conducted on a covert level, involving norms of secrecy and mutual defense against the staff.

## Linkages

These two dimensions, gratification-deprivation and patterns of control and authority, provide the hypothetical link between institutional goals and responses of the inmate group because both vary between the obedience/conformity and treatment settings. On the first dimension it is apparent that the treatment institution places much less emphasis on

degradation ceremonies, use of powerful sanctions, and the denial of impulse gratification, and much greater emphasis upon providing incentives, objectives, and experiences desired by the inmates. On the second dimension, it is obvious that the treatment institution places much less stress on surveillance, control over inmate association, restriction on freedom, a rigid model of conformity to rules, and domination and high social distance in authority relations than does the obedience/conformity institution. Analyzing the simultaneous effects of these dimensions, we are led to the following expectations:

*The Obedience/Conformity Setting.* Because of high deprivations the inmate group in an obedience/conformity institution would be organized around the functions of allocating legitimate and illicit items of value and providing mutual aid. Such functions would reflect and generate relatively negative and "prisonized" orientations toward the institution and staff. Although control and authority practices of the staff would increase the need for group solutions, the extensive control exercised would put severe enough boundaries around interaction and group formation so that group integration and solidarity would probably be relatively underdeveloped. The leadership structure, highly involved in illicit and secret activities, would tend to be negative.

*The Treatment Setting.* The inmate group in a treatment-oriented institution would be organized more voluntaristically around friendship patterns. With deprivations lower mutual aid would be less necessary, and any ameliorative system would tend to lose its market. The group would be involved in the allocation of objects of value to the group, but these would be positive rewards, given more fully in consonance with staff definitions of merit. The staff would give much freer rein to inmate association, with the result that levels of primary group integration and feelings and norms of group solidarity might be greater than in the custodial setting. This cohesiveness would not necessarily be related to opposition to the staff, however, for the inmate group would emphasize more positive norms and perspectives and greater commitment to the institution and staff. Leaders would be more positive in orientation. Finally, the more positive character of the inmate group might help generate more positive perspectives on self among the inmates.

*Re-education/Development Institutions.* As before, it is difficult to predict the exact order in re-education/development organizations, for

the fact that they are open makes it difficult to assess either the balance of gratifications to deprivations or the staff patterns of control and authority. Again, we would expect inmates of these institutions to be more like those of the treatment institutions.

## INTERPERSONAL RELATIONS

The inmate role everywhere becomes elaborated through the development of an inmate social structure and group culture. By way of illustration, observations at Dick provide the following picture of some of the major aspects of the inmates' collective life.

One major function of the inmate group was to furnish a network for the circulation of information, complaints, rumors, and legend. The component of myth was omnipresent. Dick's inmates, out of earshot of staff personnel, would revel in stories about the cottage commander who paddled in time to guitar music, the boy who withstood forty blows with smiles, the boys punished for homosexual activities by being used as dummies in football practice, the inmates who fermented fruits in the kitchen and got so very drunk, the boys who successfully faked illness in the infirmary, the boys who had stashed weapons around the institution, or the inmates who used knives to kidnap a female typist from the superintendent's office and force her to drive them away from the institution. Often the stories turned on the brutality of some staff member (the farm supervisor was said to choke boys until they bled) or the horrors of punishment yet to be experienced ("In the dungeon they're going to beat you after every meal").

Another major function involved the development of norms of mutual aid and some restriction upon aggressiveness. When staff employees were not watching there was frequent verbal and physical fighting—over places in line, sharing of cigarettes, claims upon a particular chair, and similar trivia, along with more serious aggression including sexual assaults and the use of weapons. At the same time, relationships of friendship and mutual benefit were defined by participation in the "halfer" (elsewhere known as "buddy") system. The system would begin when two boys agreed to "go halfers" with each other over cigarettes, food, or other things in short supply. Sometimes the agreement was extended among three, four, or five boys who shared

equally. In turns, halfer systems were cross-linked by friendship relations between boys in different halfer groups.[7] Mostly away from staff members' eyes, cigarettes, sex literature, money, and other items, whether procured individually or by groups of boys having access to outsiders (for example, boys working on a coal truck got outside frequently and were able to buy cigarettes), were distributed through halfer and friendship chains or through gambling, fighting, and general norms of camaraderie. Overseeing these processes, adjusting claims, and caught between the inmates' interests and the staff's surveillance and sanctions, were the inmate leaders, partially co-opted as "outline boys."

The Dick group and the outline boys system dramatized another important function of the inmate group: to keep the lid on behavior that was, from the staff's perspective, disruptive. When a boy "fouled up" and group punishment was used, he would be ostracized and would lose his halfer privileges for a period of time. In one case, after a staff member had tightened control and had suspended the monthly ice cream treat because an inmate had broken the cottage's record of having no AWOLs for a considerable period of time, the boy was beaten up in the shower by the other boys.

Another function was the use of the inmate group as a sanction against *staff* misbehavior. Dick's superintendent described an incident involving a commander who had been taking three or four boys off grounds to do painting and repairs around his home. The boys talked and got restive, he said, and then "they just tried to kill him," throwing a brick that hit him on the chest while he was standing on the playground. "The boys knew he was a phony," said the superintendent, who then fired the man despite what he described as political repercussions.

## Organizational Variation

Results on a number of questionnaire items support our hypothesis that the treatment institutions will permit and encourage more fluid, friendship-based, and positive relationships among the inmates (Table 9.1). Questions were asked about the number of other boys with whom the inmate hangs around, the number of close friends he has in the institution, whether he has more friends in the institution or back home, whether he would like to see all or most of the inmates again

**Table 9.1—Inmate Social Relations and Perspectives on Other Inmates (in percentages)**

| | Closed | | | | Open | |
| --- | --- | --- | --- | --- | --- | --- |
| | OBEDIENCE/ CONFORMITY | | TREATMENT | | RE-EDUCATIONAL/ DEVELOPMENT | |
| Relations and Perspectives | Dick | Mixter | Milton | Inland | Regis | Bennett |
| Hang around with two or more boys | 59 | 71 | 78 | 91 | 84 | 75 |
| Have two or more close friends here | 70 | 68 | 83 | 83 | 67 | 67 |
| Say more of their best friends are here rather than back home | 4 | 4 | 14 | 14 | 16 | 24 |
| Want to see all or most inmates again after release | 27 | 14 | 35 | 27 | 21 | 32 |
| Would talk to other inmates about a personal problem | 58 | 50 | 66 | 76 | 61 | 54 |
| Say you don't have to be careful around the other boys to avoid a rough time | 14 | 18 | 21 | 27 | 29 | 18 |
| No. of cases | (202–208) | (356–363) | (152–155) | (62–64) | (54–57) | (34–35) |

after release, whether he would talk with another inmate about a personal problem, and whether he agreed or disagreed with the notion that "you have to be pretty careful about what you say or do around the other boys here, or else they may give you a rough time."

The data show a consistent pattern. On every item a larger percentage of inmates in both treatment institutions reported highly developed or positive social relations than in both obedience/conformity institutions. Further, inmates of the re-education/development institutions tended to report highly developed or positive social relations more often than did those of the obedience/conformity institutions. An analysis controlling length of stay indicates that these institutional differences in social relations cannot be explained by variations in the amount of time the institutions keep their inmates. Longer stay was associated with having more close friendships at Dick, Mixter, and, perhaps, Regis and Bennett, but not at Milton and Inland, and institutional differences in friendships held up within categories of stay.

We expected to find similar institutional variations in findings on questions as to whether the inmate should try to talk others out of running away or roughing up a friend and as to whether most boys

seemed to be interested in "just getting by" in the institution. Instead, we found relatively small and inconsistent differences (with Dick having the highest proportion who *would* try to talk a friend out of running away, apparently reflecting the strong sanctions for going AWOL there). Other partial exceptions to the general pattern reported here—results on items on whether there are too many boys who push you around and whether some boys can get away with too much—were given in Chapter 8. As we indicated there, however, these findings principally seemed to reflect dilemmas of staff control under the permissive treatment model. These strains limit but do not erase the basic differences in interpersonal relations among institutions.

Theoretically, we assume that the level of social relations derives from patterns of staff behavior toward the inmates. Responses to a question on agreement or disagreement with the assertion that becoming friendly with other inmates might lead to trouble with the staff support this interpretation. About two thirds of the inmates of the obedience/conformity institutions and of Bennett agreed with this belief; in contrast, only 21 per cent at Inland and 40 to 50 per cent at Milton and Regis agreed.

## INTEGRATION AND PERSPECTIVES

In Chapter 8 it was seen that inmates of the treatment and re-education/development institutions had more positive perspectives on the organization and staff, adaptation to the institution and themselves, than did inmates of the obedience/conformity institutions. Our discussion of the inmates' collective patterns implies that inmate perspectives should vary not only with the direct experiences they have with the staff but also with their experiences within the inmate group. We may test this assumption by comparing the orientations of those who were and those who were not integrated into the inmate group. Our aim is to obtain data which will allow us to infer the dominant tone and impact of the group. If those who were integrated were more positive in perspectives than those who were not, we would infer that the inmate group exerted a positive influence; if those who were integrated were more negative than those who were not, we would infer that the group exerted a negative influence.

In this analysis we use a simple measure of integration, based on the inmates' responses to the question about the number of close friends he had among the other inmates. If the respondent said he had no friends or only one, we assume that he was not really tied into the inmate group and therefore classify him as "not integrated." If he reported having two or more friends, we assume that he had developed a set of close relationships in the larger group and classify him as "integrated." Although this operational definition is open to question regarding the likely reporting error and exclusion of other meanings of the concept of integration, it provides an understandable and empirically profitable starting point for an analysis of its consequences.

**Table 9.2—Integration into the Inmate Group and Perspectives***

| | Closed | | | | Open | |
| | OBEDIENCE/ CONFORMITY | | TREATMENT | | RE-EDUCATION/ DEVELOPMENT | |
| Integration and Perspectives | Dick | Mixter | Milton | Inland | Regis | Bennett |
|---|---|---|---|---|---|---|
| Were positive on index of perspectives toward institution and staff | | | | | | |
| Non-integrated | 36 | 36 | 31 | 55 | 84 | 36 |
| | (62) | (115) | (26) | (11) | (19) | (11) |
| Integrated† | 44 | 49 | 64 | 89 | 63 | 91 |
| | (146) | (247) | (126) | (52) | (38) | (23) |
| | $p < .05$ | | $p < .01$ | | N.S. | |
| | $Q = .22$ | | $Q = .61$ | | $Q = .17$ | |
| Gave prisonized response to question on best way to get along | | | | | | |
| Non-integrated | 73 | 73 | 72 | 60 | 72 | 60 |
| | (62) | (110) | (25) | (10) | (18) | (10) |
| Integrated | 76 | 74 | 51 | 44 | 71 | 45 |
| | (139) | (238) | (123) | (48) | (38) | (22) |
| | N.S. | | $p < .05$ | | N.S. | |
| | $Q = .04$ | | $Q = -.39$ | | $Q = -.14$ | |
| Were positive on index of self-image | | | | | | |
| Non-integrated | 31 | 37 | 35 | 44 | 30 | 33 |
| | (52) | (101) | (23) | (9) | (15) | (9) |
| Integrated | 41 | 44 | 55 | 86 | 58 | 71 |
| | (135) | (225) | (119) | (49) | (31) | (21) |
| | N.S. | | $p < .01$ | | $p < .05$ | |
| | $Q = .16$ | | $Q = .50$ | | $Q = .49$ | |

* Kendall's Q is used as a measure of the association between integration and the score or response indicated among inmates of both institutions within each organizational type.
† Those integrated report two or more close friends in the institution.

The findings (Table 9.2) give strong support to the expection that integration would have a stronger positive impact on perspectives in the treatment institutions than in the obedience/conformity institutions.[8] On the index of perspectives toward the institution and staff the association was positive in all institutions but Regis, but much higher in the treatment institutions ($Q = .61$) and Bennett than in the obedience/conformity institutions ($Q = .22$). On the second measure, about the best way to get along, there was no association in the obedience/conformity institutions ($Q = .04$) or Regis, but an inverse association between integration and prisonized response in the treatment institutions ($Q = -.39$) and Bennett. On the final measure, self-image, integration and positive response were related in all institutions, but the strength of association was high in the treatment and re-education/development institutions ($Q = .50$ and $.49$, respectively) and low in the obedience/conformity institutions ($Q = .16$). Thus, the findings show the inmate groups of the treatment institutions encouraging more positive and less prisonized perspectives on the organization, staff, and self. Patterns at one of the re-education/development institutions, Bennett, paralleled those of the treatment institutions; patterns in the other, Regis, vacillated. Further analysis indicated that variations in length of stay could not account for these organizational differences in the relationship between integration and orientation.

## INMATE SOLIDARITY

"Inmate solidarity" here refers to the development of norms, values, and orientations that emphasize general loyalty to others of the group—loyalty that goes beyond primary ties with specific persons. We have suggested that the higher deprivational levels of the obedience/conformity institution should offer a greater stimulus to the growth of solidarity but that the less restrictive patterns of the treatment environment should give solidarity greater leeway actually to develop. Our discussion also implied that to the extent that solidarity exists within the obedience/conformity context it may be associated with negative perspectives, as in the model of solidary opposition; but that in the treatment institutions no such association between solidarity and opposition should obtain. Although the concept of solidarity everywhere implies

the taking of a common stance vis-a-vis persons outside the group, it seems likely that in a group which is predominantly positive in behavior and perspectives this stance will be taken with regard to relatively benign issues (for example, demanding additional movies or ice cream).

Findings on a question asking whether the other inmates seem to dislike the place so much that they cooperate with staff members as little as possible (Table 9.3) indicate a perception of the group as

### Table 9.3—Perceptions of Inmate Uncooperativeness (in percentages)

| | Closed | | | | Open | |
|---|---|---|---|---|---|---|
| | OBEDIENCE/ CONFORMITY | | TREATMENT | | RE-EDUCATION/ DEVELOPMENT | |
| | Dick | Mixter | Milton | Inland | Regis | Bennett |
| Inmates who say all or most boys "dislike being here so much they don't want to cooperate with the adults here any more than they have to" | 40 | 36 | 27 | 13 | 29 | 20 |
| No. of cases | (203) | (356) | (155) | (64) | (56) | (35) |

more cooperative in the treatment and open institutions, with 36 to 40 per cent agreeing in Dick and Mixter and smaller proportions agreeing in the other institutions, down to only 13 per cent in Inland.

How might this difference relate to solidarity? The inmate questionnaire provided us with two major kinds of measures relevant here: a series of vignettes and questions to which the respondent had to indicate whether he approved of telling or withholding from staff information about other inmates, and two items suitable for an index of solidary orientations.

### Findings on the "Ratting" Index

There were four vignettes, dealing with whether the inmate approved of "ratting" to the staff about inmates' plans to beat up a staff member or a friend, inmate stealing from the kitchen resulting in group punishment, and an inmate's plans to run away. An arbitrary index summarizes responses to the four questions.

The results for all respondents (Table 9.4) show mostly small and fairly inconsistent differences among the closed institutions, with oppo-

### Table 9.4—Norms Against "Ratting" to Staff
### (in percentages)

| | Closed | | | | Open | |
|---|---|---|---|---|---|---|
| | OBEDIENCE/ CONFORMITY | | TREATMENT | | RE-EDUCATION/ DEVELOPMENT | |
| Inmates Who Say: | Dick | Mixter | Milton | Inland | Regis | Bennett |
| An inmate should not warn the staff of a plan to beat up an adult | 38 | 39 | 44 | 38 | 36 | 66 |
| An inmate should not tell the staff of plans to rough up the boy's friend | 36 | 32 | 37 | 27 | 40 | 45 |
| I would not tell the staff secretly who was stealing from the kitchen, when group punishment was being used | 44 | 35 | 38 | 25 | 42 | 29 |
| An inmate should not ever tell staff that another boy plans to run away | 43 | 69 | 59 | 64 | 71 | 69 |
| High opposition to telling staff on index summarizing items above | 46 | 54 | 51 | 46 | 63 | 69 |
| No. of cases | (199–209) | (326–364) | (147–155) | (52–65) | (52–57) | (33–35) |

sition to "ratting" inexplicably highest in the two open institutions. On the summary index the percentages of inmates who refused to co-operate with the staff were Dick, 46; Mixter, 54; Milton, 51; Inland, 46; Regis, 63; and Bennett, 69. Altogether, the findings give little support to the "solidary opposition" model of the inmate group. On the item about beating up an adult, over half the boys in every institution but Bennett approved of telling, and on the items about roughing up another boy and kitchen thefts, over half in all institutions approved of telling. Only on the item on another's plan to run away did substantial numbers in most institutions disapprove of telling, and even on this question in no organization did the proportion reach 75 per cent.

The vignettes seemed to have somewhat variable meanings in the different organizational contexts. The necessity for inmate secrecy is presumably greater in the obedience/conformity setting, but in this environment the amount of pressure by the staff is also greater. Although at Inland we did not observe attempts to get inmates to tell on others except during a "shakedown" following the theft of a large amount of

money from the main office, at Dick such attempts were frequent and institutionalized in the "outline boy" system, and the staff gave such special rewards as a month off the inmate's length of stay for preventing another boy from running away. (This may explain why Dick had the lowest proportion who said an inmate should never tell on another's plans to run away.) Conceivably, the unexpected findings of relatively high opposition in the open institutions may reflect a tendency of the staff not to press the inmates to tell on others—either as a result of the comparative lack of control over the boys in these institutions or of a staff belief that "ratting" is not to be demanded even in a rigid but relatively homelike atmosphere.[9]

The findings may seem to challenge our theory by implying that the different institutional settings are similar enough so that roughly comparable normative structures develop with regard to secrecy and telling on others. Findings on the association between integration into the inmate group and scores on this index present a different picture, however. The results (Table 9.5) indicate that although integration may

### Table 9.5—Integration and Scores on "Ratting" Index (in percentages)

| | Closed | | | | Open | |
|---|---|---|---|---|---|---|
| | OBEDIENCE/<br>CONFORMITY | | TREATMENT | | RE-EDUCATION/<br>DEVELOPMENT | |
| | Dick | Mixter | Milton | Inland | Regis | Bennett |
| Inmates highly opposed to staff on "ratting" index | | | | | | |
| Non-integrated | 52 | 52 | 77 | 54 | 53 | 73 |
| | (62) | (115) | (26) | (11) | (19) | (11) |
| Integrated | 44 | 56 | 45 | 44 | 68 | 65 |
| | (146) | (247) | (126) | (52) | (38) | (23) |
| | N.S. | | p < .01 | | N.S. | |
| | Q = −.01 | | Q = −.49 | | Q = .15 | |

have been related to opposition to "ratting" at Mixter and Regis, it was related to approval of "ratting" at Dick, Bennett, Inland, and especially Milton. In the latter institution only 45 per cent of the integrated inmates had "anti-ratting" scores, against 77 per cent of the non-integrated inmates. Looking at the measures of association for each of the three organizational types, we find modest or non-existent associations for the obedience/conformity institutions (Q = −.01) and re-education/devel-

opment institutions ($Q = .15$), but a strong association for the treatment institutions ($Q = -.49$). Thus integration into the inmate group in the treatment setting seems to induce willingness to talk with the staff about other inmates—certainly the reverse of the solidary opposition model.

## Findings on Solidary Orientations

Results on two questions dealing explicitly with orientations of solidarity indicate that our hypothesis that solidarity would be highest among inmates of the treatment institution is at least partially correct. The first item asked how much of the time the inmates stick together and are loyal, and the second asked how much they *should* stick together, regardless of how much they actually do. We constructed a summary index by assigning "high solidarity" scores to those who said they both do and should stick together.

The findings (Table 9.6) show a clear-cut and predicted difference

### Table 9.6—Inmate Solidarity
### (in percentages)

| | Closed | | | | Open | |
|---|---|---|---|---|---|---|
| | OBEDIENCE/ CONFORMITY | | TREATMENT | | RE-EDUCATION/ DEVELOPMENT | |
| Inmate Beliefs | Dick | Mixter | Milton | Inland | Regis | Bennett |
| The inmates do stick together all or most of the time | 42 | 40 | 48 | 58 | 50 | 48 |
| It's very important that inmates should stick together | 39 | 37 | 34 | 50 | 46 | 27 |
| Inmates high on summary index of solidarity* | 27 | 28 | 31 | 55 | 40 | 35 |
| No. of cases | (201–204) | (358–363) | (153–154) | (64) | (54–57) | (33–34) |

* Percentage who say both that the boys stick together all or most of the time and that sticking together is very important.

on the first measure between the obedience/conformity and treatment institutions. Forty-two per cent of the Dick inmates and 40 per cent of the Mixter boys said the inmates stick together all or most of the time, but 48 per cent said this at Milton and 58 per cent at Inland. No consistent pattern is seen on the second measure, on valuation of solidarity. On the summary measure, the proportion in the "high solidarity" cate-

gory varied from a low of 27 per cent at Dick to a high of 55 per cent at Inland, and showed the expected pattern for all closed institutions. Differences between Dick, Mixter, and Milton were slight, however, with Inland having the one clear pattern of high solidarity. Solidarity in the open institutions fell between the two treatment organizations.

The conclusion that solidarity need not lead automatically to opposition is further confirmed by an analysis in which we compare inmates who were high and low on the index of solidary orientations, with regard to their scores on the indices of perspectives toward the institution and staff and of "ratting," and their responses to the question about inmates' uncooperativeness. Few relationships emerged. There was a clear association between solidary orientations and positive perspectives on the institution and staff, but only within the re-education/development organizations and at Inland. There also seemed to be an association between solidarity and the view that most boys dislike the institution and cooperate minimally—but at Dick only. The findings suggest that solidarity, insofar as we were successful in measuring it, was compatible with both negative and positive perspectives within all organizational contexts.

## Observations

Interviews with inmates at Dick and Milton add to our knowledge of the limits of solidarity. At Dick there was substantial feeling among the inmates that one would *like* to help his peers but that often this was a practical impossibility. "You'll just get in trouble yourself," several boys said, and another said "You might as well chiefie [local argot for "ratting"] and get out sooner, because others will chiefie, too." Chiefing did not seem to be a particular issue here, for it was expected that under duress most boys would—even should—tell.

Asked to recount exactly what had happened at times of various runaways, Dick inmates almost never seemed to have attempted to stop the escapees. Yet they did not give reasons for this which suggested solidarity; instead, in each case the boys said the runaway was armed or too dangerously excited or had some other mitigating characteristic. In the one case where a boy had stopped a runaway the story went around that a brutal cottage commander had forced the boy to smash the runaway's head open with a rock, with all blame being put on the adult.

The boys fully distinguished between norms at Dick and at a work camp in state where older boys were sent, saying that they had heard that inmates of the work camp helped each other escape.

At Milton, "snagging" (the local term for "chiefing") was omnipresent as an issue. As we indicated in discussing staff-inmate relations, the adults there put a great deal of energy into persuading inmates to give them information on misbehavior, justifying this as therapeutically essential. The outcome at Milton seemed to be continuous ambivalence, concern, and debate over snagging—who snagged, who would, who wouldn't, I wouldn't, I think you should, and so on. The ebb and flow of crises at Milton were accompanied by periods of confrontation in the cottage meetings. In observing these sessions we often saw an initial front of strong solidarity, followed by eventual capitulation and the furnishing of names and information or confessions to the staff. On occasion the boys would maintain a solid front but later, after discussing the matter further among themselves, would come back to tell. One meeting was concerned with an incident involving a mass sexual assault in the swimming pool. As the cottage meeting went on a great initial show of resistance to talk was followed by a gradual group confessional placing most of the blame on a boy not present at the meeting. At another cottage meeting the boys said they would be beaten up if they told —but then they, too, came forward. Our observers often saw the decision to snag become legitimate in the discussions of the inmates, often justified on grounds that some competing clique (frequently the "colored kids, who mess up, make us mad, and get us in trouble") was hurting the interests of the group.

At Dick solidary opposition seemed to crumble because of the strong sanctions and control structure exercised through the outline boys. At Milton it appeared to break down more through persuasion, through the fluidity of inmates' ties to each other, and to an important extent, through acceptance of the legitimacy of cooperating with the staff and identification with staff members.

## INMATE LEADERSHIP

Our hypothesis was that relatively uncooperative and negative leadership cadres would emerge among the inmate groups in the obedience/conformity setting and that relatively cooperative and positive leadership

groups would develop among the inmate groups in the treatment environment. In all institutions inmate leaders appeared to exercise considerable influence over the other boys. Their power derived not only from the general prerogatives of leadership but also from three circumstances peculiar to the correctional organization. First, because the incoming inmate finds his status especially problematic, with respect both to the institution and to the larger society that sent him there, the leader's function in providing a role model is of great significance. Second, because the staff and inmate worlds are so bifurcated, the mediating role of the leaders is of great importance and non-leaders are dependent upon the leaders. In this role the leaders channel inmate desires, protests, and inquiries to the authorities. Third, to varying degrees inmate leaders acquire additional influence over the other boys by wielding control over the allocation of rewards, especially illicit ones.

The low level of gratification at the obedience/conformity institutions sets the stage for development of an inmate system and leadership group oriented toward compensatory and even retaliatory activities. Personnel in these institutions, faced with what is potentially a dangerous situation of rebellion, generally find themselves moving into a compromise relationship with the leaders of the threatening inmate group, granting the leaders certain rewards—contraband may be allowed to pass freely, for example, or special privileges given, or in some institutions special status. In return, inmate leaders make some effort to "keep the lid on" the other inmates. Short of the rare situations of total control of the inmates by the staff however, or the complete "sell out" of the staff members to the leaders in exchange for control, cooperation between adults and leaders in custodial institutions tends to be limited and directed toward dissimilar goals. Overtly, leaders support the institutional system because of the rewards it furnishes them personally and because it allows them control. Covertly, however, they may disseminate anti-institutional orientations and enforce an informal system opposed to the values sanctioned by the larger organizations. We would expect that in the obedience/conformity institutions leaders would appear to be even more negative and opposed to the official system than would the other inmates.

By contrast, in a situation of fewer deprivations the inmate leaders at the treatment institutions have substantially less opportunity to gain or hold power by controlling illicit rewards. Because personnel in the

treatment institutions put much less emphasis upon control, they less often need to bargain about rewards with leaders in order to gain control. In these circumstances different and more positive types of leaders are likely to be recruited. Higher status in the inmate group would tend to be granted those who effectively manage the more cooperative relationships between staff and boys. Thus in the more treatment-oriented institutions we would anticipate that leaders would be even more positive and cooperative than other members of the inmate group.

In order to test these expectations we shall look at data allowing comparisons of inmate leaders and non-leaders with regard to their perspectives. We shall also analyze information on perceptions of the leaders and of leadership behavior found dominant in the inmate group. We identified leaders on the basis of responses to a sociometric measure used on the inmate questionnaire. This was the question asked:

> What three boys are best at getting the other boys to do what they want them to do—that is, which three have the most influence among the boys? Think of the boys that you know in your cottage, in school, in the work program, or recreation.

This question appeared to provide a good general measure of leadership, capable of identifying both negative and positive types of leaders. This conclusion was reached on the basis of a correlational analysis of responses to a slightly different form of the measure and several other sociometric questions used earlier in the institutions. The other items included queries on boys who should be nominated to a council of inmates, boys who "would help you with a personal problem," boys who help others stay out of trouble or get others into trouble, and boys who are best friends. This analysis showed the influence question to be the only one with a relatively high correlation (.4 to .7) to all the other measures. Reliability is also indicated by the fact that leaders nominated on this measure usually included any we had anticipated on the basis of our observations and interviewing, and by the finding of a high association between leadership nominations made by boys and ratings on leadership made by the cottage supervisory personnel.

By "leaders" we refer to those boys who received four or more choices on the influence question. This decision is necessarily arbitrary, but it constitutes what seems to be an apparently adequate compromise be-

tween limiting the term "leader" to those very high on choices received and having enough cases to permit analysis even in the smaller institutions. So defined, leaders included, along with the elite at the top of the inmate leadership structure, those boys who exercised considerable influence, perhaps as "opinion leaders," within more limited contexts.

### Leadership and Perspectives

The data give modest support to our expectations (Table 9.7).[10] Leadership was strongly associated with holding positive perspectives on the institution and staff in the treatment institutions ($Q = .52$), reflecting a strongly positive association at Milton. There was a weaker but also positive association in data on the re-education/development institutions

### Table 9.7—Leadership and Perspectives (in percentages)

| | Closed | | | | Open | |
| | OBEDIENCE/ CONFORMITY | | TREATMENT | | RE-EDUCATION/ DEVELOPMENT | |
| Inmate Perspectives* | Dick | Mixter | Milton | Inland | Regis | Bennett |
|---|---|---|---|---|---|---|
| **Positive on index of perspectives on institution and staff** | | | | | | |
| Non-leaders | 42 | 45 | 53 | 83 | 67 | 72 |
| | (177) | (318) | (130) | (48) | (46) | (29) |
| Leaders | 37 | 48 | 80 | 88 | 82 | 83 |
| | (32) | (46) | (25) | (17) | (11) | (6) |
| | N.S. | | p < .01 | | N.S. | |
| | Q = .00 | | Q = .52 | | Q = .33 | |
| **Positive on index of self-image** | | | | | | |
| Non-leaders | 39 | 41 | 47 | 75 | 49 | 54 |
| | (162) | (287) | (120) | (44) | (37) | (26) |
| Leaders | 32 | 53 | 74 | 87 | 67 | 80 |
| | (25) | (40) | (23) | (16) | (9) | (5) |
| | N.S. | | p < .01 | | N.S. | |
| | Q = .09 | | Q = .53 | | Q = .42 | |
| **Highly opposed to staff on "ratting" index** | | | | | | |
| Non-leaders | 44 | 53 | 49 | 44 | 67 | 65 |
| | (177) | (318) | (130) | (48) | (46) | (29) |
| Leaders | 62 | 63 | 56 | 53 | 46 | 83 |
| | (32) | (46) | (25) | (17) | (11) | (6) |
| | p < .01 | | N.S. | | N.S. | |
| | Q = .26 | | Q = .14 | | Q = −.16 | |

* Q indicates the association between leadership and the score or response indicated within each institutional type.

$(Q = .33)$ and no consistent association in the obedience/conformity organizations $(Q = .00)$.

The same general findings emerge on the association between leadership and the index of self-image. Again the Milton leaders were highly positive. The Q value was .53 for the treatment institutions, .42 for the open instituions, and .09 for the obedience/conformity institutions. On the index of "ratting," leadership and opposition to staff tended to be directly associated in all institutions but Regis, but the association seemed to be stronger in the obedience/conformity institutions $(Q = .26)$ than in the treatment organizations $(Q = .14)$.

Analysis controlling the variable of integration into the inmate group indicates that these patterns·cannot be explained by the association between integration and leadership. In addition, the same basic patterns were found when we compared scores on these three indices by those boys classified as "high leaders" (boys who received 6 or more choices) and by all other inmates.

### Perceptions of Leadership

Questionnaire items that called for perceptions of inmate leadership offer an additional way of assessing the positive or negative tone of inmate leadership (Table 9.8). Results from these items also give partial support to our expectations. The first questions asked for perceptions of the specific leaders nominated by the inmate on the influence question. After writing in his nominations, each respondent was asked to rate each boy he had listed as a "good influence on the other boys" or a "bad influence on the other boys." Results on this measure show the difference predicted between the obedience/conformity and treatment pairs of institutions. Leaders were most often rated as having a good influence in the re-education/development institutions.

The other measures of perception of leadership consisted of a series of items asking about the leaders and their behavior in general. We constructed two arbitrary indices to summarize responses to these items, the first indexing responses to five items that dealt with negative characteristics of leadership, the second to four that dealt with positive characteristics.

Results on these items are not clear cut. On the first summary index

### Table 9.8—Inmate Perceptions of Leaders
### (*in percentages*)

| | Closed | | | | Open | |
|---|---|---|---|---|---|---|
| | OBEDIENCE/ CONFORMITY | | TREATMENT | | RE-EDUCATION/ DEVELOPMENT | |
| Inmate Perceptions | Dick | Mixter | Milton | Inland | Regis | Bennett |
| Leaders rated as relatively good* | 53 | 65 | 76 | 77 | 91 | 83 |
| No. of leaders | (32) | (46) | (25) | (17) | (11) | (6) |
| Inmates higher on perceptions of negative traits† | 40 | 34 | 45 | 29 | 28 | 31 |
| Inmates higher on perceptions of positive traits§ | 46 | 29 | 50 | 48 | 42 | 63 |
| No. of cases | (209) | (364) | (155) | (65) | (57) | (35) |

* After answering the influence sociometric, respondents were asked to rate each boy nominated on a six-point scale from good to bad. Figures represent percentages of leaders who received mean ratings below 3.67.

† From summary index of responses to questions asking how many of the leaders are ready to fight at most any time, have a lot of experience with crime or sex, will have little or nothing to do with adults, look for an easy way to spend their time, or go around looking for fights.

§ From summary index of responses to questions asking how many of the leaders keep other boys from getting into trouble, try to straighten out, are able to help others with problems, and get along well with staff.

the highest proportion imputing negative characteristics to leaders was found at Milton (45 per cent), with Dick (40 per cent) and Mixter (34 per cent) following, and with Inland, Regis, and Bennett having proportions of from 28 to 31 per cent. On the summary index of perceptions of positive traits, the pattern was more expected; 50 per cent at Milton and 48 per cent at Inland had positive scores, against 46 per cent at Dick and only 29 per cent at Mixter, with Regis and Bennett having proportions of 42 and 63 per cent respectively. Thus results on the first index give inconsistent or no support to our expectations, but on the second give modest confirmation.

### Concentration and Backgrounds of Leaders

Sociometric data on leadership allow us to investigate two other features, the concentration or dispersion of leadership choices and the association of leadership with background attributes. Our interest in the first of these derived from our hypothetical characterization of the leadership structure in the obedience/conformity setting as more hierarchic.

Analysis of the distribution of leadership choices fails to support the hypothesis, although not clearly refuting it. No consistent organizational differences were found in the proportions of inmates who were nominated as leaders, who received no choices, or who received very large numbers of choices. Further, no clear pattern emerged in ratios of numbers of boys nominated to numbers of choices made, although some evidence supporting our hypothesis was found in a calculation of the proportions of choices made who went to the top quartile of those nominated. These analyses were severely complicated by problems deriving from variations in organizational and living unit size, from variations in average length of stay, and from differences in the numbers of leadership choices actually made. It seems plausible that in the smaller institutions, Inland, Bennett, and Regis, the leadership structure was more visible and commonly recognized, whatever the "real" extent of concentration of leadership or potential for concentration implicit in the institutional setting.

Our interest in the association of leadership with background attributes derived from a subsidiary hypothesis, which we held at the beginning of the study. This was that inter-organizational variations in the perspectives of the leaders could be accounted for in part by variations in the patterns of recruitment to leadership of boys with certain background predispositions. The fact that background attributes could not account for perspectives among inmates in general undercuts the proposition. It was further weakened by findings on the relationship between institutional type and background attributes of the leaders. Relatively few associations emerged. We found leadership to be generally related, across all institutional contexts, to age, urban origin, and being nonwhite. Further, we found some support, mainly in the contrasts between Dick and the other organizations, for the idea that leadership is associated with the following background attributes, but only in certain settings: returnee status (boys who had been returned to the institution were more likely to be leaders in the obedience/conformity institutions); seriousness of offense and numbers of offenses (those with poorer offense records were more often leaders at Dick); and number of AWOLs (those who had run were more often leaders at Dick). The results indicated that differences we observed in leadership orientations did not derive from variations in background attributes.[11]

*Outline Boys*

Most of the informal leaders at Dick also had official status as outline boys. Staff criteria for selecting outline boys were rather vague. Clearly they had to be big and strong. They did not have to be "good" boys but they had to be at least minimally trustworthy. Outline boys could lose their status or in other ways be punished if they were caught ignoring infractions or punishing inmates themselves (although they sometimes did so without staff disapproval). For the outline boys there was considerable gain: not having to stand in line, often having later bedtimes, and for some, special privileges like driving a staff member's car on errands around the grounds.

Interviews with Dick inmates indicate that the outline-boy system was fairly successful in serving the ends of control without generating overt antagonism. Most of the inmates referred to the outline boys as "brown noses" who played some favorites and exploited others in petty ways (for example, exacting tribute of candy or cigarettes). The boys did not have strong feelings about them however; the outline boy was seen as occupying a necessary if dirty role, and if an inmate could get along with him without too much trouble that was the best he could hope for.

Occasionally the outline system would get out of control. At the time of our first survey some large, aggressive outline boys had gained unusual power in one of the cottages, and a boy known as "Chop Chop" (for reputedly having cut off his mother's head) recently had challenged the night supervisor to a fight. When the adult showed himself afraid of the challenge, the leaders took over direction of the cottage for several weeks until personnel changes could be made.

## FINDINGS ON A MAXIMUM-SECURITY UNIT

The "solidary opposition" model of the inmate group has not been useful so far, but it does seem to apply to Maxwell—the geographically and administratively separate maximum security subunit opened by Mixter three months before our second survey. We have ignored Maxwell heretofore because it had not been in operation long enough for stable

patterns of staff and inmate behavior to develop. But we shall now examine its early patterns, because of their special relevance to group formation.

The unit was custodial in that boys frequently were kept in separate, locked rooms, great stress was put on preventing runaways, and they had few recreational activities and could not go on home visits. Nevertheless, the unit's executive defined its mission as the production of change in attitudes and values. Staff encouraged some inmates to enter into individual counselling, inmates had considerable freedom within the more "open" living section, and the ratio of gratifications to deprivations was more favorable in some respects than Mixter's.

Most of the forty-six boys in Maxwell at the time had been sent there for "incorrigibility" at Mixter. Maxwell had more than twice as many inmates who had run away as had Mixter; it also had twice as many Negroes and substantially larger proportions who had lower IQs and were from urban areas. The concentration of boys with such background attributes may have had a telling outcome upon the patterns for this unit, but probably more important were the expectations inmates held before coming to Maxwell and their early experiences there. Prior to Maxwell's opening considerable speculation and fear had developed about it among the Mixter inmates, partially because some Mixter staff members were using it as a threat. Nonetheless, there was considerable *esprit de corps* in the initial group taken to Maxwell, and a "breakout" of several inmates shortly after the unit opened immediately became a significant legend. The staff then imposed exceedingly stringent security practices and sanctions and began to use freely detention rooms and tranquilizers.

The strong negativism of the first days of the unit was reduced before long. The new inmates, despite many restrictions on freedom, discovered the unit was not the "hellhole" they had anticipated, and also found the liberalized smoking privileges and headphone radios much to their liking. A survey of inmates in the unit three months after it opened disclosed that on many of the attitude questions Maxwell inmates were not particularly negative compared to those in the other institutions.[12] Thus, although Maxwell boys were only less negative than those at Dick and Mixter on the index of perspectives on the institution and staff, they were in about the middle of the distribution of organizations on two questions about adaptation to the institution, and not far

from the top in positive response on the index of the inmates' perceived self-change (Table 9.9).

### Table 9.9—Maxwell: Inmate Perspectives
### (in percentages)

| Inmates Who: | | Rank of Maxwell among Other Institutions* |
| --- | --- | --- |
| Are positive on index of perspectives toward institution and staff | 57 | 5 |
| Give a prisonized response to question on best way to get along | 71 | 3.5 |
| Give a prisonized response to question about what you must do to get out of the institution | 54 | 3 |
| Are positive on index of self-change | 58 | 2.5 |
| Score high opposition to staff on "ratting" index | 72 | 1 |
| Agree that all or most boys dislike the place and co-operate only minimally | 41 | 1 |
| No. of cases | (38–46) | |

* The seven institutions were ranked from 1 (highest percentage) to 7 (lowest) on each index used.

Maxwell boys ranked highest, however, on two measures dealing with collective opposition to staff. Fully 72 per cent of the inmates had high scores on the index of opposition to "ratting" to staff, and 41 per cent agreed that most boys dislike the place so much they would co-operate only minimally. Data on integration and perspectives show the dominant impact of the Maxwell group was negative (Table 9.10). On

### Table 9.10—Maxwell: Impact of Integration on Perspectives
### (in percentages)

| Inmates Who: | Non-integrated | Integrated | Association |
| --- | --- | --- | --- |
| Are positive on index of perspectives toward institution and staff | 64 | 54 | $Q = -.19$ |
| Give a prisonized response to question on best way to get along | 60 | 73 | $Q = .28$ |
| Are positive on index of self-change | 56 | 60 | $Q = .09$ |
| Score high opposition to staff on "ratting" index | 45 | 21 | $Q = .51$ |
| No. of cases | (9–11) | (30–33) | |

four major indices the association between integration and the holding of positive or cooperative perspectives was smaller (or inverse and larger) at Maxwell than at the obedience/conformity, re-education/develop-

ment, or treatment institutions. The association is particularly pronounced in findings on the index of sentiments against "ratting" to staff, on which the Q association between integration and cooperative response was .51.

Solidary opposition also appears in findings on the index of solidary orientations (Table 9.11). The proportion scoring high on the index

### Table 9.11—Maxwell: Inmate Solidarity and Views on "Ratting"

| | |
|---|---|
| Per cent of inmates high on index of solidary orientations | 48 |
| No. of cases | (46) |
| Ranking of Maxwell among all institutions | 2 |
| | |
| Per cent of inmates high in opposition to staff on index of "ratting" among: | |
| Those with low scores on index of solidarity | 58 |
| No. of cases | (24) |
| Those with high scores on index of solidarity | 91 |
| No. of cases | (22) |

$$Q = .75$$

at Maxwell (48 per cent) was greater than at any other institution except Inland. Most important, although data on the other organizations showed little association between solidary orientations and other attitudes, at Maxwell there was a very strong relationship between solidarity and oppositional scores on the "ratting" index (Q = .75). (In contrast, Q values in the other institutional settings were obedience/conformity, .06; treatment, −.13; re-education/development, −.07.)

Other findings indicate that solidary opposition was accompanied by relatively positive and well-developed social relationships among the inmates and by rather negative leadership. The proportion of inmates reporting two or more friends was 75 per cent, higher than in all institutions but Milton and Inland; the proportion who rejected the idea that you must be careful around other inmates to avoid a rough time was 52 per cent, by far the highest of all. Turning to the relationship between leadership and perspectives toward the institution and staff, the "ratting" index, and self-change, we find the association was more negative on the first two measures (Q = −.31 and Q = .45, respectively) than at the other institutions, although it was more positive on the third (Q = .54). The proportion of leaders nominated who were rated by the

inmates as having a relatively good influence was lower at Maxwell (29 per cent) than at any other institution, and the proportion of inmates who scored high on the index of perceptions of positive characteristics of leadership (35 per cent) was lower than at all organizations save Mixter.

Why was Maxwell the one unit in which there was an association between solidarity and negative perspectives? Findings from this unit may simply reflect the unique patterns of its first months of operation and biases in selection of the inmate population. With the passage of time, the routinization of decision-making on sending inmates to Maxwell, and the enlargement of numbers sent, some sources of hostile common ties may diminish. The findings may also reflect staff tolerance of negativism brought about by the custodial features of the institution. Because the unit's building and practices (after the initial breakout) were designed to make running away practically impossible, even with their "maximum security" orientations the staff could view inmate hostility and the development of close associations among small groups of inmates with greater equanimity than could staff at Dick or Mixter. Such a reaction would parallel the phenomena observed at some adult institutions where guards grant the inmates considerable freedom to carry on their own activities in return for assurance that the "lid will be kept on."[13] Of all the inmate groups studied, this at Maxwell seemed to approximate most closely those reported as universal in the adult correctional environment. Our findings may follow from this similarity.

## SUMMARY OF FINDINGS

The data on inmate perspectives, background attributes, and inmate groups support the following conclusions:

1. In contrast to the view that the inmate group is inevitably and uniformly cohesive and opposed to the larger organization, we found considerable variation among organizations in the perspectives and the social relations of the inmates.

2. This variation appeared to be related systematically to organizational goals—a pattern seen when we classified the institutions on the basis of levels of deprivation and authority and control.

3. Inmate background attributes did not account for the variation.

4. Specifically, inmates of the obedience/conformity institutions had relatively negative perspectives toward the institution and staff compared to those in the treatment institutions. Integration into the inmate groups of these institutions heightened this contrast.

5. Inmate primary relations and, apparently, solidarity, generally were less highly developed in the obedience/conformity setting than in the treatment environment. The one setting in which solidary opposition appeared to be really high was the maximum security unit.

6. In treatment institutions leaders appeared to have relatively positive orientations compared to non-leaders; in obedience/conformity institutions leaders appeared to have orientations more like those of other inmates.

7. Both the experiences of being institutionalized and participating in the inmate group affected inmates' perspectives on self and adaptations to the institutions. As measured by these data, obedience/conformity and treatment organizations tended to accomplish their proximate goals. By stressing covert opposition and the precept "play it cool" the inmate group of the obedience/conformity institutions encouraged behavior consistent with more custodial goals. Thus the level of "prisonized" orientations was highest among Dick and Mixter inmates. Similarly, the treatment inmate group seemed to produce in its members an orientation more consistent with the goal of achieving change—if it can be assumed that under current treatment technologies a minimally positive orientation toward the agents of change is necessary. The inmate groups in the treatment institutions more frequently encouraged the development of positive orientations and positive self-image.

8. Patterns observed in the open re-education/development institutions approximated those of the treatment organizations more than those of the obedience/conformity institutions. This was much more the case at Bennett than at Regis, a contrast not surprising in light of the differences in staff-inmate relations existing between these two organizations.

9. As between the two treatment institutions Inland generally showed more positive results on measures of perspectives and higher level of development of solidarity than did Milton. In analyses relating perspectives to patterns of the group—to integration and leadership—the Milton inmate group appeared to be at least as positive and often more positive than that at Inland, however. In understanding these differences the relative weights of such factors as Inland's status as a smaller

and private institution, with a developed program of individual treatment, against Milton's situation as a large public institution in the middle of developing its program but committed to a *milieu* approach, are difficult to assess.

These results underscore the importance of staff notions of people-changing. Although treatment staffs tended to accept the discouraging fact that inmates would often band together to circumvent or oppose official plans, obedience/conformity staffs saw such negativism as outrageous. The latter often became involved in a self-fulfilling prophecy in which, because they defined inmate association as potentially negative and disruptive, they suppressed these as much as they could. When they did so, they made it probable that whatever association did occur would be, in fact, negative. In contrast, staff at the treatment institutions found a different prophecy fulfilled. Less frequently attaching importance to threats to institutional stability and containment, they found that such threats usually did not come to fruition.

## NOTES

1. Sykes and Messinger, for example, reviewing more than thirty-five studies of correctional organizations, conclude: "Despite the number and diversity of prison populations, observers of such groups have reported only one strikingly pervasive value system . . . [which] commonly takes the form of an explicit code. . . . The maxims are usually asserted with a great vehemence . . . and violations call forth a diversity of sanctions ranging from ostracism to physical violence. . . . The chief tenets . . . [include] those maxims that caution: *Don't interfere with inmate interests,* which center of course in serving the least possible time and enjoying the greatest possible number of pleasures and privileges in prison. The most inflexible directive [is] *Never rat on a con.* . . . The prisoners must present a united front against their guards no matter how much this may cost in terms of personal sacrifice" (Gresham M. Sykes and Sheldon L. Messinger, "The Inmate Social System," in Richard A. Cloward, *et al., Theoretical Studies in Social Organization of the Prison* [New York: Social Science Research Council, 1960], pp. 5–8).

2. For example, Lloyd E. Ohlin and William C. Lawrence, "Social Interaction among Clients as a Treatment Problem," *Social Work,* 4 (April, 1959), 3–14. Similar treatments of the inmate group in juvenile correctional organizations may be found in Cloward, "The Correctional Institution for

Juveniles: A Discussion of Selected Problems," paper read at the New York School of Social Work seminar on juvenile institutions, 1956; and George P. Grosser, "The Role of Informal Inmate Groups in Change of Values," *Children,* 5 (January–February, 1958), 25–29. Other analyses suggesting that the inmate system in these institutions operates principally to oppose or circumvent the organization's aims include Howard Polsky's study of a cottage in a treatment institution, reported in "Changing Delinquent Subcultures: A Social Psychological Approach," *Social Work,* 4 (October, 1959), 3–16; Polsky, *Cottage Six—The Social System of Delinquent Boys in Residential Treatment* (New York: Russell Sage Foundation, 1962); and Ohlin's observations on a training school for girl delinquents, "Reduction in Role Conflict in Institutional Staff," *Children,* 5 (March–April, 1958), 65–69.

3. Variation in inmate attitudes and behavior underlies the whole notion of prisonization. See Donald Clemmer, *The Prison Community* (New York: Rinehart, 1958). Also the various studies of social types in the prison, for example, Clarence Schrag, "Social Types in a Prison Community," unpublished M.A. thesis (University of Washington, 1944), and his "Leadership among Prison Inmates," *American Sociological Review,* 19 (February, 1954), 42—in which he writes of "a number of dissentient minorities [that] resist, at least to some extent, the dominant influence of the typical leader group."

4. Stanton Wheeler, "Socialization in Correctional Communities," *American Sociological Review,* 26 (October, 1961), 697–712; Peter C. Garabedian, "Social Roles and Processes of Socialization in the Prison Community," *Social Problems,* 11 (Fall, 1963), 139–152; and Garabedian, "Legitimate and Illegitimate Alternatives in the Prison Community," *Sociological Inquiry,* 32 (Spring, 1962), pp. 172–184. See also the discussion of the inmate society as made of three subcultures dependent on latent identities, in John Irwin and Donald R. Cressey, "Thieves, Convicts and the Inmate Culture," *Social Problems,* 10 (Fall, 1962), 142–155; along with the contributions by Wheeler, Schrag, and Donald L. Garrity to Cressey (ed.), *The Prison: Studies in Institutional Organization and Change* (New York: Holt, Rinehart and Winston, 1961).

5. The inmate system is seen as providing new, deviant standards to allow the inmates to assuage guilt by "rejecting their rejectors"—see Lloyd W. McCorkle and Richard Korn, "Resocialization within Walls," *The Annals,* 293 (May, 1954), 88–98—or to achieve compensatory status and to benefit from contraband and illegitimate activities (Ohlin and Lawrence, *op. cit.*), and to defend against aggression and exploitation by other inmates (Sykes and Messinger, *op. cit.*). The latter authors, even though they seem to assume that the inmate group is inevitably cohesive and opposed to official

goals, also suggest that the extent of deprivation and degradation might predict the inmate group's response (p. 19).

6. Even this technique is in doubt. See Richard McCleery's account of an adult maximum security unit, "Authoritarianism and the Belief System of Incorrigibles," in Cressey (ed.), *The Prison: Studies in Institutional Organization and Change* (New York: Holt, Rinehart and Winston, 1961), pp. 260–306.

7. The halfer relationship also implied reciprocal obligations to provide general help to partners and a vague expectation that one would help his halfer in a fight, if staff members were not around. The general feeling was that one had no real claim on his halfer when it came to fighting, however, since staff punishment was likely to be so severe.

8. We report findings on the three major measures of perspectives that showed statistically significant relationships between integration and orientation in at least one of the major institutional settings. We applied statistical tests and Q measures of association to provide criteria for asserting and assessing findings when complex multivariate analysis made decisions about patterns difficult.

9. Some preliminary interviewing at Mixter seemed to indicate that solidary opposition was pronounced in some of the Mixter cottages, ones that staff saw as tougher because they contained larger numbers of Negroes or boys thought to be more committed delinquents. Analysis of the scores on the "ratting" index by the proportions with various background attributes in the respondent's cottage produced results partially consistent with this assumption: Uncooperative views of "ratting" were more frequent in cottages with larger proportions of non-whites, older boys, and inmates from urban areas, although there was no relationship to numbers of boys with many offenses or numbers of returnees.

10. Again we report findings on the major measures of perspectives on which statistically significant associations were found in any of the institutional settings.

11. For the detailed findings, see David Street, "Inmate Social Organization: A Comparative Study of Juvenile Correctional Institutions," unpublished Ph.D. dissertation (Ann Arbor: The University of Michigan, 1962), pp. 119–126.

12. Responses to a question about what the inmate thought of the institution before he arrived were the most negative in Maxwell, whereas responses to a following question asking what he now thought of the institution were the most positive in this unit. Further, when we asked Maxwell inmates to judge whether the new unit or Mixter was "better" on a series of items, more preferred Maxwell on all counts. The items referred to food,

school, rooms, living unit, trouble with other boys, amount of help received from adults, and discipline and rules. This finding did not mean the respondents would have preferred to be in Maxwell than in Mixter. Eighty-two per cent said they would rather have stayed in Mixter—a finding that may chiefly reflect the fact that their release date was now further away. The inmates' reaction to Maxwell was like that of the boys in the maximum security cottage at Milton, who said they generally liked it better because they received "special attention" and got cigarettes and coffee more frequently.

13. Analysis of response in three separate living units in operation at Maxwell indicates that the viability of social relations and solidarity was at its lowest, and perspectives were most negative, in the "closed" living unit—in which staff exercised very tight control, restricting some inmates to their individual rooms at all times. This confirms the interpretation that whatever the stimuli, in a situation of high control the inmate group would be disabled and cohesive patterns could not develop. The closed unit also was where inmates were placed when they first arrived, however, so that these findings may also reflect the short average stay of its residents.

# Organizational Change

# Chapter 10

# CHANGE BETWEEN SURVEYS

Because we observed the six organizations from time to time over a two year period and collected questionnaire data twice, twelve months apart in each institution, we are able to look at various issues of organizational stability and change. We can ask how and why the organizations were changing and which ones were more prone to change —including change induced by the study and by sessions held between surveys to feed back our findings.

## THE EXECUTIVE SEMINAR

The feedback sessions provided an opportunity for learning more about the executives and organizations in general along with seeing how the information we furnished might be used as a basis for intentional change. The four institutions in the same state, Mixter, Regis, Bennett, and Inland, received findings in the "executive seminar," a series of seven day-long sessions held in the comfortable private dining room of a centrally located hotel. These four institutions were surveyed in April and May of 1959 and 1960, and the seminar was held from October, 1959, to March, 1960. The executive of each institution attended, along with one of his chief subordinates.

The sessions usually included a brief general statement by one of the researchers, a quick review of the previous meeting by another, and presentations and discussions of sets of tables and other materials—which by the last meeting filled a 125-page book. We provided basic information about the institutions (including formal goals), data on inmate backgrounds and attitudes, information on staffs and staff subgroups, and findings on relations between staffs and inmates. Anonymity was provided by coding the tables, each executive being told only his own code, and organizational size being given only as large or small. Executives found it difficult and unnecessary to maintain any semblance of secrecy, however, and soon began identifying their organizations.

A different format was used in the case of the out-of-state institutions, Milton and Dick, which were surveyed in July and October, respectively, of 1959 and 1960. Data books from the executive seminar, together with various amplifications, were sent to these institutions in the spring of 1960. Then two researchers visited each organization for a two-day session, conducted in a manner similar to that of the executive seminar. The executive and whichever subordinates he selected were present.

Participation was high, which surprised us at the time. Although we had suggested the likelihood of the seminar in our first contacts with the executives, we had no certainty that it would gain substantial involvement. Reasons for the high participation seemed to include recognition by the executives of inadequacies in their own information, especially on how their institutions compared to others; for some, a genuine desire for aid in coping with the problems of their institutions; and for others, an urge to control interpretations of the data. Another major attraction seemed to come from the fact that the executives constituted, to some extent, a reference and membership group. They were interested in who was doing what and in the careers of individual administrators, and they interchanged a great deal of information and showed high sensitivity to one another's opinions. Other bases for participation probably were the attraction of the fringe benefits of excellent food and drink and, in the case of one executive, the feeling that his parent organization expected him to attend.

## Deficit of Information

The executives had a critical deficit of information. Even data drawn directly from institutional files often were viewed as new and surprising information. The executives had intimate knowledge of specific individuals and situations and their institutions had expended substantial energy in collecting information, but few generalized understandings resulted. They were uncertain and differed about which might be the most significant types of information, but most were hesitant to forego collecting information of any kind.

These problems did not restrain them from making confident statements about their populations, however. This "knowledge" often was cited as necessitating particular practices. For example, the executives

saw the orientations of their personnel as largely determined by levels of resources available to the institution and therefore largely inaccessible to manipulation.

Although the information we provided was of substantial interest, it threatened the executives' preconceptions and sense of mastery. It weakened one of their chief claims to competence, intimate knowledge of institutional realities. A frequent response was to challenge the reliability and validity of the findings. Often other participants countered these challenges, however, and a norm slowly developed that data were not to be questioned except for face validity or apparent inconsistencies with other findings. At length, participants sometimes were induced to make accommodations in their belief systems—at least temporarily.

Perhaps the most glaring deficit of information referred to inmate behavior after release. Executives had only fragmentary knowledge of whether or not changes seen in the institution were sustained later. Each institution heard about a few former inmates, usually through letters or visits from releasees who had developed positive relations with certain staff members. Also, each institution had its proportion of returnees—a figure the executives were very sensitive about when we reported it routinely with other descriptive measures. Participants were quick to disclaim the returnee rate as an adequate index of effectiveness, pointing out that some institutions refused to readmit inmates, and strongly condemned public groups that used it as a measure of effectiveness.

In the absence of information about eventual outcomes, executive perspectives turned toward behavior and events within the institution. Many of the participants' anecdotes and luncheon conversations centered around minor crises, and frequently they were called to the telephone or arrived late because of day-to-day incidents demanding attention. The other executives responded on such occasions with sympathetic understanding, and all expressed the belief that there is "no rest for the administrator."

*Orientations Toward Change*

We did not find it easy to direct the executives' attention to indications of likely long-run effects. We continually emphasized findings having pertinence for outcomes and, in reaction, the participants revealed their competing commitments to goal achievement and organizational main-

tenance, the uncertainties in their operational strategies, and their frequent assumption that inmate outcomes are largely determined by their personal attributes. Findings of inconsistent or undesired patterns usually evoked great interest and expressions of surprise, especially in the case of data revealing discrepancies between the goals of executives and those of other personnel, and findings on staff loyalty to the organization and commitment to working with children. One executive crashed his fist on the table and angrily exclaimed that he would not tolerate the sentiments he had learned of, and another was seen after one session bracing his chauffeur against the wall and demanding to know how *he* felt about the institution and its purposes.

In general, the executives seemed to be guided by one of two major orientations. Executives who had the *resigned conservatism* orientation were largely satisfied with current levels of organizational attainment. Demands or expectations of others for higher achievement were regarded as inappropriate because of limitations set by resources and the intractability of inmates. These executives readily proposed concrete improvements which could be undertaken only if resources were increased. Typically, such improvements were additions to present services and contemplated no significant departures from current practices. In this view the executive's obligation was to define the needed resources; the parent organization had the responsibility of obtaining and making them available.

Executives with the *dissatisfied innovation* orientation were far less content with current levels of organizational achievement and sought improvement in directions they already had charted. These executives also cited needs for new resources but did not believe that failure to secure them vitiated all possibility for advance. They accepted responsibility for mobilizing as well as defining needed resources and contemplated somewhat greater innovation if new resources were forthcoming. Within existing circumstances they found many opportunities to enhance operational patterns, and they were interested in new information and techniques.

*Formulation of Alternatives*

The executives referred to many external sources, including public interest groups, parent organizations, professional associations, and other

juvenile institutions in order to define their situations and assess achievement. The process of comparing the institutions represented at the seminar was generalized to include other institutions throughout the nation. Comparisons were oriented toward four foci. First, there was some interest in the goals and outcomes currently sought by other institutions. For example, all executives expressed awareness of the general trend away from "correctional" and toward "residential treatment" orientations. Second, the executives were interested in how their peers defined their situations and how they developed defensive strategies with regard to environmental pressures, resources, and population patterns. Third, the executives, especially those who had more innovative outlooks, were interested in modifications in structure and procedure made in other institutions. Fourth, executives sought to anticipate the probable outcomes of alternatives developed elsewhere. They were reluctant to consider innovations when outcomes were relatively unknown.

Early in the seminar the participants actively worked to establish themselves and their organizations by exchanging information. We had overestimated the level of conventional knowledge they already had about one another's institutions and underestimated the importance of its exchange. One result was that during the first sessions the participants exchanged and absorbed information in ways which reinforced existing definitions of their situations and validated the images they wished others to accept. An implicit rank order emerged among the institutions represented in the study: at the lower end of the ranking were the large public institutions, believed to be less committed to treatment goals and disadvantaged by scarce resources, and at the upper end were the small private institutions, committed to treatment and presumably enjoying favorable resources. After we addressed ourselves to challenging this ranking, primarily through the introduction of more and more findings that undermined its basic premises, it dissipated—but this occurred only gradually.

Early in the seminar the executives also tended to see only limited alternatives to the resolution of organizational problems. The "resigned conservatives" sometimes saw none and the "dissatisfied innovators" tended to see only one or two. Few were confident about the consequences of any of the alternatives. In part, this reflected reasonable doubt evoked by the revelation of the deficit of information about their own institutions. In addition, the superficiality of their knowledge of

other institutional programs reduced reliance on others' solutions and the special pleading of defensive strategies obscured the comparability of organizations.

Over time, the presentation of comparative findings and the perspectives of the research staff seemed to alter this situation. The group's discussion of problems in the integration of treatment and management practices can serve as an example. All participants were concerned about incompatible practices and cleavages among personnel. Dissimilarities in structure at first seemed too great for joint discussion, but the group eventually saw that the same issues, differently resolved, were present in all institutions. The participants began to speak of our findings, particularly data on staff tensions, the distribution of power, and inmate responses to staff members, as consequences of the various structural alternatives. They came to discern several distinct structural patterns, varying as to the level at which integration was achieved and the positions of major subgroups, and they began to assess the consequences or "costs" of each pattern.

*Stimulation of Change*

Our interest in stimulating and facilitating change within the institutions was advanced when, during the fifth session, we responded to requests for a more general framework by presenting a set of ideal type-models of juvenile institutions and a summary of all the variables about which data were being reported. The models were labeled containment, obedience, unstable mixed goals, individual treatment, and milieu treatment. Although none of the disciplines from which the executives came or drew knowledge presented comprehensive models for institutional design, the executives readily grasped the meaning of the scheme. They noted many similarities between their own institutions and the models without seeming to confuse the two. In the sixth session, when we presented new materials in terms of the models, the participants increasingly began to view inmate attitudes and behavior as significant measures of institutional functioning, and sought to link these with particular patterns of organization and operations. Presentation of data indicating that inmate responses were not inevitable outcomes of background attributes this time had some persuasive effects. Discussion moved toward exploration of various modifications, including alterations in staff orien-

tations, which might alter inmate responses in ways likely to have a positive carry-over.

During the final session we introduced few new findings but presented a list of preconditions to desired changes in the inmates. We attempted to write criteria relating to the general goal of effecting changes commensurate with the inmates' well-being and adherence to legal norms without referring to specific goals or technologies. We listed the following conditions as requisite to change: First, avoidance of pain and the securing of alternative sources of gratification; second, perception of the institution as oriented toward change and supportive of attempts to change; third, learning alternative ways of behaving and responding to maximize gratifications; fourth, internalization of changes as attitudes, values, perceptual orientations, ego skills, and self-understanding. This formulation focused attention on inmate responses as the primary index of effectiveness and provided a basis for integrating diverse sets of data.

On this basis the executives were able to clarify their ideas of desirable goals and match these with effects indicated by the data. This process was in contrast to their usual emphases on the accommodation of the inmates and manifest behavior. The executives did question particular aspects of the list and were skeptical of what could be done with their limited resources, but eventually they began to discuss practices and structures that seemed to lead to desirable and undesirable inmate responses. During the last sessions, the executives also were led to discuss the introduction and management of organizational change. Although no executive appeared to shift from resigned conservatism to dissatisfied innovation, all became more optimistic about the potentials for deliberate change.

Our guiding assumption for the seminar, made explicit in retrospect, was that increased effectiveness requires the continual introduction and management of organizational change by the executives. We attempted to define and impart a rationalistic strategy as the basis for executive leadership. The essential elements of the strategy, as we pursued it in the seminar, were as follows: First, clarification of institutional goals and specification of desired effects on inmates. Second, identification of units and means for action to implement goals. Third, assessment of the consequences, both intended and unintended. Finally, identification of alternatives for action and estimation of their consequences.

## MEASURES OF STABILITY AND CHANGE

It is difficult to predict on a theoretical basis what effects the feedback processes and other forces should have had in a short period of time. Assessments of actual change transpired or changes underway or proposed may be made on the basis of our observations during the second survey, interviews with executives and other personnel, and results of comparable questions asked in both surveys.

Earlier interviews with executives together with the experiences of the seminar had indicated that the executives of Dick, Mixter, and Bennett held resigned-conservative attitudes toward change. The executive of Regis was more innovative but, like the other three, was relatively content with his program. At these institutions the executive and his subordinates were more or less satisfied with the data from the survey, justified those findings they felt implied criticism of institutional performance, and said they had made few if any changes in their programs as a result of the seminar. In contrast, the executives and assistant directors of Milton and Inland were dissatisfied innovators, continuously seeking to improve their programs, more willing to accept critical data from the reporting sessions, and ready to talk of changes they would or might make on the basis of the seminars.

Shifts in patterns of staff and inmate response to comparable questionnaire items were analyzed to obtain rough measures of change between surveys. This procedure was more meaningful for the staff data, for many of the significant dimensions of the inmate responses had been tapped only on the second survey. We collapsed responses to questions where there were more than two alternatives in such a way as to provide roughly equal dichotomous distributions for the total sample of respondents, and we identified one part of the dichotomy as favoring a treatment-oriented response or in other ways a "positive" response. To provide a criterion for asserting change we arbitrarily chose a cutting point of ten percentage points change between responses to an item in the first and second surveys. Results of this analysis are presented in Table 10.1 for staff questions in the closed institutions only (unfortunately, the staff questionnaire was not used a second time in Regis or Bennett) and Table 10.2 for inmate questions in all six of the institutions.

Our overall findings indicate that except at Inland little dramatic and

**Table 10.1—Changes of 10 Per Cent or More on Comparable
Staff Questions from Survey I to Survey II**

| | OBEDIENCE/ CONFORMITY | | TREATMENT | |
|---|---|---|---|---|
| | Dick | Mixter | Milton | Inland |
| **Attitudes toward delinquents** | | | | |
| (11) items) | | | | |
| Negative change | 2 | 0 | 2 | 0 |
| No change | 5 | 10 | 7 | 7 |
| Positive change | 4 | 1 | 2 | 4 |
| **Attitudes toward inmates** | | | | |
| (3 items) | | | | |
| Negative change | 0 | 0 | 0 | 0 |
| No change | 3 | 3 | 3 | 3 |
| Positive change | 0 | 0 | 0 | 0 |
| **Sanctions questions** | | | | |
| (6 items) | | | | |
| Negative change (harsher sanctions) | 0 | 3 | 1 | 0 |
| No change | 3 | 3 | 5 | 6 |
| Positive change | 3 | 0 | 0 | 0 |
| **Tension questions** | | | | |
| (5 items) | | | | |
| Negative change (more tension) | 3 | 0 | 1 | 0 |
| No change | 2 | 5 | 1 | 2 |
| Positive change | 0 | 0 | 3 | 3 |
| **Goal question** | | | | |
| (1 item) | | | | |
| Negative change (less treatment-oriented) | 0 | 0 | 0 | 0 |
| No change | 0 | 1 | 1 | 1 |
| Positive change | 1 | 0 | 0 | 0 |
| **Job involvement and satisfaction** | | | | |
| (2 items) | | | | |
| Negative change | 0 | 0 | 0 | 0 |
| No change | 1 | 1 | 2 | 1 |
| Positive change | 1 | 1 | 0 | 1 |
| **All 28 items** | | | | |
| Negative change | 5 | 3 | 4 | 0 |
| No change | 14 | 23 | 19 | 20 |
| Positive change | 9 | 2 | 5 | 8 |

consistent change occurred from one year to the next. Findings follow
individually for each institution.

*Dick*

As we expected, the survey had little effect upon Dick. We heard of
few instances where the questionnaire had provoked staff discussion of

**Table 10.2—Changes of 10 Per Cent or More on Comparable
Inmate Questions from Survey I to Survey II**

|  | Open | | | | Closed | |
|  | OBEDIENCE/ CONFORMITY | | TREATMENT | | RE-EDUCATION/ DEVELOPMENT | |
|  | Dick | Mixter | Milton | Inland | Regis | Bennett |
|---|---|---|---|---|---|---|
| **Attitudes toward institution, staff, and other inmates (13 items)** | | | | | | |
| Negative change | 0 | 0 | 0 | 1 | 6 | 4 |
| No change | 13 | 10 | 11 | 8 | 4 | 5 |
| Positive change | 0 | 3 | 2 | 4 | 3 | 4 |
| **Leadership characteristics (8 items)** | | | | | | |
| Negative change | 1 | 0 | 0 | 1 | 2 | 0 |
| No change | 7 | 8 | 8 | 7 | 6 | 7 |
| Positive change | 0 | 0 | 0 | 0 | 0 | 1 |
| **Attitudes toward self (6 items)** | | | | | | |
| Negative change | 1 | 1 | 4 | 2 | 3 | 1 |
| No change | 5 | 5 | 2 | 3 | 1 | 4 |
| Positive change | 0 | 0 | 0 | 1 | 2 | 1 |
| **All 27 items** | | | | | | |
| Negative change | 2 | 1 | 4 | 4 | 11 | 5 |
| No change | 25 | 23 | 21 | 18 | 11 | 16 |
| Positive change | 0 | 3 | 2 | 5 | 5 | 6 |

institutional realities or aims. Jackson, the executive, had anticipated the data would tell him little about the institution and, although he readily cooperated in almost all phases, he used conversations with us chiefly to discuss the virtues of his institution and his views about the general field.

When shown the models presented at the seminar, Jackson readily chose the obedience model as best fitting his institution and approved of it. One item that disturbed him was the apparent low degree of commitment to children held by his personnel. We told him that although he himself believed that inmates, like one's own children, should be both loved and punished depending upon their behavior, many staff understood only the latter part of the message. Further, we pointed out that the staff overwhelmingly felt there should be a training program to show them how to handle potential truants, instead of an increase in negative sanctions or security measures. Using such items as these, we

attempted to dislodge the executive and his top assistants from their secure beliefs.

Initially denying the importance of institutional differences, Jackson was at times struck by the range of programs and results obtained in some of the other institutions and debated these matters with interest. His chief subordinates, however, persistently defended the existing program with rationalizations of the data or challenges to their accuracy. It appeared that the executive, isolated from almost all developments in the field, found the sessions more stimulating than did his subordinates, but the results of the first survey had no apparent impact upon his plans. As far as we know, the findings were not communicated to other staff members beyond the assistant director, chaplain, and social service director. The school principal, who was the only member of the executive core critical of the program, may have seen the report, but he was not invited to the sessions by the executive.

The year between the surveys saw some changes occurring within the institution and in its political environment, however. Although newspaper criticism of the "dungeons" had not caused the executive to close them down initially, he did close them some two months after the first survey—approximately eight months after the newspaper criticism. When asked why, Jackson mentioned political considerations. The impending election may have brought pressure from the party. It is also possible that use of the cells during the cold, damp winter months— without heat or even a bench to lie on—was considered unwise. It is even possible that the persistent though tactful inquiries of the research staff had some influence.

The only personnel change of note was that the social service director had left to take a better paying job and was replaced by a newspaper woman who held, in addition, an important position in the executive's political party. She proved to be more industrious and effective in her efforts to speed up the discharge process once a boy had been approved for release by the staff and executive. She also worked closely with Jackson in political matters and had access to state political leaders. (The staff appreciated this difference, for in the second survey the percentage reporting that the social service director had considerable influence on the way the institution was run rose by 26 per cent.)

A final change was mounting uncertainty about the tenure of many of the staff. It was increasingly apparent that the party in power had

an excellent chance of losing the election, which would mean that most personnel would lose their jobs. This may have accounted for an increase in tension among all role groups measured on the second survey.

Other than the increase in tension, the analysis of staff questions repeated in the second survey (Table 10.1) shows little change. Three of the sanctions questions reflected positive changes (less severe sanctions favored), but in two of these an error in wording apparently produced more favorable responses. In general there was a tendency to positive change, but mainly in attitudes toward delinquents and sanctions. Changes in inmates (Table 10.2) were smaller and, if anything, in a negative direction.

This was to be expected. With a simple model of rehabilitation and without significant pressure from the environment, including the parent organization, there was little occasion for change.

*Mixter*

At Mixter neither the survey, the executive seminar, nor other events (with one exception) led to many changes in the questionnaire responses of staff and inmates or any changes in organization or program. Hanna, the executive, who characterized himself as having "held the line" for years in the face of severe deprivations and external pressures, believed that "under the circumstances" he could not risk making even those internal changes he felt should be made. The exception was the establishment of the Maxwell security unit, which at the time of the second survey had removed from Mixter about fifty of what were defined as the most recalcitrant inmates.

In Hanna's view, the impact of the survey upon the institution was negative. Initially reluctant to participate, he circumscribed the activities of the research staff at many points. He felt that both staff and boys would be upset and as evidence cited the effects of state police investigations in the past.[1] When questioned about the seminar a few months after the last session, Hanna said that he had not learned anything from the data he did not already know but that the information was of some value, since he could use it with the staff as corroboration for what he had been telling them all along. (There was some inconsistency apparent here, for he had repeatedly disputed in the seminar the meaning and adequacy of the data on his institution.) He also felt that

a comparative study was not possible, since "no two organizations are ever alike" and even Mixter changed a great deal from month to month. Nevertheless, the director of social service, who also participated in the reporting sessions, felt that he had learned much that was new about the organization. Hanna's defensive strategy may have been due in part to the fact that he had known before the reporting sessions occurred that he was to be transferred to another institution a few months after the sessions. He said, "I decided to play the devil's advocate."

No changes were reported as having been made as a direct or indirect result of either the survey or reporting sessions. Hanna reported that as a result of the one important change that did occur in the year, the opening of Maxwell four months before the second survey, it was possible to open up two cottages that had been closed. He also claimed that because of Maxwell the truancy rate had dropped "tremendously," although it had risen again to near its previous level a few months later; that the number of waivers to the court, a method of transferring older boys from the jurisdiction of the probate courts to the adult criminal courts, had dropped to almost zero; and that cottage parents reported there was far less fighting in the cottages and the boys were easier to handle. The executive remarked that few people had believed him when he said about 10 per cent of the boys took up about 60 per cent of the staff time, but now it was clearly proved. He said the inmates themselves felt the change. Previously many boys ran away because they were afraid of the tough, hostile boys. With these inmates removed, the atmosphere had improved and security precautions could be reduced.

The results of the second survey provide little support for these assertions. Results of a special question asking personnel to agree or disagree that "the new (security) unit has made our work with the boys much easier," are revealing. Only 38 per cent of the staff agreed with the statement, and the percentage of the administrative group checking "strongly agree" was seven times as large as the next most favorable staff group (86 per cent compared with 12 per cent). Aside from the administration, those groups with the most custodial philosophy (night men, detail supervisors, and maintenance men) were the most enthusiastic.

The new unit appeared to have no appreciable effect upon the responses of the staff to other questions. Less than a fifth of the questions had distributions that changed 10 per cent or more between surveys, and

the positive and negative changes were about equal (Table 10.1). Indeed, despite the removal of more than fifty hostile and aggressive boys from the program, half the sanctions questions showed increases in *negative* responses of 10 per cent or more.

Inmate responses, however, seemed to show a small positive gain (Table 10.2). Of the twenty-seven comparable items, three changed 10 per cent or more in a positive direction and one in a negative direction. Responses to questions on leadership characteristics did not change, despite the apparent removal of many negative leaders. Two items dealing with inmates' relations with one another changed positively: boys were more likely to feel they could be friendly with one another without fear, but only by 11 per cent, and they were more likely to talk a boy out of running, again by 11 per cent. Thus, neither inmates nor staff showed substantially different responses to reflect the changes presumably brought about by the new security unit. As one cottage parent put it, although some disruptive boys were removed to Maxwell, "it seemed as if new ones were here to take their places right away."

## Regis

Mitchell of Regis, like Jackson of Dick and Hanna of Mixter, had felt the survey would give him little new information. The effect of the survey operation probably was not great. The executive enjoyed describing his program and giving his philosophy, but usually was unaffected by critical probes in the interviews. Similarly, there was little in the seminar sessions that seemed to cause him to re-examine his program in any basic sense. He was greatly upset that his staff showed little commitment to children, but he readily and approvingly identified his institution as fitting the "obedience model" presented in the seminar.

It is possible, however, that the seminar precipitated some subsequent changes in the institution. Mitchell took steps to insure that brothers who were assigned to the institution in the future would be those who showed some interest in working with youth—men studying psychology, for example, or social work. Further, as a result of an improvement in the institution's financial situation but perhaps also partly because of the research project, he obtained another full-time social worker, whose task was to work with parents and to help inmates with post-institutional adjustment. Finally, after seeing that the runaway rate

had almost tripled in three years (in part because the institution was accepting more delinquent children) and struck by the policies of the other institutions, which accepted back most of their truants, Mitchell liberalized the Regis policy on boys who ran away.

Mitchell was very interested in the seminar sessions themselves and wished they could continue. It seems possible that this experience provided him with a reference group that induced him to broaden his conception of the role of clinical personnel.

Staff questions were not repeated at Regis. Results of the second inmate questionnaire show considerable change (Table 10.2). Of twenty-seven questions, there was change on responses to sixteen; five of these were positive, eleven negative. Negative changes occurred on six of the thirteen questions dealing with attitudes toward other boys and the institution and staff in general; on two of the eight about leadership characteristics; on three of the six dealing with self-conceptions. We do not know why. Results of new questions used during the second survey indicated the existence of a more negative inmate system at this institution than we had imagined, but perhaps this reflected change between years. It seems possible that more negative inmate norms were gradually developing at the institution. which could not be managed with the philosophy of "wear them out before they wear you out," or with the prevalent view that any kind of leadership is bad.

*Bennett*

Ramsey of Bennett, who was somewhat surprised that we wished to include his institution in the sample because he felt that most of the inmates were only nominally delinquent, was alerted by the seminar to many similarities between his inmates and those of other institutions and to common structural and staff problems. He was surprised to learn, for example, that many of his boys felt the "best way to get along here" was "to do what you are told, and do it quickly." He then spent several evenings in the cottages talking with the boys to find out if this was really the way they felt, and if so, why. Although he had been aware that the social worker had little constructive contact with either inmates or the rest of the staff the survey brought this home to him forcefully, and he attempted to deal with this problem by holding staff meetings. He sought advice from the research staff on handling these problems and

help in securing a replacement for the social worker, who was about to resign. Ramsey also came to feel that perhaps more clinical services were needed for the inmates; heretofore he had believed that only 5 to 10 per cent might require such services.

Again, we have no questionnaire data on staff change. Findings on the inmate responses (Table 10.2) show change on eleven of the twenty-seven items. On five the boys moved in a negative direction, and on six they moved in a positive direction. Negative changes occurred primarily on those questions dealing with situations in which the respondent could choose between supporting inmates or staff. The largest positive changes occurred in their preference for staying here or going elsewhere (24 per cent) and in their response to the "best way to get along" question (34 per cent). It is possible that the discussions the executive had with the boys regarding these issues, taking place within three or four months of the second survey, had some effect upon their responses.

It appeared that Ramsey, like his counterpart at Regis, intended to continue with the goals and staff practices he already favored, although participation in the research project had opened up some limited alternatives. This executive, nearing retirement and committed basically to handling boys whom he considered primarily dependent and neglected, foresaw no major changes in his institution over the next five years.

*Milton*

The impact of the first survey itself upon Milton seemed to be considerable. Because its results could not be presented and discussed until a few weeks before the second survey, it was the primary stimulus to change introduced by the research that we could see. Interviews with the executive cores of both Milton and Inland, in contrast to those of the other four institutions, often turned into discussions in which the "respondent" examined and discussed various philosophies and program alternatives with the "interviewer" and sought his ideas and criticisms. Members of the executive core at both institutions were enthusiastic about the survey—they said it was something they had wanted to do themselves or to have done. Similarly, after turning in the questionnaires, personnel frequently discussed individual items with one an-

other and with the research staff. The executive, Perkins, said he was attempting to use the research staff to obtain an outside evaluation.

Interviews and written questions regarding the academic school prompted Perkins and Taylor, the assistant director, to start an in-service training program for school personnel. "There was a good deal of discussion of tensions around here after you left," the director said. The executive core had been aware of this as a problem area, and the survey gave further impetus to action. In some other areas in which we probed, however, core members felt that difficulties were due to the newness of the program. Although the integration of clinical and cottage parent staff had started more than two years before, the decision to put clinical coordinators in full charge of each cottage had been made only three months before the first survey. This change played a large part in their interpretations of the results.

During the year between the two surveys the institution was able to effect greater control over inmate intake, with the consequence that its inmate population declined by over 10 per cent. Extensive community relations programs were carried out with such groups as Parent-Teacher Associations throughout the state. There was no unfavorable publicity, and raises in pay were obtained for some of the staff. Most of the changes, however, were internal and centered around crises in relationships among individuals or groups. At the beginning we had noted a high level of tension among staff members; it remained quite high, judging from the number of personnel conflicts that occurred between the two surveys. Several staff members were fired or resigned; petitions were circulated to remove one department head; all but three of the academic teachers were leaving, with considerable criticism directed against the principal; relations between a head cottage parent and the clinical coordinator were very strained and the topic of considerable discussion and analysis; some of the older, more custodial staff employees were "acting out"; a crisis developed over a highly organized system of sexual activities discovered among the boys in one cottage; a clinical coordinator had been reassigned to a new cottage and other changes in personnel assignment were made. Boys wrote freely in the institution's paper about crises: the articles included a penetrating analysis of "chaos" in one cottage, and an account of the defiant, open truancy of a large group of boys. Since the paper was supervised by a

disaffected member of the "old guard," it tended to publish trenchant criticism. These problems made obvious the relevance of the survey data.

The reaction to the data from the first survey was initially quite defensive. Gradually, executive core members agreed there was greater emphasis upon discipline and punishment among the staff members than they had anticipated or wanted and that the whole area of informal inmate relations had been neglected. They were disturbed by negative attitudes of inmates and inmate leaders and by their own failure to cope with oppositional informal organization. They sought further contacts with the research staff and decided they should focus more upon some of the "sociological" implications of their treatment plan. They felt, however, that the second survey would show large reductions in tension and that staff personnel would indicate they were clearer about their roles and responsibilities.

Comparison of staff questionnaire responses in the two surveys (Table 10.1) indicates some reduction in tension, particularly between teachers and cottage parents and between teachers and social service personnel, apparently reflecting the in-service training program for teachers. A question about the clarity of institutional practices was repeated at Milton (although not in the other institutions, so it is not included in Table 10.1) but the distributions were almost identical. The teachers did show a substantial positive shift, but this was offset by a decline in the amount of clarity perceived by some other groups. Thus the program had not "settled down" as the executive core had predicted. Over all twenty-eight questionnaire items, responses to five changed positively and four negatively.

Inmate responses seemed to become somewhat more negative (Table 10.2). There were two positive and four negative increases. All four negative changes occurred on questions dealing with attitudes toward self—a remarkable shift for which we have no explanation.

The impact of the data reporting sessions was potentially large but because the second survey took place the following month we had little opportunity to see modifications in program. Both the executive and the clinical director were more ready to accept the accuracy and relevance of the survey findings than were other members of the executive core. Although the research staff indicated a perspective divergent from that of the psychiatrists and psychologists in the executive core, includ-

ing the clinical director, the high interest in the survey and the data reported suggested there would be some impact upon the program.

## Inland

Personnel at Inland were very interested in participating in the study, said they found the survey stimulating, and showed intense interest in the results. As at Milton, the executive core sought to use the study as a resource.

The major change to take place at Inland between surveys was the resignation of the director, Wright, and the promotion of the assistant director, Burns, to his post. This occurred during the period of the seminar. Since Wright and Burns were in basic agreement regarding general institutional goals and program, there was no major reorientation. The change was important in several respects, however. Wright had not been well liked by the staff or inmates, and his resignation also removed the irritation of additional minor measures designed to promote cleanliness, order, and activities whose principal aim was to appeal to the public. Burns had begun to direct the appeal to professional publics, and proceeded to establish close working relations with academic and clinical professionals in universities and nearby treatment facilities.

The conjunction of the executive seminar with the Wright resignation accelerated a change that was already contemplated. The institution had sought for some time to employ a person familiar with therapeutic group management to improve the inmates' interpersonal relations and to bridge the gap between the clinical staff and cottage parents. Data from the survey underlined difficulties in these areas, and the vacancy in the assistant director's position stimulated a search for a person who could fill these needs and at the same time hold a position of high authority. The research staff helped obtain a group worker, who filled a new "program-coordinator" position. He did not start work until two weeks before the second survey, but further changes had already preceded his arrival. Contact between the clinicians and the cottage parents was increased; cottage parents were given in-service training in group management and were now expected to handle behavior problems directly and to be more active in structuring inmate activities; a vocational counselor was hired; efforts were made to integrate the teachers

further into the program and to acquaint them with group management techniques. These changes reflected a shift from an almost exclusive reliance upon individual casework. Both Wright and Burns had been impressed with the intent and structure of the milieu program developed at Milton.

The changes that occurred at Inland are reflected in staff data from the second survey (Table 10.1). Of the twenty-eight items, there was change in response to eight—all in the positive direction. Lowering of tensions apparently followed upon the change in the executive and efforts to increase understanding among members of different units. Responses to questions on the influence and help of staff groups (not reported in the table) also indicate change. The percentage of personnel feeling that the social service staff members were "a lot of help in advising how to work with boys" increased from 43 to 67; there was a 17 per cent rise in the proportion who felt the influence of teachers was considerable, a 24 per cent rise regarding the influence of the school principal, and a 26 per cent rise in regard to the cottage parents. The proportion indicating that the (new) director had a great deal of influence increased from 62 to 93 per cent. A major reorientation of the program seemed to be reflected in these changes. Both cottage parents and teachers became more integrated, and social service personnel, who met regularly with cottage parents, were perceived as more helpful. These changes in attitudes occurred despite the fact that responses were so concentrated at the positive end that not much change could occur.

Changes on the inmate questionnaire did not reflect these extensive changes among staff members. Many of the program modifications could have effects on the inmates only later. On the questionnaire (Table 10.2) there were nine changes, five positive and four negative.

*Summary*

Social scientists have often noted that studying a social object can change it, and this was evident in our research. To varying degrees at each institution the research provoked discussions among personnel, some extensive and heated and making staff members aware of divergencies in perspectives on goals and means. With the survey acting as a catalyst Inland undertook major changes in its program, and Milton indicated similar plans. The feedback sessions also were change-inducing for

Milton and Inland and, to a much smaller degree, for Regis and Bennett.

Finally, the institutions did not exist in a research vacuum. Inmates continued to come and go; courts made their demands; personnel resigned or were removed; new facilities opened up; parent organizations applied new pressures and local communities continued to exert their influence. Some of these pressures and changes had far reaching consequences, although others were absorbed by the institutions with little effect. The treatment-oriented institution appeared to be most sensitive to these internal and external forces.

## NOTES

1. In actuality, we noted no such effect upon staff and inmates, and in the vast majority of the cases we received willing and sometimes enthusiastic cooperation throughout the lengthy research period. Those staff members we had least contact with—cottage parents on the night shift and some maintenance personnel—were the least likely to return their completed questionnaires, but the overall response rate was high. The staff questionnaire in particular created some discussion as to institutional realities and proper procedures, although there was less of this than at Milton and Inland. Some members of the executive core, however, challenged the adequacy and reliability of the questionnaire, and their cooperation was reluctant.

*Chapter 11*

# CONCLUSIONS

## OVERVIEW OF THE STUDY

The foregoing analysis can be thought of as an expression of the sociology of knowledge. We have viewed the juvenile correctional institution as a people-changing organization, in which the lack of objective measures of effectiveness invites the pre-eminence of a variety of competing belief systems. Tied to various goals, these belief systems infuse and provide criteria for day-to-day operations and furnish a rationale for defending the organization against ambiguities and conflicts from within and without. The research questions that arose concerned not only the consequences of commitment to different sets of beliefs and goals but also the conditions under which these organizations can sustain or adapt old models or develop new ones.

Any comparative study having this range of research techniques will produce some findings that are clear-cut and others that are ambiguous. Altogether, however, the results consistently confirm and give substance to our guiding propositions—about the implications of different goals for operating patterns and staff behavior and perspectives; about the crucial role of the executive in formulating goals and developing internal and external strategies; and about the ways inmates should be affected by varying institutional environments.

The findings strongly refute the notion that the alienating qualities of the correctional institution or the previous experiences of the staff and inmates make them totally unmalleable. Background characteristics were important in screening staff and inmates in most of the institutions. In no way, however, could these characteristics account for such differences as we found among Dick, Mixter, and Milton—all state institutions having rather low rates of pay for line personnel and re-

ceiving a "mixed bag" of types of inmates. Differences in the organizations' handling of the inmates had measurable and, for the treatment institutions, desired effects upon the inmates and the inmate collectivity.

Findings on the inmates also indicate that the re-education/development institutions can make some of the apparent gains of the treatment model without all of its costs, at least for some populations and in an open format. However, the degree to which the relatively positive responses at Regis and Bennett depended on the fact that these institutions, largely for reasons of historical and financial accident, sent their boys out to community schools is unknown. The question of whether a re-education/development model could be sustained in a completely closed setting or would "backslide" into an obedience/conformity approach is also empirically unanswerable.

## THE IMPLEMENTATION OF TREATMENT

The goal of treatment becomes more pervasive throughout the corrections field but its implementation remains elusive. Before our first survey was conducted, Robert Vinter and Morris Janowitz wrote a paper presenting a series of hypotheses about the consequences of the introduction of "segmented therapeutic practices."[1] By this term they referred to the piecemeal injection of counselling and other treatment programs into institutions that remain basically custodial. As major outcomes of segmented treatment they foresaw mobilization of local community criticism of permissiveness; generation of unrealistically high expectations for achievement in the parent organization, which would jeopardize the executive's security in office; generation of an unstable bifurcation of staff groups; creation of inconsistencies in handling the inmates; and conversion of therapeutic practices into mechanisms for supporting custodial goals.

These predictions do not fit with precision the patterns of any one of the institutions in our sample. Mixter most clearly approximated the segmented model. In this institution, although local community antipathy was very high and the executive lost his job after failing to satisfy the expectations of the parent welfare organization, bifurcation and inconsistency in staff-inmate relations were not very great—precisely because treatment programs and personnel were so easily subordi-

nated to custodial ends. In the other institutions attempts to implement treatment either were so minimal (in Dick, Regis, and Bennett) or had gone so far (in Milton and Inland) that little overt segmentation appeared.

Despite their lack of exact applicability, the predictions define basic organizational problems which our observations indicate must be handled if treatment is to be implemented in a genuine way. Our findings also suggest some crucial approaches to these problems. First, sufficient power must be given to staff units and members who celebrate the treatment ideal so that operations will be ever under their control, thus resolving inconsistencies, preventing bifurcation, and insuring that decisions are made under criteria of rehabilitation rather than containment or convenience. Throughout its history of attempts at reformation, Mixter had never redistributed power in a thoroughgoing way. Therefore it remained essentially an obedience/conformity institution. In contrast, the treatment institutions had largely accomplished this change, although in different ways. Inland had merely downgraded the roles of all but its clinical staff until there could be no challenge. Milton, with less freedom of action, achieved the change only tortuously and with continuing conflict—by forging a managerial role for its clinicians in the cottage committees after its initial attempts at treatment had resulted in high bifurcation.

Second, implementation of treatment requires special external efforts to fend off hostility from the local community and to gain support from parent organizations and other agencies that furnish resources, legitimation, cooperation, or inmates. Needs for support are much broader than merely increased money for additional personnel. While Mixter's staff felt forever hamstrung by community attitudes, Inland and Milton staff members were out "selling" their institutions. Inland capitalized on a nearly professional public relations program, its favorable geographical location (which permitted runaways to leave by bus without disturbing the local community), and later on its rising status in professional circles. Milton built support through grass-roots work with legislators and by using to advantage its relationship with the nearby psychiatric center.

Third, treatment programs necessitate a high degree of organizational flexibility. There must be substantial tolerance of disruptions of routine, ambiguities in criteria for staff and inmate performance, and conflict

among personnel groupings and between staff and inmates. This requires considerable decentralization of decisions over means—although decisions over ends must be monopolized by those who have high commitments to treatment. The Milton cottage committee structure furnishes a prototype for reconciling managerial with rehabilitative and particularistic standards.

Fourth, executive leadership is crucial to producing change. The significant skills of the treatment executives were in part entrepreneurial, but they also had to do with creating a sense of urgent mission to overcome the drift toward custodialism among the staff members. These executives spoke of expansive goals, used terms that evoked a sense of unceasing effort, and demanded that staff members share their idealistic and innovative orientations and participate willingly in the transformation of the enterprise.

Finally, our data suggest many of the limits upon the capacities of correctional organizations and executives to accomplish major changes, as well as of the treatment model to provide a wholly satisfactory ideal for innovation. All institutions suffered from the tendency toward routinization, the deficit of information on organizational processes and outcomes, and the inability to integrate all staff, particularly the teachers, into the total program. Especially important was the fact that the perspectives of the mental health field from which the treatment model flows induced a concern with emotional problems and two-person therapy that was inadequately addressed to organizational realities and design even in the "milieu" treatment institution. Although the positive results of treatment appeared to require the use of an "adaptive" approach to inmate social organization, in which the staff fosters positive group relations and informal leadership, staff members in the treatment institutions were only beginning to grasp the general ramifications of this approach.

Most important, none of the institutions was truly successful at producing changes appropriate to the lives the inmates would lead on the outside. The results of the obedience/conformity institution appeared to be clearly negative, of course, for the experience of being dominated cannot be expected to produce positive personality changes or to increase one's capability for legal conformity in an open, individualistic, and achievement-oriented society. The effects of the more conventional and open programs of the re-education/development institu-

tions appeared mixed, but on balance they seemed to show improvement or at least the preservation of personal skills and emotional controls needed after release.

The consequences for the inmates of the treatment institutions appeared to be even more positive, with greater development of personal and social controls and the acquisition of some skills in problem-solving and self-understanding. There is some question, however, about the relevance and utility of these skills for the offenders' future life situations and about whether or not such skills can be maintained without considerable reinforcement after release. Even in the treatment institutions, the inmates' experiences were little articulated with post-discharge processes. That this was due to limitations in design rather than in resources is indicated by the lack of attempt to make post-discharge plans with inmates, to provide anticipatory training for handling problems of community re-entry, or to furnish post-discharge services.

Correctional institutions lack the organizational capacity to handle the provision of post-release services adequately. However, these organizations could profitably seek to specify the changes sought in the inmates from a longer time perspective and to work to mesh their programs more fully with processes and agencies involved in re-integrating the inmates into the community. Our observations indicate that serious thinking along these lines was beginning in the treatment institutions, and it is likely that the expansive designs of these organizations will ultimately compel them to face this issue forcibly. Both in theory and reality there appear to be many alternative opportunities for breaking out of the unilateral strategy by cooperating with community and other agencies to assure a better sequence of resocialization activities.

## NOTES

1. "Effective Institutions for Juvenile Delinquents: A Research Statement," subsequently published in *Social Service Review,* 33 (June, 1959), 118–131.

# Appendixes

*Appendix A*

# THE STAFF QUESTIONNAIRE

The staff questionnaire was administered in all six institutions during the first survey and, in revised and shortened form, repeated in all but Regis and Bennett during the second. In each organization, shortly before its administration the executive sent out a memorandum or communicated informally about the purposes of the study and the need to fill out the questionnaire. We passed out the questionnaires to groups of employees in some instances and individually in others, repeating and elaborating explanations of the study.

Each questionnaire had a face sheet bearing the respondent's name. After filling out the form, the respondent was to tear off the face sheet and, so we would know he had turned in a questionnaire, place it along with the questionnaire in a sealed box. At some of the institutions several contacts and letters to individual staff members were necessary to secure fairly complete coverage. In the distant institutions late questionnaires were returned by mail after we had left, and additional reminder letters and phone calls were occasionally necessary. Staff members were assured that we had no interest in their names, that no one from the institution would see individual questionnaires, and that all questionnaires were anonymous. All this was true, but it was also necessary to arrange for matching of questionnaires with file data obtained on individual staff members. Some employees at some institutions, particularly at Mixter, refused to complete the questionnaire, a number saying that individuals could be identified by handwriting or personal data.

Response percentages were as follows: First survey, Dick, 95; Mixter, 85; Regis, 100; Bennett, 100; Milton, 91; Inland, 93. Second survey, Dick, 72; Mixter, 94; Milton, 83; Inland, 91. The substantial number of refusals at Mixter on the first survey occurred mainly among night supervisors (nine of thirty-one refusing) and cottage parents (nine of

forty-three refusing). The night men were the personnel with whom we spent the least time, and many of the cottage parents who did not turn in questionnaires were isolated from the others and more autonomous, being responsible for the closed discipline or orientation cottages. Two cottage parents who did not turn in questionnaires were fired later for maltreatment of boys. The distribution of responses at Mixter therefore probably underestimates custodial orientations.

In the second survey, by the time we left the distant institutions, Dick and Milton, substantial numbers of staff had still not turned in their questionnaires. Subsequent letters of appeal were not very successful, especially at Dick, where, the executive told us, a negative election result a month after our visit killed employee interest in general in doing their work. Non-respondents at Dick were spread out over all positions.

Nine per cent of the questionnaires were check-coded. The overall rate of error was .0125, undoubtedly based on the almost exclusive use of close-ended questions.

The basic questionnaire, the one used in the first survey, follows.

*The University of Michigan*
*Ann Arbor, Michigan*

A STUDY OF INSTITUTIONS FOR JUVENILES

We need your cooperation to get at some important information. You can assist us in a study we are making of the ways in which different institutions that work with children operate. We wish to know about some of your activities, how you feel about your job, and your opinions about juvenile delinquency. This study is being supported by a grant from the National Institute of Mental Health, United States Public Health Service.

Each member of the staff of several institutions is being asked to fill out this questionnaire. Your answers will be *completely confidential and anonymous,* so feel free to answer the questions frankly. It is important that we know just how the employees here feel about these various things. Please don't discuss the questionnaire with anyone who has not finished filling out theirs. We want only your *personal* reactions. Please answer all of the questions.

We think you will enjoy filling out this questionnaire and thinking about the questions. Any comments or ideas which you have will be appreciated; just write them in.

Thank you for your cooperation in our study. Your assistance will be of benefit to many agencies working with children.

NAME _____

When you have finished the questionnaire, rip this page off. Put this sheet and the questionnaire in the box in the office. We will then know who has turned in the questionnaire while preserving anonymity.

A. *Ideas about juvenile delinquents*

Thinking about delinquents in general—that is, children who get into trouble and come to the attention of the authorities—we would like to know how you feel about the following statements. There are no right or wrong answers. All we want to know is what *you* feel about the statement. If you "strongly agree," check the line below Strongly Agree. If you "agree," check the line below Agree, and so forth.

287

1. We can try but it is difficult to understand the peculiar behavior of delinquents.

| Strongly Agree | Agree | Unsure | Disagree | Strongly Disagree |
|---|---|---|---|---|
| 1_____ | 2_____ | 3_____ | 4_____ | 5_____ |

[NOTE: Questions 2 through 17 had the same format of response patterns; these are omitted here to conserve space.]

2. Because of his past behavior a delinquent should not expect to have his needs considered as much as an adult's may be.
3. Understanding may be important in helping delinquents but what is really needed is strictness and firmness.
4. Most juvenile delinquents are in no condition to make decisions even about every day living problems.
5. Unless you take precautions, a delinquent may attack you.
6. The chances that a delinquent will straighten out are very slight.
7. Most delinquents are rejected children who need help.
8. Delinquents have to be punished if they're going to learn correct behavior.
9. Sympathetic understanding is the key to helping delinquents.
10. Normal kids horse around some, but most delinquents are always horsing around.
11. Most juvenile delinquents can't be trusted.
12. Most delinquents will respond to genuine friendship.
13. Society is going to have to be a lot tougher than it has been if it is going to cut down on delinquency.
14. One of the things a delinquent needs is a chance to express his feelings without being punished.
15. The trouble with delinquents is that they haven't learned to treat adults with respect and obedience.
16. Most delinquents can't even be friends among themselves, let alone with adults.
17. Firmness will help delinquents to learn right from wrong.

B. *About the boys*

Below are some statements about the *boys you have here*. Write in the answer that comes *closest* to the way you think things actually are.

1. What per cent of the boys here are below normal intelligence? _____%
2. a) What per cent of the boys here are assaultive and hostile? _____%

b) What per cent of the boys have neurotic problems,
feelings of inadequacy, or are withdrawn? \_\_\_\_%

3. Sometimes boys hang around in cliques and informal groups in the institution. Are all of these groups bad—that is, do all make your job harder and have a bad influence on the boys?

    1\_\_\_\_ All are bad      3\_\_\_\_ Only a few are bad
    2\_\_\_\_ Most are bad      4\_\_\_\_ None are bad

3a. If *some* groups *are not bad,* are they generally helpful to you in working with the boys or don't they affect your job at all?

    1\_\_\_\_ All are helpful      4\_\_\_\_ Few are helpful
    2\_\_\_\_ Most are helpful      5\_\_\_\_ They have no effect
    3\_\_\_\_ Some are helpful

4. Do you agree or disagree with the following statements:

A. "The boys who get the most out of their stay here keep to themselves and don't get too close to the other boys."

\_\_\_\_ *Strongly Agree*      \_\_\_\_ *Agree*
\_\_\_\_ *Disagree*      \_\_\_\_ *Strongly Disagree*

B. "The best way for a boy to get along here is to do what he's told and to do it quickly."

\_\_\_\_ *Strongly Agree*      \_\_\_\_ *Agree*
\_\_\_\_ *Disagree*      \_\_\_\_ *Strongly Disagree*

C. "All boys should receive the same discipline for breaking a rule."

\_\_\_\_ *Strongly Agree*      \_\_\_\_ *Agree*
\_\_\_\_ *Disagree*      \_\_\_\_ *Strongly Disagree*

5. Would you say that the leaders among the boys around here are a bad or good influence upon the other boys? (*Check one*)

    1\_\_\_\_ Always a *bad* influence
    2\_\_\_\_ Usually a *bad* influence
    3\_\_\_\_ Sometimes a *bad* influence
    4\_\_\_\_ Usually a *good* influence on the other boys
    5\_\_\_\_ Always a *good* influence

6. What about problems of boys running away? (*Check one*)

    1\_\_\_\_ Almost all of the boys would run at some time if we didn't keep a close watch on them.
    2\_\_\_\_ Many boys would run, but some wouldn't.
    3\_\_\_\_ Some would run away, but most wouldn't even if we didn't keep a close watch on it.
    4\_\_\_\_ Very few would run away even if we didn't keep a close watch.

5_____ Running away is no problem; we don't have to keep a close watch on the boys.

7. How many of the boys can a worker realistically expect to change for the better? (*Check one*)

A_____ Few will become better.

B_____ About the same number will become better as don't change.

C_____ Most will change for the better, but some won't.

8. How many of the boys will become worse? (*Check one*)

A_____ None will become worse.

B_____ Few will become worse.

C_____ Some will change for the bad; but most won't.

D_____ Most will become worse; but some won't.

C. Different institutions for delinquents have different ideas of what their purposes are. Below are a set of statements about purposes.

1. Our purpose is to punish delinquent behavior.

2. Our purpose is to teach boys good social habits.

3. Our purpose is to train and educate these boys.

4. Our purpose is to change a boy's social attitudes and values.

5. Our purpose is to help each boy gain an understanding of the kinds of things that got him into trouble.

6. Our purpose is to protect the home community for a period of time.

(A) Now look over the list and write down the numbers of the *two statements* which in your opinion best describe what the director thinks are the purposes of Blank School.

(1)_____          (2)_____

(B) Which two statements are furthest away from what the director thinks are the purposes of the institution?

(1)_____          (2)_____

(C) Which *two* statements *best* describe the way things *actually are* at this institution?

(1)_____          (2)_____

(D) Which *one* statement *least* applies to the way things *actually are*?

(1)_____

(E) Which two statements best describe how *you think* things should be operated?

(1)_____          (2)_____

Now, in your own words, what do you think the purpose of Blank School is? _____

D. Below are a group of stories about things that happen at institutions for boys. After each story check the one alternative which is closest to what *you would do* if the situation came up here at Blank School.

1. A boy truants and is gone for a day. The police bring him back. He has broken a couple of windows to get into a garage, but he has not stolen anything. The boy has truanted once before. He has made a fairly good adjustment to the institution, aside from his truancy.

   _____ Try to find out why he ran, talk with him about his behavior and put him back into the program.

   _____ Talk to him about it; put him back in the program, but have everyone keep an eye on him.

   _____ Ask him why he ran, then put him in isolation or in a closed program until you are fairly sure that he has learned his lesson.

2. A boy starts a fight with another boy and gives him a black eye. The boy who starts the fight has been very quiet before and has never gotten into a fight. The other boy has been teasing him.

   _____ Try to help them settle it, but fighting can't be permitted and the boy must learn this; his privileges must be cut down.

   _____ Fighting has to be prevented; transfer the boy to another cottage or assignment.

   _____ Work with the two boys, try to get them to see why their behavior is bad; but don't punish the boy who started the fight.

3. A boy starts to complain about how he is being treated here. He gets very aggravated and swears at you. He has done this before and you had spoken to him about it.

   1_____ Slap him.

   2_____ Call the head supervisor; penalize him, since swearing can't be allowed.

   3_____ Tell him that if he keeps it up he'll have to do extra work.

   4_____ Listen to him; try to calm him down once more, and talk with him about it.

4. A boy does not want to go to a meeting of a club group that he has joined. He has gone regularly before, but he refuses to this time and begins to get upset and shout when he is told to go. He says that he just doesn't feel like it.

   _____ Tell him he can withdraw from the group if he gets permission from the person in charge of club activities, but he has to go tonight.

   _____ Warn him that his privileges will be taken away if he does not go.

_____ Talk with him about it, but leave it up to his decision whether he goes.

5. A boy is talking too loudly while playing a game. Several times before you have spoken to him about his loud talking. Usually he quiets down for awhile but then starts talking too loudly again.

1_____ Slap him the next time he talks too loud.

2_____ Talking loud tends to excite other boys so report him to the supervisor—penalize him.

3_____ Bawl him out; because loudness can't be permitted.

4_____ Find out how the other boys feel about it; if he doesn't bother them too much, talk to him about it but don't make an issue out of it.

6. You have asked a boy to help another boy clean a room. He says he doesn't want to. You have gotten along well with him in the past.

_____ Order him to do it; otherwise he'll be penalized.

_____ Ask him to do it for you, if he wants to keep your friendship.

_____ Reason with him; explain why he should do it.

E. In each of the following sets of items check the *one item* which comes closest to describing what you think the director (superintendent) expects from the employees here. Read all of the alternatives in a set before you check one.

SET 1. He expects personnel:

1_____ to have close relationships with the boys, so that we can get to understand the boys.

2_____ to be close to the boys, but not so close that our status and authority will be questioned.

3_____ to keep distant from the boys; otherwise we will both lose our objectivity and not be able to maintain our authority.

4_____ He doesn't care what kind of relationship we have.

SET 2. He expects personnel:

1_____ to maintain order at all times; otherwise the boys will get out of control.

2_____ to let the boys have freedom to express themselves; but we have to keep a close watch over it.

3_____ to let the boys set their own limits, except if it gets dangerous; otherwise the boys won't learn to control themselves.

4_____ He's not concerned about whether the staff let boys have freedom to express themselves or not.

SETS 3, 4 AND 5 FOR COTTAGE PARENTS ONLY, OTHERS SKIP TO F

SET 3. He expects the cottage parents:

_____ to give the boys who help keep control special privileges.

_____ to treat all the boys alike, in order to be fair.

_____ to treat each boy according to his needs.

SET 4. He expects the cottage parents:

1_____ to keep all of the boys in sight when they are with the boys; a boy shouldn't be allowed out of sight.

2_____ to allow any boy to be out of sight if he feels that the boy can be trusted.

3_____ to allow a boy to be out of sight if the boy wants to; in most situations the boys don't have to be watched that closely.

4_____ it doesn't matter to the superintendent how cottage parents regulate the movement of the boys.

SET 5. He expects cottage parents:

1_____ to meet the parents when they visit the institution if the parents want to meet them.

2_____ to avoid meeting the real parents if at all possible.

3_____ to attempt to see the real parents when they come visiting.

4_____ it doesn't matter to him whether cottage parents meet the real parents or not.

F. Staff have different tasks at any institution. We would like your opinion on the following statements about the staff. Read all of the alternatives in a set before you check one.

1. Is it easier to get these boys interested in learning here than in a regular school?

_____ It is tougher here.

_____ It would be just as tough teaching these boys in a regular public school.

_____ It is easier teaching these boys here.

2. How much disciplinary power over boys do the cottage parents need to do their job right?

_____ They need a *lot of disciplinary power* to do their job right.

_____ They need *some disciplinary power*.

_____ They need *very little disciplinary power*.

3. How important are the cottage parents to the institution?

_____ No matter what everyone else does, if the cottage parent doesn't do his job right the organization doesn't function properly.

_____ It is important that the cottage parent's job is done right, but no more important than the clinic's or the school's.

_____ Even if the cottage parent doesn't do a good job, the teacher and the counselor can accomplish a lot.

4. How much influence do each of the following groups have in making decisions about *how the boys should be handled?*

|  | 1<br>*Very little<br>influence* | 2<br>*Some<br>influence* | 3<br>*About the<br>same as<br>anyone else* | 4<br>*A good<br>deal of<br>influence* |
|---|---|---|---|---|
| Social Service, psychologists | _____ | _____ | _____ | _____ |
| Teachers | _____ | _____ | _____ | _____ |
| Cottage parents | _____ | _____ | _____ | _____ |
| Detail supervisors | _____ | _____ | _____ | _____ |

5. How important is the Social Service in running the institution?

_____ Blank School could run O.K., even if we didn't have the social service workers.

_____ Social service workers are fairly important in running the institution.

_____ Without good social service workers it would be almost impossible for us to do a good job.

6. How much help are the people in Social Service in advising how to work with the boys?

_____ *A lot of help* in advising us.

_____ *Some help* in advising us.

_____ *Little help* in advising us.

7. In general, how much say or influence in *the way Blank School is run* would you say each of the following individuals or groups has? (*Put one check on each line*)

|  | 1<br>*A great<br>deal of<br>say* | 2<br>*A lot<br>of say* | 3<br>*Some<br>say* | 4<br>*Little<br>say* | 5<br>*Very<br>little<br>say* |
|---|---|---|---|---|---|
| (Parent Organization) | _____ | _____ | _____ | _____ | _____ |
| The Director (Superintendent) | _____ | _____ | _____ | _____ | _____ |
| Assistant Director | _____ | _____ | _____ | _____ | _____ |
| The Head of Social Service | _____ | _____ | _____ | _____ | _____ |
| The School Principal | _____ | _____ | _____ | _____ | _____ |
| The Head of Home Life | _____ | _____ | _____ | _____ | _____ |

G. 1. Most new staff tend to let the boys get away with too much until they have been here awhile.

1_____ Strongly agree; they're not strict enough.

2_____ Agree

3_____ They're neither over-strict nor under-strict.

4_____ Disagree

5_____ Strongly disagree; if anything they're too strict.

2. The institution ought to pay more attention to the working conditions of their employees, and worry a little less about the boys.

1_____ Strongly Agree    4_____ Disagree

2_____ Agree             5_____ Strongly Disagree

3_____ Unsure

3. Considering the kind of boy we have here, we are doing a good job if we can get a boy to adjust to the institution.

1_____ Strongly Agree    4_____ Disagree

2_____ Agree             5_____ Strongly Disagree

3_____ Unsure

4. It would help a lot if we had more ways of rewarding and praising boys for learning good behavior.

1_____ Strongly Agree    4_____ Disagree

2_____ Agree             5_____ Strongly Disagree

3_____ Unsure

5. The program we have now is about as good as it can be; we don't need any more treatment programs.

1_____ Strongly Agree    4_____ Disagree

2_____ Agree             5_____ Strongly Disagree

3_____ Unsure

6. Regardless of the rules, each staff person tends to use his own judgment in handling the boys.

1_____ Strongly Agree    4_____ Disagree

2_____ Agree             5_____ Strongly Disagree

3_____ Unsure

7. From time to time changes in methods, practices and procedure are introduced by the Administration (director, assistant director). In general, *do you think* these changes lead to better ways of doing things?

1_____ They are always an improvement.

2_____ Most of the time they are an improvement.

3_____ Sometimes they are an improvement.

4_____ They seldom are an improvement.
5_____ They never improve things.
6_____ I can't judge.

8. If you were a member of a committee to advise the director of the institution, which of the following statements about new treatment programs would you approve? (*Check one only*)

_____ No new treatment program should be started if custodial security precautions would have to be lowered.

_____ Treatment programs can be started even though a moderate increase in number of escapes might result.

_____ Custodial considerations are secondary in setting up a treatment program (except for the clearly dangerous offender).

9. If the institution was having trouble with runaways and you were on a committee to decide what to do about it, which of the following answers would you recommend? (*Check one only*)

1_____ Give the staff more opportunity to discipline, even though really hurting a boy should not be tolerated.

2_____ Put some of the boys into a closed program.

3_____ Institute a training program with staff so that they can learn how to make the boys want to stay here.

4_____ Try and get people in the community to support your program and procedures.

H. *About your job*

1. How long would you like to work at this institution? (*Check one*)

_____ I'd like to stay until I retire or until I don't have to work any more.

_____ I wouldn't mind staying but I'd leave for a better job.

_____ I'd like to leave soon.

2. How satisfied are you with your chances for advancement at Blank School. (*Check one*)

1_____ Not at all satisfied with my chances for advancement.

2_____ Little satisfied.

3_____ Fairly satisfied with my chances for advancement.

4_____ Very well satisfied.

5_____ I don't care about my chances for advancement.

3. How does Blank School compare with other places in which to work?

1_____ Much better than most.

2_____ Better than most.

3_____ About the same as most.

4_____ Somewhat poorer than most.

5_____ Much poorer than most.

4. On the whole would you say that in Blank School there is any tension between the following pairs of groups? (*Check one for each pair*)

| | 1<br>A great deal of tension | 2<br>Consid-erable tension | 3<br>Some tension | 4<br>Very little tension | 5<br>No tension at all |
|---|---|---|---|---|---|
| Teachers and Social Service | _____ | _____ | _____ | _____ | _____ |
| Social Service and Cottage Parents | _____ | _____ | _____ | _____ | _____ |
| Cottage Parents and Teachers | _____ | _____ | _____ | _____ | _____ |
| Employees and the (Parent Organization) | _____ | _____ | _____ | _____ | _____ |
| Employees and the Director | _____ | _____ | _____ | _____ | _____ |

5. You may not have any plans about changing jobs, but what kind of job would you like if you did change jobs? (*Put a check next to each job*)

| | Would not accept | Accept | Favor |
|---|---|---|---|
| 1. A job that gave a chance to work with children | _____ | _____ | _____ |
| 2. A civil service job | _____ | _____ | _____ |
| 3. A job in the penal system, in corrections | _____ | _____ | _____ |
| 4. A job in a factory, or in a business | _____ | _____ | _____ |
| 5. A job that paid more money no matter what the field | _____ | _____ | _____ |

*Now go back and circle the number in front of the one you* MOST *favor.*

6. Which one of the following statements comes closest to your feelings?

A_____ Just as long as you do your job well and follow the rules it isn't so important how you feel about children.

B_____ To do a good job it's better for a worker to have a lot of feeling for children.

C_____ A worker can't do a good job at all without a real feeling for children.

7. Workers in any organization may feel loyalty to their fellow workers, their community, the children they are responsible for, the institution, or their profession. How much loyalty do you feel to each of these?

|  | A little loyalty | Some loyalty | A good deal of loyalty |
|---|---|---|---|
| a. The institution | _____ | _____ | _____ |
| b. Fellow workers | _____ | _____ | _____ |
| c. The children I am responsible for | _____ | _____ | _____ |
| d. The community | _____ | _____ | _____ |
| e. My professional group | _____ | _____ | _____ |

*Now go back and circle the one that you feel the* MOST *loyalty toward.*

8. Some people are deeply involved in their job. Such a person may think about his job constantly. A second person may view his job simply as a way to earn a living. How strongly do you feel involved in your job? (*Check one*)

1_____ Not involved at all; chiefly a way to earn a living.
2_____ Slightly involved.
3_____ Moderately involved; an important part of my life.
4_____ Strongly involved.
5_____ Very strongly involved; one of the most important things in my life.

9. In general, do you think *the institution* is highly regarded in the community or not?

_____ The institution is highly regarded in the community.
_____ Most people don't feel one way or the other about the institution.
_____ Most people think the institution is bad for the community.

10. What appear to be the complaints about Blank School by people in the community? (Put a "1" before the most important criticism and a "2" before the next most important.)

1_____ Truancy.
2_____ Behavior of boys at community events.
3_____ The community thinks we're too tough on the boys.
4_____ Fear and dislike of the boys.
5_____ Dislike of some of the staff.
6_____ The community thinks we're too easy on the kids.

11. Some juvenile correctional institutions use volunteers from the com-

munity to help with parts of the program. Do you think they are (or would be) helpful?

1\_\_\_\_ Very helpful

2\_\_\_\_ Somewhat helpful

3\_\_\_\_ Do not make any real difference in the program

4\_\_\_\_ May often create problems for us

12. The public may have varying ideas about the importance of helping people who require specialized care. How do you think the *public* ranks the importance of helping each of the following? (Put a "1" in front of the most important one, a "2" in front of the next most important and so on.)

1\_\_\_\_ Persons on public wel-     3\_\_\_\_ Physically handicapped
     fare programs              4\_\_\_\_ Adult criminals

2\_\_\_\_ Mentally retarded        5\_\_\_\_ Juvenile delinquents

13. Rank the following occupations by how highly regarded they are in the community. (Put a "1" before the most highly regarded, and so on through "10.")

\_\_\_\_ Teacher             \_\_\_\_ Children's supervisor in

\_\_\_\_ Unskilled worker          an institution

\_\_\_\_ Salesman              \_\_\_\_ Doctor

\_\_\_\_ Social worker          \_\_\_\_ Truck driver

\_\_\_\_ Skilled machinist       \_\_\_\_ Policeman

                                   \_\_\_\_ Office clerk

14. When you get together socially with friends who don't work here, how likely is it that you will talk to them about things that happen at work?

1\_\_\_\_ I'm almost sure to talk about things that happen at work.

2\_\_\_\_ There's a pretty good chance I will.

3\_\_\_\_ I probably won't talk about them.

4\_\_\_\_ I'm almost sure not to talk about things that happen at work.

5\_\_\_\_ I don't have any friends who don't work here.

15. Do you feel that you have an accurate picture about what is going on at Blank School?

1\_\_\_\_ I have a completely accurate picture; everything that is going on at Blank School can be understood.

2\_\_\_\_ A very accurate picture.

3\_\_\_\_ A fairly accurate picture; some things can be understood.

4\_\_\_\_ Not so accurate a picture.

5\_\_\_\_ I have a very poor picture; very little of what is going on can be understood.

NEXT TWO PAGES FOR THE CLINIC STAFF
ONLY. OTHERS SKIP TO I

16. Regarding the families of the children, how many do you see while a boy is at Blank School?

1\_\_\_\_ None             3\_\_\_\_ About half
2\_\_\_\_ A few      4\_\_\_\_ Most      5\_\_\_\_ All

17. Of those family members that you see, about how frequently do you usually see them during the boy's stay in the institution?

1\_\_\_\_ Once             3\_\_\_\_ Three or four times
2\_\_\_\_ Twice            4\_\_\_\_ Five or more times

18. How many of the boys do you hear about after they leave here?

1\_\_\_\_ Never hear about them
2\_\_\_\_ Hear about a few boys
3\_\_\_\_ Hear about half of them
4\_\_\_\_ Hear about most of them
5\_\_\_\_ Hear about all of them

19. Of these boys that you hear about after they leave, how are you informed?

|  | Most | Some | A few |
|---|---|---|---|
| Reports at staff meetings or official memoranda | \_\_\_\_ | \_\_\_\_ | \_\_\_\_ |
| Follow-up reports by probation officer or social worker | \_\_\_\_ | \_\_\_\_ | \_\_\_\_ |
| Other staff members mention it | \_\_\_\_ | \_\_\_\_ | \_\_\_\_ |
| The boys or their parents write | \_\_\_\_ | \_\_\_\_ | \_\_\_\_ |
| The boys come back to visit | \_\_\_\_ | \_\_\_\_ | \_\_\_\_ |
| The boys are committed here again | \_\_\_\_ | \_\_\_\_ | \_\_\_\_ |

20. What types of work or services do you think individual volunteers or volunteer groups can assist with?

_____    _____
_____    _____
_____    _____

21. Indicate about how many times you have spoken before community groups regarding juvenile delinquency or child welfare during the past two years:

1\_\_\_\_ None             3\_\_\_\_ Two or three times
2\_\_\_\_ Once             4\_\_\_\_ Four or more times

22. Think back over the last few days. How many boys have you seen in your office each day?

Average number \_\_\_\_\_

23. About how long was your average contact with a boy?

Average length of time _____

24. Below is a list of reasons why a boy might come to a social worker's office. Check the number of boys who come to your office for each of the reasons:

| | Many do | Some do | None do |
|---|---|---|---|
| 1. To get a change in work or school assignment | _____ | _____ | _____ |
| 2. To find out about home visits | _____ | _____ | _____ |
| 3. To find out about when they are going to be released | _____ | _____ | _____ |
| 4. To talk about some trouble which they have gotten into in Blank School | _____ | _____ | _____ |
| 5. To talk about their family problems | _____ | _____ | _____ |
| 6. To talk about the kinds of problems they have which got them into trouble | _____ | _____ | _____ |

### FOR ALL STAFF

I. *Personal data.* In these questions we would like to know a little about your background. We are not interested in your particular answers but only in the general pattern for all personnel. Please answer all questions.

1. _____ Male          _____ Female

2. How old are you?

   1_____ less than 25          6_____ 45–49
   2_____ 25–29          7_____ 50–54
   3_____ 30–34          8_____ 55–59
   4_____ 35–39          9_____ 60–64
   5_____ 40–44          10_____ 65 and over

3. Education (*Check the number of years of school completed*).

   1_____ 3 or less years          5_____ completed high school
   2_____ 4–6 "          6_____ 1–3 years of college
   3_____ 7–9 "          7_____ completed college
   4_____ 10–11 "          8_____ graduate study

   Have you taken any night school or extension courses?

   _____ Yes          _____ No

   If so, what courses? _____

   If you went to college, what was your major field of study? _____

If you went on for graduate study, what degrees did you earn?
(1)_____ (2)_____ In what fields? (1)_____ (2)_____

4. What is your marital status?

_____ Single                 _____ Widowed
_____ Married                _____ Separated
_____ Divorced

If you are married, does your wife (or husband) work here?
_____ Yes            _____ No
If yes, in what position? _____

5. How long have you worked at the institution? _____
What jobs have you held in the institution? State the *one* you are in now as Number 1, the one before that as Number 2, and so on. Next to each job write in the number of years you have been in (or were in) each position.

|          |                | Afternoon | Night | Months or years |
|----------|----------------|-----------|-------|-----------------|
| Job (1)  | _____  | _____     | _____ | _____           |
| Job (2)  | _____  | _____     | _____ | _____           |
| Job (3)  | _____  | _____     | _____ | _____           |

What were the last two jobs you had before you came to work here?
Last job _____
Second last job _____
Have you had any other similar kind of work to the job you have now? (For example, in a prison, social agency, mental hospital, institution, court, etc.)
_____ Yes        _____ No        Where? _____

6. Are you a member of any union or employee group?
_____ Yes            _____ No
If so, please list.
(1) _____        (3) _____
(2) _____

7. Are you a member of any groups or clubs outside of work?
_____ Yes            _____ No
PLEASE LIST: (For example, business and civic groups, political clubs, churches, church-related groups, veterans' groups, neighborhood groups, PTA, sports and athletic groups, honorary societies, and lodges.)

|                                     | Check if active |
| *Name of Organization*              | (*Attend half or more of meetings*) |
| _____  | _____ |
| _____  | _____ |
| _____  | _____ |
| _____  | _____ |
| _____  | _____ |

8. Are you a member of any technical or professional organizations?

_____ Yes       _____ No

PLEASE LIST:

(1) _____       (3) _____

(2) _____

Have you been to any meetings of these in the last year?

_____ Yes       _____ No

9. Do you live on the grounds? (Have a room or apartment here?)

_____ Yes       _____ No

10. What was your salary last year? (Not including your husband's or wife's?)

$ _____

11. Race

_____ Caucasian       _____ Negro       _____ Oriental

12. Religion

_____ Protestant       _____ Catholic       _____ Jewish

If Protestant, what denomination? _____

13. Do you get together socially more often with people who work here or with people who work elsewhere?

_____ More often with people who work here

_____ About equally divided

_____ More often with people who work elsewhere

14. If you do spend *some* of your *free time* with other employees, what positions do they hold? (On the first line put the *position* of the person you see most, on the second line the person you see next most, and on the third line the person you see third most.)

POSITION:

Person (1) _____       Person (3) _____

Person (2) _____

The questionnaire used in the second survey contained the following major new questions: *

Regardless of what anyone says, the best way for a boy to get along here is to: (*Check one*)

1_____ Stay out of the way of the adults but get away with what he can
2_____ Don't break any rules and keep out of trouble
3_____ Show that he is really sorry for what he did
4_____ Try to get an understanding of himself

Regardless of how much tension you yourself feel, if there is any tension between some of the groups named above [Question H-4] what is the reason for it?

A. If you think there is any tension between *cottage parents* and *social service* it is because: (*Check as many as you like*)

_____ (a) Social service workers feel cottage parents don't understand how to work with the boys.

_____ (b) Social service workers think that the cottage parents are too hard on the boys.

_____ (c) Social service workers feel that the cottage parents don't do enough for the boys.

_____ (d) Cottage parents feel the social service workers don't give them enough information about the boys.

_____ (e) Cottage parents feel the social service doesn't do enough to help the boys.

_____ (f) Cottage parents feel the social service workers believe what the boys tell them too often.

_____ Other (*write in*) _____

B. If you think there is any tension between *teachers* and *social service or psychologists* is it because: (*Check as many as you like*)

_____ (a) Teachers feel that social service and psychologists don't give them enough information about the boys.

_____ (b) Teachers feel that social service and psychologists don't try to control the boys enough.

_____ (c) Social service and psychologists feel the teachers don't try to understand the boys.

* The complete questionnaire used in the second survey is reproduced in *The Comparative Study of Juvenile Correctional Institutions: A Research Report* (Ann Arbor: School of Social Work, University of Michigan, 1961), pp. 694–704.

_____ (d) Social service and psychologists feel the teachers don't work hard enough with the boys.

_____ Other (*write in*) _____

C. If you think there is any tension between *teachers* and *cottage parents* is it because: (*Check as many as you like*)

_____ (a) Teachers feel the cottage parents *don't* discipline the boys enough.

_____ (b) Teachers feel the cottage parents discipline the boys *too much*.

_____ (c) Teachers feel the cottage parents don't encourage the boys enough.

_____ (d) Cottage parents feel the teachers don't discipline the boys enough.

_____ (e) Cottage parents feel the teachers don't work with the boys enough.

_____ (f) Cottage parents feel the teachers don't watch the boys closely enough.

_____ Other (*write in*) _____

D. If you think there is any tension between the *employees* and the *administration* is it because: (*Check as many as you like*)

_____ (a) The employees feel the administration wants them to be easier on the boys.

_____ (b) The employees feel the administration wants them to control the boys more.

_____ (c) The employees feel the administration doesn't work hard enough to get them better salaries and working conditions.

_____ Other (*write in*) _____

E. If you think there is any tension between the *employees* and the (*Parent Organization*) is it because: (*Check as many as you like*)

_____ (a) Employees feel the (Parent Organization) wants them to be easier on the boys.

_____ (b) Employees feel the (Parent Organization) doesn't try to get more things for the boys.

_____ (c) Employees feel the (Parent Organization) wants them to control the boys more.

_____ (d) Employees feel the (Parent Organization) doesn't do enough to get them better pay and working conditions.

_____ Other (*write in*) _____

*Appendix B*

# SCALE AND INDEX CONSTRUCTION
# FOR STAFF DATA

The seventeen items from which the scales of normal relations, understanding, and discipline were adapted came from several
sources, especially the Custodial Mental Illness Ideology Scale.* Fourteen of the items yielded significant differences between the more custodial and more treatment-oriented staff groups under the Kolmogorov-
Smirnov Two-Sample Test. Guttman scaling techniques, following
machine processing procedures, were used.† Four of the fourteen
items had proportions of over 80 per cent in the positive response categories and therefore did not meet minimum error criteria for the acceptance of items with extreme proportions. Ten items were used in the
three scales, with a single item being used in both the understanding
and discipline quasi-scales. Scaling procedures and distributions of
responses for all staff members in the first survey are presented in
Tables B.1, B.2, and B.3. Table B.4 gives the same information for the
prisonization scale.

### Table B.1—Scale of Normal Relations

| Scale Type | | Item Number 10 16 11 | | | Non-Scale Types | Perfect Scale Types | Total | Per Cent |
|---|---|---|---|---|---|---|---|---|
| No trust possible | I | — | — | — | 14 | 66 | 80 | 21 |
| | II | x | — | — | 32 | 50 | 82 | 22 |
| | III | x | x | — | 14 | 61 | 75 | 20 |
| Trust possible | IV | x | x | x | 10 | 127 | 137 | 37 |
| | | | | | 70 | 304 | 374 | 100 |

Coefficient of Reproducibility .94

* Doris C. Gilbert and Daniel J. Levinson, " 'Custodialism' and 'Humanism'
in Mental Hospital Structure and in Staff Ideology," in Milton Greenblatt, Daniel
J. Levinson, and Richard H. Williams, *The Patient and the Mental Hospital*
(New York: Free Press, 1957), pp. 20–35.
† Jackson Toby and Marcia L. Toby, "A Method for Selecting Dichotomous
Items by Cross Tabulation," in M. W. Riley, J. W. Riley, Jr., and J. Toby, *Socio-
logical Studies in Scale Analysis* (New Brunswick: Rutgers University Press,
1954).

| ITEM | Positive Position | Per Cent |
|---|---|---|
| 10. Normal kids horse around some, but most delinquents are always horsing around | 3,4,5 | 71 |
| 16. Most delinquents can't even be friends among themselves, let alone with adults | 4,5 | 57 |
| 11. Most juvenile delinquents can't be trusted | 4,5 | 49 |

### Table B.2—Scale of Understanding

| Scale Type | | Item Number 9 | 3 | 1 | Non-Scale Types | Perfect Scale Types | Total | Per Cent |
|---|---|---|---|---|---|---|---|---|
| Understanding difficult | I | — | — | — | 13 | 38 | 51 | 14 |
| | II | x | — | — | — | 134 | 134 | 36 |
| | III | x | x | — | 13 | 71 | 84 | 23 |
| Understanding the key | IV | x | x | x | 37 | 64 | 101 | 27 |
| | | | | | 63 | 307 | 370 | 100 |

Coefficient of Reproducibility .94

| ITEM | Positive Position | Per Cent |
|---|---|---|
| 9. Sympathetic understanding is the key to helping delinquents | 1,2 | 79 |
| 3. Understanding may be important in helping delinquents, but what is really needed is strictness and firmness | 3,4,5 | 44 |
| 1. We can try but it is difficult to understand the peculiar behavior of delinquents | 4,5 | 29 |

### Table B.3—Scale of Discipline

| Scale Type | | Item Number 14 | 8 | 3 | 13 | 15 | Non-Scale Types | Perfect Scale Types | Total | Per Cent |
|---|---|---|---|---|---|---|---|---|---|---|
| Discipline | I | — | — | — | — | — | 15 | 39 | 54 | 16 |
| | II | x | — | — | — | — | 20 | 60 | 80 | 23 |
| | III | x | x | — | — | — | 15 | 35 | 50 | 15 |
| | IV | x | x | x | — | — | 33 | 17 | 50 | 15 |
| | V | x | x | x | x | — | 16 | 22 | 38 | 11 |
| | VI | x | x | x | x | x | 29 | 45 | 74 | 21 |
| | | | | | | | 128 | 218 | 346 | 101 |

Coefficient of Reproducibility .92

| ITEM | Positive Position | Per Cent |
|---|---|---|
| 14. One of the things a delinquent needs is to express his feelings without being punished | 1,2 | 74 |
| 8. Delinquents have to be punished if they're going to learn behavior | 3,4,5 | 54 |
| 3. Understanding may be important in helping delinquents, but what is really needed is strictness and firmness | 3,4,5 | 44 |
| 13. Society is going to have to be a lot tougher than it has been if it is going to cut down on delinquency | 4,5 | 40 |
| 15. The trouble with delinquents is that they haven't learned to treat adults with respect and obedience | 4,5 | 34 |

### Table B.4—Prisonization Scale

| Scale Type | | Item Number 4a | 4c | 4b | Non-Scale Types | Perfect Scale Types | Total | Per Cent |
|---|---|---|---|---|---|---|---|---|
| High prisonization | I | — | — | — | 30 | 68 | 98 | 27 |
| | II | x | — | — | 28 | 76 | 104 | 28 |
| | III | x | x | — | — | 62 | 62 | 17 |
| Low prisonization | IV | x | x | x | 4 | 100 | 104 | 28 |
| | | | | | 62 | 306 | 368 | 100 |

Coefficient of Reproducibility .94

| ITEM | Positive Position | Per Cent |
|---|---|---|
| 4a. The boys who get the most out of their stay here keep to themselves and don't get too close to the other boys | 3,4 | 72 |
| 4c. All boys should receive the same discipline for breaking a rule | 3,4 | 52 |
| 4b. The best way for a boy to get along here is to do what he's told and to do it quickly | 3,4 | 37 |

The Sanctions Index is an arbitrary index constructed by adding together scores from five story vignettes. A low score was given a punishing or penalizing response, a high score was given a response that did not penalize. For each story we have included the response alternatives and their weights. Numbers on the left refer to the number of the story as presented in the questionnaire. Total scores ranged from three to fifteen.

| Story Number | Response Alternative | Score |
|---|---|---|
| D 1. | Try to find out why he ran, talk with him about his behavior and put him back into the program. | 3 |
| | Talk to him about it; put him back into the program, but have everyone keep an eye on him. | 2 |
| | Ask him why he ran, then put him in isolation or in a closed program until you are fairly sure that he has learned his lesson. | 1 |
| D 2. | Try to help settle it, but fighting can't be permitted and the boy must learn this; his privileges must be cut down. | 1 |
| | Fighting has to be prevented; transfer the boy to another cottage or assignment. | 2 |
| | Work with the two boys, try to get them to see why their behavior is bad; but don't punish the boy who started the fight. | 3 |

D 3.   Slap him.                                                                     0
       Call the head supervisor; penalize him, since swearing can't
       be allowed.                                                              1
       Tell him that if he keeps it up he'll have to do extra work.   2
       Listen to him; try and calm him down once more, and talk
       with him about it.                                                    3
D 5.   Slap him the next time he talks too loud.                      0
       Talking loud tends to excite the other boys so report him to
       the supervisor—penalize him.                                    1
       Bawl him out; because loudness can't be permitted.        2
       Find out how the other boys feel about it; if it doesn't
       bother them too much, talk to him about it but don't
       make an issue out of it.                                            3
D 6.   Order him to do it; otherwise he'll be penalized.             1
       Ask him to do it for you, if he wants to keep your friend-
       ship.                                                                       2
       Reason with him; explain why he should do it.               3

When a respondent failed to make a choice on one of the items his score from item D 4. was used. This query had its wording changed for each institution; it was used in the index—to increase the number of respondents with full index scores—only as a last resort.

D 4.   Tell him he can withdraw from the group if he gets per-
       mission from the person in charge of club activities, but
       he has to go tonight.                                                 1
       Warn him that his privileges will be taken away if he does
       not go.                                                                    2
       Talk with him about it, but leave it up to his decision
       whether he goes.                                                      3

*Appendix C*

# THE INMATE QUESTIONNAIRE

Prior to final revisions before the first survey, inmate questions drawn up after informal interviewing at Mixter and Inland were pre-tested, first orally and then in written form, at two institutions outside our sample. For the second survey the inmate questionnaire was revised again and substantially expanded.

Ordinarily, the questionnaire was administered to groups of fifteen to thirty-five boys in classrooms or cottages. The inmates were told about the nature of the study, the importance of their cooperation, and the fact that their responses would be seen by no one in the institution. Usually we pointed out that the questionnaire was not a test, that there were no right or wrong answers, and that we wanted to find out how they "really felt" in order to write a book on how these organizations could be improved. (Frequently boys would ask the title and say they wanted to buy a copy when it was published.) They were also told to keep their answers to themselves and that they would receive a bottle of pop as a token of our gratitude. Although we had to use a device to identify respondents in order to analyze the association of responses with background attributes and leadership, no names appeared on the questionnaires.

On a few occasions we administered the questionnaire to larger groups, and in most institutions we administered a few questionnaires to groups of two to five slow readers who needed special help. With only unimportant exceptions, we were able to complete the administration in a single day.

The occasional presence of staff members, and difficulties in controlling talking among the inmates, presented special problems. The first problem was much easier to handle in the more treatment-oriented institutions, where personnel were usually ready to leave. In general it was less serious than the second, for even when they stayed in the

room we could usually keep them from talking or getting close enough to see the inmates' responses. The problem of talking may have been serious on a few items, usually open-ended ones or items provoking hilarity. Frequently the modal responses were not those discussed most loudly, however. The consensus of the several persons who administered questionnaires was that the inmates generally accepted us for what we were: persons from outside the institution who could be trusted to keep their responses secret from staff.

The percentages of inmates filling out questionnaires were as follows: First survey, Dick, 90; Mixter, 97; Regis, 97; Bennett, 100; Milton, 91; Inland, 97—total, 94. Second survey, Dick, 95; Mixter, 98; Regis, 98; Bennett, 100; Milton, 96; Inland, 93; Maxwell, 100—total, 97. There were few or no outright refusals. Those we missed were physically ill, unable to read, thought to be too disturbed to participate, or simply "lost" administratively.

We check-coded every fourth questionnaire from the first survey. The percentage of error was 1.2 for the close-ended questions, 4.9 for the open-ended items, and 1.9 overall. On the second survey we check-coded every fifth questionnaire from Dick, Mixter, Milton, and Inland. The percentage of error was 1.3 for close-ended questions, 4.8 for open-ended ones, and 1.3 overall.

The questionnaire used in the second survey follows.*

* The questionnaire used in the first survey, containing more detailed socio-metric items and several projective questions, is reproduced in *The Comparative Study of Juvenile Correctional Institutions: A Research Report* (Ann Arbor: School of Social Work, University of Michigan, 1961), pp. 725–734.

*The University of Michigan*
*Ann Arbor, Michigan*

Your answers to these questions will be seen only by the research people from The University of Michigan. No one at Blank School or any other place will see them.

1. We would like your opinion about these things at Blank School. Check for each one whether you agree, disagree, or are unsure.

   (a) We get enough food at meals.

   _____1 Agree          _____5 Disagree          _____3 Unsure

   [NOTE: Questions b through k had the same format of response patterns; these are omitted here to conserve space.]

   (b) There are not enough things to do during free time.

   (c) We are not allowed to smoke enough.

   (d) The food does not taste as good as what I'm used to.

   (e) Some adults here are too strict.

   (f) Boys should be able to suggest changes in work programs, smoking rules, and activities.

   (g) The adults here are pretty fair.

   (h) Adults here are not strict enough with certain boys.

   (i) There are too many boys here who push other boys around.

   (j) Some boys can get away with too much.

   (k) Boys here get enough help in preparing for jobs they want in the future.

2. When you talk with your social worker, which of these things do you talk *mostly* about? (*You may check more than one*)

   _____1 Home visits

   _____2 Parole or release date

   _____3 Change in cottage or work assignment

   _____4 Punishment or losing privileges

   _____5 Why I get into trouble here

   _____6 What I will do after I am released

   _____7 How I get along with my family

   _____8 Why I got into trouble in the past

   _____9 Personal problems that bother me

312

3. When you first found you were going to be sent here, what did you think about this place? Did you think it would be a good place or a bad place?

_____1 Good place       _____3 Bad place

_____2 Neither good nor bad       _____4 Very bad place

4. What do you think about this place *now?* Is it better than you expected or worse than you expected?

_____1 A lot better than I expected

_____2 Better than I expected

_____3 About the same as I expected

_____4 Worse than I expected

_____5 A lot worse than I expected

4a. What kind of work does your father or stepfather—or whoever supports your family—do for a living? (*Please be specific*)

5. For some boys, some things like the food and sports here may be better than what they have at home. How about you? Are things like these better or worse for you here than they were at home?

_____1 Very much better       _____4 Worse

_____2 Better       _____5 Very much worse

_____3 About the same

6. Some boys who get into trouble are sent to one place and some are sent to another. If you were back home and had your choice to come here or go to some other institution where they send boys who get into trouble (not your home, or a boarding home), which would you choose?

_____1 Come here       _____5 Go to some other institution

6a. How close are you to the cottage parent you know best?

_____1 Very close       _____3 Not very close

_____2 Close       _____4 Not close at all

7. How do you feel about this?

You have to be careful about the boys you get friendly with around here. To stay out of trouble with the adults you have to keep to yourself.

_____1 Strongly agree       _____3 Disagree

_____2 Agree       _____4 Strongly disagree

8. Some boys make good after they're released; others don't and are returned to an institution. What do you think your chances are to make good? (*Check one*)

_____1 Excellent chance to make good

_____2 Fair chance to make good

_____3 My chances are about 50–50

_____4 I may not make good

_____5 Little chance to make good

9. *In your own words,* write in what you think a boy has to do to get a parole or discharge from here.

10. How many months do you think *most* boys stay here before they get out?

_____ months

11. How about *you?* How long do you think you will stay here?

_____1 A lot less time than most     _____4 A little longer than most

_____2 A little less time than most     _____5 A lot longer than most

_____3 About the same as most

12. Do you think you know pretty well how the adults here feel about how long you will have to stay here?

_____1 I am sure how I stand with the adults

_____2 I think I know how I stand with the adults

_____3 It's hard to say how I stand with the adults

_____4 I have no idea of how I stand with the adults

13. Boys do different things after they are released. What do you think *you* will do after you are released? (*Check one*)

_____a I'll be careful and behave myself

_____b I won't get caught again

_____c There's a lot to learn, but I think I can make good

_____d I will live it up, and hope I don't get sent back here

14. Some say that *most* boys are interested in just getting by while they are here and don't care to learn about why they did the things that got them into trouble or how to change. Do you agree or disagree?

_____1 Strongly agree     _____4 Disagree

_____2 Agree     _____5 Strongly disagree

_____3 Neither agree nor disagree

15. Do you usually hang around here with several guys, a few, mostly with one boy, or with none?

_____4 Four or more guys     _____2 One guy

_____3 Two or three guys     _____1 None

16. How about *close* friends? Some boys have close friendships with other boys here and some boys don't. How many of the other boys here are close friends of yours?

_____1 None     _____3 Two or three

_____2 One     _____4 Four or more

17. Are more of your best friends here, or are more of your best friends back home?

_____1 More friends are here

_____5 More friends are back home

_____3 About the same here as back home

18. How many of the boys you have met here would you like to see again after you get out?

_____1 All or almost all          _____4 A few

_____2 Most                       _____5 None

_____3 Some

18a. Have you been helped here to prepare for future jobs you would like to have?

_____1 I have received a lot of help

_____2 I have received some help

_____3 I have received little help

_____4 I have not received any help in preparing for the future

19. Do you think that you need help from someone so you can change and stay out of trouble?

_____1 Yes                _____5 No

20. Do you think some of the adults here can help you find out why you get into trouble and help you change?

_____1 Adults here can help me a lot

_____2 Adults here can help me some

_____3 Adults here can help me a little

_____4 Adults here can't help me at all

21. How many times have you gone on a home visit since you came here? (If none, write in 0.)

_____

22. How many times in the last two months have you gone away from the institution with a group of boys for something like a sports event, movie, or tour? (If none, write in 0.)

_____

23. What three boys are best at getting other boys to do what they want them to do—that is, which three have the most influence among the boys? Think of the boys that you know in your cottage, in school, in the work program, or recreation. Please write in their first and last names.

1 _____          3 _____

2 _____

24. Now take the *first* boy you named on the page before this. Do you think he is mostly a *good influence* on the other boys—for example, is he fair with all the boys? Does he help other boys stay out of trouble?

OR

Do you think he is mostly a *bad influence* on the other boys—for ex-

ample, does he bully the others, shove some of the weaker boys around, or get his own way whether he is right or not?

(a) Think of the *first* boy you listed. Is he:

_____1 Always a good influence
_____2 Mostly a good influence
_____3 More of a good than a bad influence
_____4 More of a bad than a good influence
_____5 Mostly a bad influence
_____6 Always a bad influence

(b) Now think of the *second* boy you listed. Is he:

_____1 Always a good influence
_____2 Mostly a good influence
_____3 More of a good than a bad influence
_____4 More of a bad than a good influence
_____5 Mostly a bad influence
_____6 Always a bad influence

(c) Now think of the *third* boy you listed. Is he:

_____1 Always a good influence
_____2 Mostly a good influence
_____3 More of a good than a bad influence
_____4 More of a bad than a good influence
_____5 Mostly a bad influence
_____6 Always a bad influence

25. Supposing you had a friend back home who was committing some burglaries and car thefts. He was caught once and put on probation. He got caught again. Do you think it would straighten him up if he was sent here?

_____1 It probably would          _____5 It probably wouldn't

26. (a) How much would you say that your stay here has helped *you*?

_____1 A great deal          _____4 Very little
_____2 Quite a bit           _____5 None
_____3 Some but not much

   (b) If it has helped you, is it mostly because: (*Check one*)

_____1 I have learned my lesson
_____5 I have learned something about myself and why I get into trouble

27. Suppose you had been feeling sad for several days and are very upset about a personal problem. Are there any *boys* here you would go to and talk with about the things that made you sad?

_____1 Yes          _____5 No

28. All of us do things at times or act in certain ways so that people become angry or disappointed with us. At other times we do things which

they like very much, or they are glad when we act a certain way. What sort of things do people like *best* about you?

29. What sorts of things do people like *least* about you?

30. (a) Of all the people you have ever met, known, or know now—which of them would you want most to be or to be like when you're older?

    (b) Why do you think you would rather be like that person than other persons you know?

31. Boys who are here think different things about themselves. Check the statement that comes *closest* to what you think about yourself. (*Check only one*)

    _____a Someone who got a raw deal
    _____b Someone with personal problems
    _____c Someone who knows what the score is and how to play it cool
    _____d Someone who doesn't let anyone push him around
    _____e Someone who is trying to straighten out

32. Which one of the adults here has the most say about what happens to you while you're here?

    _____ (name of person)

33. Which one of the adults here has the most to say about when you get out of here?

    _____ (name of person)

34. Suppose a group of boys took a dislike for a boy you knew, and decided to rough him up for no particular reason. If a friend of the boy learned about their plan, what should he do?

    (a) Should he warn an adult?
    _____1 Yes                    _____5 No
    (b) Should he try to talk the group out of it?
    _____1 Yes                    _____5 No

35. Suppose a group of boys are planning to get even with a night man here that no one likes, by beating him up. Should a boy warn some adult here about it?

    _____1 Yes                    _____5 No

36. Suppose a group of boys from your cottage started stealing food from the kitchen and eating it themselves. When the adults found that food was being stolen they said that until they found out what boys were taking the food, the whole cottage would be restricted.

    Suppose you knew who was in the group that was stealing the food. If you got the chance to tell an adult without anyone else knowing, would you do so?

    _____1 Yes          _____5 No          _____3 Maybe

37. Suppose a boy you knew fairly well was planning to run away tonight, or not come back from a home visit.
   (a) Would you try to talk him out of it?
   _____1 Yes  _____5 No
   (b) Do you think a boy should ever tell an adult here that another boy is planning to run?
   _____1 Yes  _____5 No
38. What do your family and friends back home think of this place? Do they think it is: (Check one)
   _____1 A place that *helps* boys in trouble
   _____3 A place to *send* boys who get into trouble
   _____5 A place to *punish* boys for something wrong they did
39. Think about yourself now—what do *you* think about this place? (Check one)
   _____1 A place that *helps* boys in trouble
   _____3 A place to *send* boys who get into trouble
   _____5 A place to *punish* boys for something wrong they did
40. Do you think this is true or not? Boys dislike being here so much that they don't want to cooperate with the adults here any more than they have to.
   _____1 True for all boys  _____4 True for a few boys
   _____2 True for most boys  _____5 Not true at all
   _____3 True for some boys
41. How long have you been in the cottage you live in now?
   _____1 Two weeks or less  _____5 Five or six months
   _____2 One month  _____6 Seven to eleven months
   _____3 Two months  _____7 A year or more
   _____4 Three or four months
42. Most cottages have different groups of boys who stick closely together and don't have much to do with the other boys. How many groups like this does your cottage have?
   _____1 There are three or more groups
   _____2 There are two groups
   _____3 There is one group
   _____4 There are no groups at all
43. Do you belong to one of these groups?
   _____1 Yes  _____5 No
44. If you are in one of these groups, what boy in your group is most often listened to by other members of the group? (Please write in first and last name)

   _____

45. If you were going to be moved to another cottage, would you rather stay in the cottage you are in now or be moved?

_____1 Definitely would move

_____2 Probably would move

_____3 Wouldn't make any difference

_____4 Probably would stay here

_____5 Definitely would stay here

46. Regardless of what the adults here say, the best way to get along here is to: (*Check one*)

_____1 Stay out of the way of the adults but get away with what you can

_____2 Don't break any rules and keep out of trouble

_____3 Show that you are really sorry for what you did

_____4 Try to get an understanding of yourself

46a. I'd be better off if I lived in a smaller cottage with fewer boys.

_____1 Agree                    _____3 It doesn't make

_____5 Disagree                  any difference

47. Some boys say that you have to be pretty careful about what you say or do around the other boys here, or else they may give you a rough time. What do you think about this?

_____1 You have to be very careful about what you say and do around the other boys

_____3 You have to be somewhat careful

_____5 You don't have to be careful

48. How old are you?

_____

49. What school grade are you in here?

_____

50. What work detail are you on?

_____

51. How much of the time do you think most of the boys here really stick together, and are loyal to each other? Do they stick together and are they loyal:

_____1 All of the time          _____4 A little of the time

_____2 Most of the time         _____5 Never

_____3 Some of the time

52. Regardless of how much the boys actually do stick together now, how much do you think they *should* stick together? Do you think it's very important that the boys stick together and be loyal to each other, or don't you think it makes much difference?

_____1 It's very important  _____4 It doesn't make any difference
_____2 It's fairly important  _____5 It would be better if the boys
_____3 It's a little important  kept to themselves

53. Do you agree or disagree?
The adults here really don't care what happens to us; they're just doing a job.

_____1 Strongly agree  _____3 Disagree
_____2 Agree  _____4 Strongly disagree

54. Now think of the leaders among the boys here—the boys that the other boys will listen to or obey. It doesn't matter if you think they are good leaders or bad leaders, or if some of them are good and others are bad. We are interested in all kinds of leaders. There are bound to be some boys who have more influence over other boys, so think of them and answer these questions:

How many of the leaders here:

(a) Are ready to fight other boys at most any time?

_____1 All or most leaders
_____3 About half and half
_____5 Few or no leaders

[NOTE: Questions b through i had the same format of response patterns; these are omitted here to conserve space.]

(b) Have had a lot of experience with crime or sex before they came here, or act like they did?

(c) Have little or nothing to do with the adults here?

(d) Keep other boys from getting into trouble?

(e) Try to straighten out and get something good out of the place?

(f) Are able to help with personal problems other boys have?

(g) Get along well with the staff?

(h) Look for an easy way to spend their time without caring about changing their ways?

(i) Go around looking for fights?

55. Now, one last question:
What do you think is the worst thing a boy could do?

# FACTOR ANALYSIS AND INDEX
# CONSTRUCTION FOR INMATE DATA

We made various factor analyses of inmate data in order to check our estimates of what the major dimensions should be and to guide us in constructing indices. Most relevant here are the results of an analysis of the responses to forty items or combinations of items, made by the 931 who completed second survey questionnaires in the six institutions plus Maxwell. Correlations and factor analysis were done on an IBM 704 computer, using programs furnished by the data-processing section of the Institute for Social Research, University of Michigan. The principal axes, or principal components, procedure was used. The factors and loadings are those that emerged as rotation by the varimax technique turned out additional factors until at least 95 per cent of the variance in the matrix of correlation coefficients of all variables was explained. The coefficients are Pearson r's, based upon numerical values assigned to the various categories of the question responses. While the procedure of assigning such values in order to approximate interval scale measurement and of correlating the variables *en masse* without paying attention to their distributions is questionable, it appears to have been adequate to the largely exploratory purposes at hand.

The factor analysis produced seven factors. Two or more variables had loadings of .4 and above on each of the first six factors to emerge. Ordering the results by the size of the loadings, we reproduce these variables and factors in Table D.1. The table also shows summary labels we have given the factors, indicative of the dimensions that appear to underlie them. Factor I appears to measure cooperative views with regard to the staff and organization, with high loadings found on the four items dealing with telling adults on other boys. Loadings above .4 were also discovered on the question about talking another boy out

## Table D.1—Factor Loadings of .4 and Above

| Variables* | FACTORS | | | | | |
|---|---|---|---|---|---|---|
| | Cooperative Views | Integration and Solidarity | Perception of Leaders' Pos. Qualities | Perception of Leaders' Neg. Qualities | Leadership | Perspectives on Inst. & Staff |
| | I | II | III | IV | V | VI |
| Q.35 Tell staff of plan to beat up adult | −.691 | | | | | |
| Q.34a Tell re plan to rough up boy | −.666 | | | | | |
| Q.37b Tell re boy's plan to run | −.595 | | | | | |
| Q.37a Try to talk boy out of run | −.570 | | | | | |
| Q.26a How much has stay helped | −.488 | | | | | .409 |
| Q.36 Tell re kitchen stealing | −.460 | | | | | |
| Q.20 Adults here can help me | −.460 | | | | | .413 |
| Q.15 How many boys hang around with | | −.584 | | | | |
| Q.16 How many close friends | | −.553 | | | | |
| Q.51 How much boys stick together | | .425 | | | | |
| Q.18 How many want to see again | | .400 | | | | |
| Q.54f Leaders help with problems | | | −.684 | | | |
| Q.54d Leaders keep others from trouble | | | −.666 | | | |
| Q.54e Leaders straighten out | | | −.644 | | | |
| Q.54g Leaders get along with staff | | | −.479 | | | |
| Q.54a Leaders ready to fight | | | | −.616 | | |
| Q.54i Leaders look for fights | | | | −.547 | | |
| Q.54b Leaders have experience with crime & sex | | | | −.508 | | |
| Q.23 Influence choices received | | | | | −.707 | |
| Q.44 Clique choices received | | | | | −.695 | |
| Q.39 Is this a place that helps? | | | | | | .593 |
| Q.6 Rather be here or in some other institution | | | | | | .534 |
| Q.3,Q.4 Summary, good-bad place | | | | | | .531 |
| Q.53 Adults don't care re us | | | | | | −.507 |
| Q.1g Adults are pretty fair | | | | | | .474 |

* With question numbers (see Appendix C for questionnaire).

of running and on two items on whether or not the institution can help the boy and how much it has helped. Factor II appears to measure integration into the inmate group and solidarity. Factors III and IV measure perceptions of leaders in general, with regard to positive qualities of leadership in the first case and negative qualities in the second. Factor V measures leadership choices received. Finally, Factor VI appears to tap general perspectives on the institution and staff, with high loadings appearing on several questions about being helped in the institution and on orientations toward the adults.

These findings gave us confirmation that we could view cooperative-non-cooperative and positive-negative perspectives on the institution and staff, integration and solidarity, leadership, and qualities of leadership as major dimensions that could characterize the inmates. A similar conclusion had been reached on some of these dimensions (those we measured earlier) on the basis of factor analyses of data from the first survey.*

Both theoretical criteria and the results of the factor analysis guided the construction of indices. The indices were arbitrary; we simply took the items we decided should make up an index, dichotomized the potential responses, assigned a score of 0 or 1 to each of the response categories of each item, and added up scores for each component item to obtain a summary score for each respondent. Had the factor analysis shown substantial variations in the values of the loadings among different items used in the same index, we would have weighted the numerical scores of the various items differentially.

* For the complete factor-analysis results, see *The Comparative Study of Juvenile Correctional Institutions: A Research Report* (Ann Arbor: School of Social Work, University of Michigan, 1961), Chapter 17 and Appendix H. This report also gives results of two factor analyses made of data from the first survey. The first included several background attributes. We found that these attributes clustered by themselves, ordinarily not having high loadings on factors that correlated highly with attitudes. Furthermore, when we repeated the analysis without the background variables, we found the structure of factors, and often the values of the loadings themselves, virtually unchanged. We also made a factor analysis of the proportions of inmates living in the different cottages of the institutions who responded in given ways. This analysis yielded five factors and, generally, much higher loadings than those found in the analysis of data on individuals. It was very difficult to give any clear-cut theoretical definition to the dimensions denoted by the factors, however, and the associations among variables often seemed to reflect principally interinstitutional variations rather than "true" associations among scores.

The indices were constructed as follows:

*Index of Perspectives Toward the Institution and Staff.* The index of perspectives summarizes responses to the seven questions with loadings of .4 and above on Factor VI. One point was given for the responses indicated on the following questions:

| | |
|---|---|
| Is this a place to help, send or punish boys? | —help |
| Rather be here or in some other institution | —here |
| Summary: Did you think this would be a good or a bad place, and what do you think about it now? | —positive responses (improved perception) |
| The adults here don't really care what happens to us. | —disagree |
| Adults here are pretty fair. | —agree |
| Adults here can help me. | —can help a lot |
| How much has your stay here helped you? | —great deal, quite a lot |

We considered as generally positive those boys with scores of 4 or higher.

*Index of "Ratting."* The ratting index summarizes responses to four of the seven items with loadings of .4 and above on Factor I. The four selected (listed with the results of this index in Chapter 9) have a clear theoretical association, for all refer to telling staff on other boys. One point was given for each *yes* answer. Scores of 2 or less were considered as generally uncooperative.

*Index of Perceptions of Positive Characteristics of Leadership.* The positive perceptions index summarizes responses to the four items with loadings of .4 and above on Factor III. One point was given for a response of "all or most leaders" on each of the questions. Total scores of 1 and above were classified as positive.

*Index of Perceptions of Negative Characteristics of Leadership.* The negative perceptions index summarizes responses to the three items with correlations of .4 and above on Factor IV, plus two other items (questions 54c and 54h—see Appendix C) on negative qualities of leadership inadvertently left out of the factor analysis. Tabular analysis showed that responses to these two questions were highly associated with those to the three we had included. Again one point was given for saying "all or most leaders" on each item. We considered scores of 2 and higher negative.

*Appendix E*

# PUBLICATIONS AND DISSERTATIONS
# CONNECTED WITH THE RESEARCH

Oscar Grusky, *Treatment Goals and Organizational Behavior: A Study of an Experimental Prison Camp,* unpublished Ph.D. dissertation, The University of Michigan, 1957.

Robert D. Vinter and Roger Lind, *Staff Relationships and Attitudes in a Juvenile Correctional Institution* (Ann Arbor: The University of Michigan School of Social Work, 1958).

Oscar Grusky, "Role Conflict in Organization: A Study of Prison Camp Officials," *Administrative Science Quarterly,* 4 (March, 1959), 452–72.

Robert D. Vinter and Morris Janowitz, "Effective Institutions for Juvenile Delinquents: A Research Statement," *Social Service Review,* 33 (June, 1959), 118–31.

Oscar Grusky, "Organizational Goals and the Behavior of Informal Leaders," *American Journal of Sociology,* 65 (July, 1959), 59–67.

Robert D. Vinter, "The Social Structure of Service," *Issues in American Social Work,* Alfred J. Kahn, ed. (New York: Columbia University Press, 1959).

Mayer N. Zald, "The Correctional Institution for Juvenile Offenders: An Analysis of Organizational 'Character,'" *Social Problems,* 8 (Summer, 1960), 57–67.

Robert D. Vinter and Morris Janowitz, "Decision-Making Problems of the Institutional Executive," *Proceedings of the National Association of Training Schools,* 1960.

Mayer N. Zald, *Multiple Goals and Staff Structure: A Comparative Study of Correctional Institutions for Juvenile Delinquents,* unpublished Ph.D. dissertation, The University of Michigan, 1960.

Robert D. Vinter, *et al., The Comparative Study of Juvenile Correctional Institutions: A Research Report* (Ann Arbor: The University of Michigan School of Social Work, 1961).

Mayer N. Zald, "Power Balance and Staff Conflict in Correctional Institutions," *Administrative Science Quarterly*, 7 (June, 1962), 22–49.

Mayer N. Zald, "Organizational Control Structures in Five Correctional Institutions," *American Journal of Sociology*, 68 (November, 1962), 335–45.

Bernard Berk, *Informal Social Organization among Inmates in Treatment and Custodial Prison Camps: A Comparative Study*, unpublished Ph.D. dissertation, The University of Michigan, 1961.

Rosemary C. Sarri, *Organizational Patterns and Client Perspectives in Juvenile Correctional Institutions: A Comparative Study*, unpublished Ph.D. dissertation, The University of Michigan, 1962.

David Street, *Inmate Social Organization: A Comparative Study of Juvenile Correctional Institutions*, unpublished Ph.D. dissertation, The University of Michigan, 1962.

Charles Perrow, "Reality Shock: A New Organization Confronts the Custody-Treatment Dilemma," *Social Problems*, 10 (Spring, 1963), 374–82.

Mayer N. Zald, "Comparative Analysis and Measurement of Organizational Goals: The Case of Correctional Institutions for Delinquents," *Sociological Quarterly*, 4 (Summer, 1963), 206–30.

Robert D. Vinter, "Analysis of Treatment Organizations," *Social Work*, 8 (July, 1963), 3–15.

Mayer N. Zald and David Street, "Custody and Treatment in Juvenile Institutions," *Crime and Delinquency*, 10 (July, 1964), 249–56.

David Street, "The Inmate Group in Custodial and Treatment Settings," *American Sociological Review*, 30 (February, 1965), 40–55.

Robert D. Vinter and Rosemary C. Sarri, "The Juvenile Court: Organization and Decision-Making and Implications of Research Findings for Action Strategies," *Juvenile Court Hearing Officers Training Manual* (Ann Arbor: The University of Michigan Institute of Continuing Legal Education, 1965).

Rosemary C. Sarri and Robert D. Vinter, "Group Treatment Strategies in Juvenile Correctional Programs," *Crime and Delinquency*, 11 (October, 1965), 326–40.

Bernard Berk, "Organizational Goals and Inmate Organization," *American Journal of Sociology*, 71 (March, 1966), 522–34.

Albert J. Reiss, Jr., Rosemary C. Sarri, and Robert D. Vinter, "The Detroit Pre-Release Guidance Center: A Research Report," *Federal Pre-Release Guidance Centers* (Washington, D.C.: Correctional Research Associates, forthcoming).

# INDEX

Adaptation, 204–6
Authority relations, 161–66

Background characteristics
  of inmates, 212–20
  of staff, 107–9
Beliefs, 18–21
Bendix, Reinhard, 15
Bennett, 25, 34–35
Berk, Bernard, 326
Blau, Peter, 40
Block, Herbert, 221
Broom, Leonard, 39, 66

Change between surveys, 264–77
Clemmer, Donald, 211, 221, 252
Cloward, Richard A., 66, 251
Conflict, 125–32
Control of inmate association, 174–77
Cottage parents, 179–81
Cottrell, Leonard, Jr., 39, 66
Cressey, Donald R., 15, 40, 190, 252, 253

Daily round, 153–58
Departmental structure, 114–23
Dick, 24, 27–29
Differentiation, 159–61
Discipline scale, 143–46, 307
Dissertations, 325–26
Drucker, Peter, 39
Dual department structure, 120–22

Environmental relations, 67–88
Etzioni, Amitai, 39, 40
Executive behavior, 45–132
  autonomy, 46–47
  backgrounds and goals, 65
  executiveship, 45–46
  external strategies, 67–88
  goal definition, 48–65
  internal strategies, 93–106
Executive seminar, 257–63
External strategies, 67–88

Factor analysis, 321–23
Flynn, F. T., 221
Formal organization, 114–22

Garabedian, Peter C., 212, 221, 222, 252
Garrity, Donald L., 252
Gerth, Hans, 39
Gilbert, Doris C., 306n
Goal formulation, 48–65
Goffman, Erving, 15, 40, 190
Gouldner, Alvin, 39, 66
Gratifications and deprivations, 224–27
Greenblatt, Milton, 132, 306n
Grosser, George P., 252
Grusky, Oscar, 325

Henry, Jules, 132
Hypotheses, 22, 198–99

Implementation
  general problems, 177–88
  of treatment, 279–82
Indeterminate means, 13–14
Index construction
  for inmates, 321–24
  for staff, 306–9
Inland, 25, 36–39
Inmate backgrounds, 212–20
Inmate group, 222–51
  general characteristics, 222–23
  interpersonal relations, 227–30
  leadership, 239–45
  solidarity, 232–38
  summary of findings, 249–51
  theoretical scheme, 223–27
Inmate perspectives, 195–220
  on adaptation, 204–6
  by background attributes, 217–20
  on institutional features, 201–2
  on institution and staff, 199–201
  by integration, 230–32
  by length of stay, 209–12
  on self, 206–9
  on staff supervision, 203–4
Inmate-staff ratios, 106–7
Institutional models, 21–22
Integration, 230–32
Internal strategies, 93–106
Interpersonal relations, 227–30
Inward perspectives, 10–11
Irwin, John, 252

Janowitz, Morris, 40, 279, 325
Juvenile correctional institution, 7–15

Kahn, Alfred J., 325
Korn, Richard, 252

Lawrence, William C., 251, 252
Leadership, 239–45
Length of stay
  and perspectives, 209–12
  variation, 196–97

Levinson, Daniel J., 132, 306
Lind, Roger, 325
Litwak, Eugene, 132

McCleery, Richard, 66, 253
McCord, Joan, 221
McCord, William, 221
McCorkle, Lloyd W., 252
McEwen, William, 39
March, James G., 15, 189
Maxwell, 32, 245–49
Merton, Robert, 39, 66
Messinger, Sheldon L., 251, 252
Milieu treatment, difficulties, 181–88
Mills, C. Wright, 39
Milton, 25, 35–36
Mixed goal model, 21–22
Mixter, 24, 29–32
Multiple department structure, 117–20

Normal relations scale, 143–46, 306–7

Obedience/conformity model, 21
Offense records, 215–17
Ohlin, Lloyd, 66, 89, 251, 252
Organizational change
  executive seminar as stimulant to, 257–63
  between surveys, 264–77
Organizational effectiveness, 195–97
Organizational goals, 16–22, 45–65
  beliefs and, 18–21
  conceptions of, 17–18
  formulation of, 45–65
  multiple, 13–14
Organizational structure, 106–32
Outline boys, 245

Parsons, Talcott, 17, 39, 40
People-changing organizations, 3–7
Perceptions of leadership, indices of, 242–43, 320

Perrow, Charles, 15, 39, 40, 189, 326
Personnel cadres, 11–13
Perspectives toward institution and staff, index of, 199–201, 324
Polsky, Howard, 252
Powelson, Harvey, 15
Power distribution, 123–25
Prisonization scale, 176–77, 308
Publications and dissertations, 325–26

Questionnaires
  inmate, 310–20
  staff, 287–305

Rapoport, R., 190
Rapoport, R. N., 190
"Ratting" index, 233–36, 324
Re-education/development model, 21
Regis, 24, 32–34
Reiss, Albert J., Jr., 326
Research design
  administration of questionnaires, 285–86, 310–11
  coding reliability, 286, 311
  general, 22–26
  inmate factor analysis and indices, 321–24
  numbers of cases, 41
  staff scales and indices, 306–9
Rewards and sanctions, 166–74
Riesman, David, 14, 15
Riley, J. W., Jr., 306n
Riley, M. W., 306n
Role definitions of staff, 108–13
Rosow, I., 190
Runaways, 197

Sanctions, 166–74, 308–9
  index, 169–71, 308–9
Sarri, Rosemary C., 208–9, 326
Scales, 306–9

Schrag, Clarence, 252
Scott, W. Richard, 40
Selection of institutions, 23–25
Self-image, 206–9
Selznick, Philip, 40, 66
Shils, Edward, 40
Simon, Herbert, 66
Simple department structure, 114–17
Sketches of institutions, 26–39
Solidarity, 232–38
"Solidary opposition" model, 222–27, 232–38, 244–49
Staff background characteristics, 107–9
Staff control and authority, 225–27
Staffing patterns, 106–8
Staff-inmate relations, 151–88
Staff perspectives
  on delinquents, 142–46
  on goals, 137–40
  on jobs and careers, 148–49
  on rehabilitative potential, 146–48
  on treatment programs, 140–42
  on volunteers, 142
Street, David, 253, 326
Sykes, Gresham M., 251, 252
Systems of social control, 151–53

Task definitions, 108–13
Technologies, 11–13
Tension, 125–32
Theoretical framework
  general, 17–22
  on inmates, 223–27
Thompson, James, 39
Toby, Jackson, 306n
Toby, Marcia L., 306n
Treatment
  model, defined, 21
  implementation of, 279–82

Understanding scale, 143–46, 307
Unilateral strategy, 8–10

Vinter, Robert D., 15, 279, 325, 326

Weber, George H., 190
Weber, Max, 17, 39

Wheeler, Stanton, 211, 212, 221, 222, 252
Williams, Richard H., 132, 306n

Zald, Mayer, 15, 39, 325, 326